"Great are the Words of Isaiah"

"GREAT ARE THE WORDS OF ISAIAH"

Monte S. Nyman

Salt Lake City, Utah

Library of Congress Catalog Card Number: 79-57137
ISBN 0-88494-910-9

Fifth Softcover Printing, 1998

Printed in the United States of America

Key to Abbreviations

AQ	Joseph Fielding Smith, *Answers to Gospel Questions*, 5 vols. (Salt Lake City: Deseret Book Company, 1979)
CHC	B. H. Roberts, *A Comprehensive History of the Church*, 6 vols. (Provo, Utah: Brigham Young University Press, 1965)
CR	Conference Report
DS	Joseph Fielding Smith, *Doctrines of Salvation*, 3 vols. (Salt Lake City: Bookcraft, Inc., 1967-73)
DNTC	Bruce R. McConkie, *Doctrinal New Testament Commentary*, 3 vols. (Salt Lake City: Bookcraft, Inc., 1966-73)
HC	*History of the Church*, 7 vols. (Salt Lake City: Deseret Book Company, 1973)
IE	*Improvement Era*
JS-H	*Joseph Smith—History*
JST	Joseph Smith Translation of the Bible (often referred to as the "Inspired Version")
JD	*Journal of Discourses*, 26 vols.
KJV	King James Version of the Bible
MA	*Messenger and Advocate*
MS	*Millennial Star*
RSV	Revised Standard Version of the Bible
ST	Joseph Fielding Smith, *The Signs of the Times* (Salt Lake City: Deseret Book Company, 1963)
TPJS	*Teachings of the Prophet Joseph Smith*
Works	*Orson Pratt's Works*

Contents

1 Search the Prophecies of Isaiah: A Commandment

On two different occasions, the resurrected Lord and Savior admonished the Nephites to search the prophecies of Isaiah which they had before them (see 3 Nephi 20:11; 23:1). On the second occasion, he made it a *commandment* unto them to "search these things diligently; for great are the words of Isaiah" (3 Nephi 23:1).

The significance of this commandment is highlighted by the fact that, as far as the record goes, Isaiah was the only book among the writings of the ancient prophets which the Savior specifically commanded the Nephites to search. That the commandment was to be extended to the latter days, and especially to the readers of the Book of Mormon, is shown by the Savior's charge to the Nephites to record his words so that they could go forth unto the Gentiles: "Therefore give heed to my words; write the things which I have told you; and according to the time and the will of the Father they shall go forth unto the Gentiles" (3 Nephi 23:4).

Jesus further declared that those who would hearken to his words (which included the commandment to search Isaiah)—and would repent and be baptized—would be saved (see 3 Nephi 23:5a). Is our salvation dependent upon our diligence in heeding the commandment to search Isaiah? This possibility has been suggested by Elder Bruce R. McConkie:

> If our eternal salvation depends upon our ability to understand the writings of Isaiah as fully and truly as Nephi understood them—and who shall say such is not the case!—how shall we fare in that great day when with Nephi we shall stand before the pleasing bar of Him who said: "Great are the words of Isaiah"? (*Ensign*, Oct. 1973, p. 78.)

The Savior followed his specific admonition to search Isaiah with a general admonition to "search the prophets, for many there be that testify of these things" (3 Nephi 23:5b). An inference from this instruction is that various other prophets had also testified of the things of which Isaiah had written, but that none of them had spoken so thoroughly "as touching all things concerning my [Christ's] people which are of the house of Israel" (3 Nephi 23:2) as had Isaiah.

Jewish tradition regards Isaiah as the chief prophet of his period. With the above statement, the Savior seems to broaden that distinction, perhaps even to the entire period of the prophets from Samuel to Malachi.

The Nephite prophets also considered Isaiah to be an extremely important prophet. They included over 30 pages of Isaiah's writings in the current 522-page edition of the Book of Mormon, despite the difficulty of engraving on metal plates (see Jacob 4:1) and the restriction of including even less than "a hundredth part" of the available material in their abridgment (see Jacob 3:13). This illustrates the priority which the Book of Mormon compilers gave to the words of Isaiah. While approximately one-third of the biblical writings of Isaiah are quoted in the Book of Mormon, the prophet Moroni admonished his future readers to search also the rest of the prophecies of Isaiah (see Mormon 8:23). This extends the Savior's commandment to include the entire book of Isaiah, not just those parts recorded in the Book of Mormon. Thus the readers of the Book of Mormon have been admonished and even commanded by the Lord Jesus Christ, and by the Nephite prophet who was given stewardship over the ancient plates, to search the prophecies of Isaiah.

The Book of Mormon contains three basic reasons for searching the prophecies of Isaiah. Two of these reasons were given by the Savior in justification of his statement, "Great are the words of Isaiah." The first one was that "he spake as touching all things concerning my people which are of the house of Israel; therefore it must needs be that he must speak also to the Gentiles" (3 Nephi 23:2). While the Savior was among the Nephites, he declared that much of what Isaiah and other prophets had written concerning the house of Israel was yet to be fulfilled:

> Behold, I do not destroy the prophets, for as many as have not been fulfilled in me, verily I say unto you, shall all be fulfilled.
>
> And because I said unto you that old things have passed away, I do not destroy that which hath been spoken concerning things which are to come.
>
> For behold, the covenant which I have made with my people is not all fulfilled; but the law which was given unto Moses hath an end in me. (3 Nephi 15:6-8.)

After identifying various groups of the house of Israel and declaring his visits or intended visits among them, the Savior told of the gospel's being taken to the Gentiles. He said that through the Gentiles the house of Israel would again be brought to a knowledge of him. He also spoke of the day when the Gentiles would sin against his gospel, at which time the gospel would be taken from them and he would remember his covenant unto Israel. He said further that if the Gentiles would repent, they would be numbered among the house of Israel; otherwise they would be trodden under foot by Israel (see 3 Nephi 16:4-16). The Savior also stated that the Father had commanded him to give the land of the Americas unto "this people" (who were descendants of Joseph) as their inheritance (see 3 Nephi 15:12-13). When these things came to pass, said Jesus, the words of the prophet Isaiah would be partially fulfilled (see 3 Nephi 16:17-20).

On the second day of his ministry among the Nephites, the Savior declared again that the Father's covenant unto Israel would be fulfilled in the day when Isaiah's prophecies were fulfilled. He then outlined how these promises would be brought to fulfillment, both on the American continent, which was the land given to Joseph, and in the land of Jerusalem; he quoted freely from Isaiah's writings to substantiate this outline (see 3 Nephi 20:11-22:17). It was at the conclusion of these teachings, wherein the Savior had quoted from the prophet Isaiah, that he gave the commandment to search Isaiah's prophecies.

Nephi, the son of Lehi, confirmed his father's words concerning the house of Israel and the Gentiles in the latter days (see 1 Nephi 15:7-18) by quoting to his brothers the words of Isaiah: "And I did rehearse unto them the words of Isaiah, who spake concerning the restoration of the Jews, or of the house of Israel; and after they were restored they should no more be confounded, neither should they be scattered again" (1 Nephi 15:20a).

Jacob, the brother of Nephi, also bore testimony that Isaiah spoke concerning all of Israel, and he encouraged his people to liken Isaiah's words unto themselves: "And now, the words which I shall read are they which Isaiah spake concerning all the house of Israel; wherefore, they may be likened unto you, for ye are of the house of Israel. And there are many things which have been spoken by Isaiah which may be likened unto you, because ye are of the house of Israel." (2 Nephi 6:5.)

Therefore, a major reason for searching Isaiah's prophecies, as declared by the Savior and confirmed by Nephi and Jacob, is that Isaiah spoke concerning all the house of Israel and the covenants unto them which were to be fulfilled in the latter days. As the fulfillment of these covenants was to center around the Lord's dealings with the Gentiles, we can see that we are living in the very day when Isaiah's prophecies concerning Israel are coming to pass. The modern-day apostle Orson Pratt, after quoting and commenting on several of Isaiah's prophecies, stated: "We have read these words of the ancient Prophet, in order that the Latter-day Saints may call to mind how completely the Lord is fulfilling every jot and every tittle . . . of that which he caused to be spoken, by the power of the Holy Ghost, through his ancient Prophets" (*JD*, 18:153).

The Savior provided a second justification for his declaration concerning the greatness of Isaiah's words: "And all things that he spake have been and shall be, even according to the words which he spake" (3 Nephi 23:3).

Jacob, the brother of Nephi, bore a similar testimony of the certainty of Isaiah's prophecies as he spoke unto the people of Nephi: "And now, behold, I would speak unto you concerning things which are, and which are to come; wherefore, I will read you the words of Isaiah. And they are the words which my brother has desired that I should speak unto you. And I speak unto you for your sakes, that ye may learn and glorify the name of your God." (2 Nephi 6:4.)

In equating Isaiah's words with "things which are, and which are to come," Jacob is also equating them with the Lord's definition of *truth* as given to the Prophet Joseph Smith (see D&C 93:24). That Isaiah was noted for speaking and writing truth is confirmed by the Jewish historian Josephus:

> . . . he was, by the confession of all, a divine and wonderful man in speaking truth; and out of the assurance that he had never written what was false, he wrote down all his prophecies, and left them behind him in books, that their accomplishment might be judged of from the events by posterity. (Flavius Josephus, *Josephus: Complete Works*, trans. William Whiston [Grand Rapids, Mich.: Kregel Publications, 1972], Antiquities of the Jews, 10. 2.2.)

To those who seek truth—especially the truths concerning the fulfillment of the Lord's covenants with the house of Israel—the words of Isaiah are an authentic and excellent source of knowledge. The Savior's divine stamp of approval regarding the authenticity of these writings should motivate one to search the prophecies of Isaiah.

The third reason given in the Book of Mormon for searching the words of Isaiah is that he bore testimony of Christ. The Savior declared to the Nephites that the law and the prophets (which would have included Isaiah) truly testified of him (see 3 Nephi 15:10). And Nephi looked to Isaiah as the primary source to persuade his people to believe in Christ:

> And I did read many things unto them which were written in the book of Moses; but that I might more fully persuade them to believe in the Lord their Redeemer I did read unto them that which was written by the prophet Isaiah; for I did liken all scriptures unto us, that it might be for our profit and learning.
>
> Wherefore I spake unto them, saying: Hear ye the words of the prophet, ye who are a remnant of the house of Israel, a branch who have been broken off; hear ye the words of the prophet, which were written unto all the house of Israel, and liken them unto yourselves, that ye may have hope as well as

> your brethren from whom ye have been broken off. . . . (1 Nephi 19:23-24.)

Later, Nephi quoted again from the words of Isaiah. In a preface to this quotation, he declared that Isaiah had seen the Redeemer, even as Nephi and Jacob had, thus establishing God's words by three witnesses.

> And now I, Nephi, write more of the words of Isaiah, for my soul delighteth in his words. For I will liken his words unto my people, and I will send them forth unto all my children, for he verily saw my Redeemer, even as I have seen him.
>
> And my brother, Jacob, also has seen him as I have seen him; wherefore, I will send their words forth unto my children to prove unto them that my words are true. Wherefore, by the words of three, God hath said, I will establish my word. Nevertheless, God sendeth more witnesses, and he proveth all his words. (2 Nephi 11:2-3.)

Nephi's desire to use the words of Isaiah is perhaps best explained by the Prophet Joseph Smith's teachings about the knowledge given to one who receives the Second Comforter:

> The visions of the heavens will be opened unto him, and the Lord will teach him face to face, and he may have a perfect knowledge of the mysteries of the Kingdom of God; and this is the state and place the ancient Saints arrived at when they had such glorious visions—Isaiah, Ezekiel, John upon the Isle of Patmos, St. Paul in the three heavens, and all the Saints who held communion with the general assembly and Church of the Firstborn. (*TPJS*, p. 151.)

Nephi wrote that his soul delighted in proving to his people that Christ would come, as typified by the law of Moses and "all things which have been given of God." His soul also delighted in the covenants which the Lord had made to his fathers; in the grace, justice, power, and mercy of "the great and eternal plan of deliverance from death" which Christ would carry out; and in proving to his people that "save Christ should come all men must perish." Therefore, he wrote the words of Isaiah that others might also rejoice in the same knowledge of Christ which he had (see 2 Nephi 11:4-8).

Abinadi bore witness to the wicked priests of King Noah that Moses and "even all the prophets who have prophesied ever since the world began" had "spoken more or less" concerning the coming of Jesus Christ.

> Have they not said that God himself should come down among the children of men, and take upon him the form of man, and go forth in mighty power upon the face of the earth?
>
> Yea, and have they not said also that he should bring to pass the resurrection of the dead, and that he, himself, should be oppressed and afflicted? (Mosiah 13:34-35.)

To support this witness, Abinadi quoted to them what is now designated chapter 53 of Isaiah (Mosiah 14).

As stated on its title page, the purpose of the Book of Mormon is to convince "the Jew and Gentile that JESUS is the CHRIST, the ETERNAL GOD." Of the 425 separate verses of Isaiah which are quoted in the Book of Mormon, 391 say something about the attributes or mission of Jesus Christ. While many of the other passages in Isaiah also testify of Christ, those used by the Book of Mormon prophets exemplify why they and the Savior quoted freely from Isaiah in support of their overall objective. These passages also demonstrate a major reason why we should search the prophecies of Isaiah—so that they can testify to us of Jesus Christ.

Thus, the words of Isaiah should be studied today because the Lord has commanded us to search them diligently. This commandment was given because of the greatness of Isaiah's words in outlining the fulfillment of God's covenant with Israel in the latter days, in declaring words of truth which shall all be fulfilled, and in testifying of the attributes and mission of the Lord Jesus Christ.

How to Understand Isaiah 2

Nephi, the son of Lehi, recognized that Isaiah was a difficult book for his people to understand (see 2 Nephi 25:1), even though they had left Jerusalem only 100 years or so after Isaiah concluded his writings. Nearly 2,600 more years have passed since that time, so if it was hard for Nephi's people (who came from the same geographical area and lived in the same general time period as did Isaiah) to understand the words of the ancient prophet, it would seem they must be even more difficult for us to understand today. However, the passage of time is not the only thing which makes Isaiah hard to understand. To come to an understanding requires that we diligently *search* Isaiah's words, as the Savior commanded. To search is to carefully and thoroughly examine in an effort to discover. To search is also to inspect or explore possible places of concealment.

Nephi provided a three-pronged formula for comprehending Isaiah's writings: (1) understand "the manner of prophesying among the Jews"; (2) be "filled with the spirit of prophecy"; and (3) live in the days when the prophecies of Isaiah are fulfilled (see 2 Nephi 25:1, 4, 7). Applying one or more of these approaches will help us in searching the words of Isaiah, and we can thereby gain understanding—although it will probably come "line upon line" and "precept upon precept," as Isaiah defined the process of receiving revelation (see Isaiah 28:10).

Understand the Manner of Prophesying Among the Jews

Nephi said that Isaiah was hard for many of his people to understand because "they know not concerning the manner of prophesying among the Jews" (2 Nephi 25:1). Nephi's people might have known more on this subject, but he had not taught them many things concerning the Jews, "for their [the Jews'] works were works of darkness, and their doings were doings of abominations" (2 Nephi 25:2). His reluctance to teach concerning the Jews was probably a preventive measure to avoid introducing similar works and abominations among his people. Nevertheless, Nephi himself understood Isaiah's words, and the Jews to whom these words were addressed also knew their meaning (see 2 Nephi 25:5-6).

Nephi indicated that other people could understand Isaiah by being taught "after the manner of the things [prophecies] of the Jews" (2 Nephi 25:5). However, preventing the introduction of abominations and works of darkness among our people today would still seem desirable. Through the Book of Mormon, we can learn the message of Isaiah without having those works of darkness introduced. We have the advantage of Nephi's interpretive commentary upon various passages of Isaiah, which help he gave in such a manner that he knew "that no man can err" (2 Nephi 25:7). Nephi's commentary was based upon his knowledge of "the regions round about" Jerusalem and "the judgments of God, which hath come to pass among the Jews" (2 Nephi 25:6). This suggests that a study of the geography of the land, as well as the history of the people and their manner of writing, would also help us today in understanding Isaiah. Knowledge of the geography and history could be obtained from the scholars of the world, but these scholars do not necessarily know of the judgments of God which have come upon the Jews. However, the words of Nephi and others who quoted and commented upon Isaiah's writings, recorded in the Book of Mormon, would reveal the judgments which came upon the Jews. This would be especially true of the Savior's teachings which were based upon Isaiah's writings. The Book of Mormon text quotes 425 separate verses of Isaiah (21 of these are duplicated, making a total of 446), and it provides many verses of explanation. The quoted passages are taken from 24 of the 66 chapters in Isaiah; 19 chapters are completely quoted, and 2 other chapters are nearly complete. All this material is a great source for shedding light on the words of Isaiah. In fact, the Book of Mormon is the best single commentary available on the book of Isaiah. In the words of Elder Bruce R. McConkie:

> The Book of Mormon is the world's greatest commentary on the book of Isaiah.
>
> And may I be so bold as to affirm that no one, absolutely no one, in this age and dispensation has or does or can understand the writings of Isaiah until he first learns and believes what God has revealed by the mouths of his Nephite witnesses as these truths are found in that volume of holy writ of which he himself swore this oath: " . . . as your Lord and your God liveth it is true." (D&C 17:6; *Ensign*, Oct. 1973, p. 81.)

One reason why the Book of Mormon is such an excellent resource to help us understand Isaiah is that it preserves a better text. This text of Isaiah was taken from the brass plates of Laban and copied onto the plates from which the Book of Mormon was translated; it is at least five hundred years older than the oldest manuscript of the Isaiah text available today. The discovery of the Dead Sea texts of Isaiah was very significant because it moved the date of earliest Isaiah manuscripts from A.D. 900 (the Masoretic text) to about 100 B.C., the date of the Dead Sea Scroll texts. The plates of brass from which Nephi copied the text of Isaiah would have been recorded by at latest 600 B.C., when Lehi and his party left Jerusalem. This places the Book of Mormon text of Isaiah within 100 to 150 years of the time of the original writing, making it closer to the time of the original writing than any other Old or New Testament manuscript. Therefore, this text is probably more accurate than any other account of Isaiah, so retentions in the Book of Mormon text should be given prime consideration.

A second reason why the Book of Mormon is so valuable in helping us understand Isaiah is that it provides a number of commentaries on his writings. These commentaries are necessary because the book of Isaiah is written much as were the parables of Jesus, so that those who would diligently search the prophecies of Isaiah would know the mysteries of the kingdom of heaven, while those who failed to search them would not have these mysteries revealed unto them (see Matthew 13:10-17). It does not seem just a coincidence that the Savior quoted from the prophet Isaiah to describe those who would not understand his parables (compare Matthew 13:14-15, Isaiah 6:9-10).

Another source to help us understand "the manner of prophesying among the Jews" is the Doctrine and Covenants. As Joseph Smith received revelations from the Lord Jesus Christ, those revelations were often phrased in the language of the prophets. The Lord stated in his Preface to the Doctrine and Covenants (section 1) that his purpose in giving commandments to Joseph Smith and others was that they might proclaim them to the world, "that it might be fulfilled, which was written by the prophets" (D&C 1:18). The language of the ancient prophets is used throughout the revelations recorded in the Doctrine and Covenants, showing us the relevance of the prophets to our own day and also helping us understand the message of those prophets. At least sixty-six different quotations from the book of Isaiah are used in the Doctrine and Covenants, and several of these are used more than once. There are possibly other phrases based on Isaiah, but those sixty-six can be positively identified (see Appendix D). There are phrases, and often whole verses, which show the context and meaning of the Isaiah text. They are taken from thirty-one different chapters of Isaiah, ranging from chapter 1 through chapter 66. A comparison of these passages with the book of Isaiah should also help us understand Isaiah better.

There is still another source to which one may look to understand "the manner of prophesying among the Jews." The apostles of the New Testament era left their testimony to the world, and in witnessing of the Savior and his gospel they frequently called upon the words of Isaiah to substantiate their teachings. Forty-two different passages from the book of Isaiah are quoted in the New Testament; some were quoted by the Savior himself, and others by such men as Peter, Paul, and John. Many of these passages are repeated, providing a total of at least fifty-four instances in which passages from Isaiah are quoted or commented upon to give us insight into their meaning. There are also several other passages which may be quotations, paraphrases, or expressions about the text of Isaiah (see Appendix D). The forty-two passages mentioned above are quoted from twenty-five of the sixty-six chapters of Isaiah in the current Bible; they range from the beginning to the end of his writings, thus giving Isaiah a broad coverage. These, too, are a great source for an understanding of the words of Isaiah.

Before leaving this subject of understanding the manner of prophesying among the Jews, we must give a word of caution. Nephi said that he "did liken all scriptures unto us, that it might be for our profit and learning" (1 Nephi 19:23; see also 19:24 and 2 Nephi 6:4-5). To "liken" a scripture to a different situation than that in which it originated is not always to learn the original message of that scripture. To correctly interpret a scriptural passage is to learn its original meaning; thus biblical criticism endeavors to find the original texts and meanings of Old and New Testament writings. There is a distinction between the interpretation of a scripture and some personal application of the same scripture to show a principle or lesson. It should also be pointed out that we learn from the Book of Mormon that scriptures can sometimes have a dual interpretation—that is, some prophecies were originally intended to apply to two or more different times, places, or situations.

In summary, there are three excellent sources to help us learn "the manner of prophecying among the Jews" and thus learn the meaning and message of the words of Isaiah. These sources—the Book of Mormon, the Doctrine and Covenants, and the New Testament—provide quotations and commentaries from forty-two of the sixty-six chapters in the current text of Isaiah. There are also allusions and paraphrases from eight of the other twenty-four chapters. Thus Isaiah is broadly commented upon by these three sources. No more reliable or enlightening sources are available, and Latter-day Saints would do well to search these scriptural commentaries along with the book of Isaiah itself to obtain a deeper and fuller understanding of the great words of Isaiah.

Be Filled with the Spirit of Prophecy

The second part of Nephi's formula for understanding the words of Isaiah is to be "filled with the spirit of prophecy." The spirit of prophecy and of revelation comes through searching the scriptures and through much prayer and fasting (see Alma 17:2-3). As we live worthy of this blessing, and as we examine carefully and thoroughly every word, phrase, sentence, verse, paragraph, and chapter in the scriptures, the Spirit will bear witness of their meaning and application to our lives (see John 5:39, also 2 Nephi 32:2-5).

Latter-day Saints also have the inspired words of modern-day prophets and apostles to help them interpret the writings of Isaiah. In a revelation given in November 1831, the Lord declared that he had called Elder Orson Hyde to expound "all scriptures" unto those he taught, and that this was to be "an ensample unto all those who were ordained unto this priesthood." The Lord further declared that, as the priesthood holders were to go forth expounding all scriptures, "whatsoever they shall speak when moved upon by the Holy Ghost shall be scripture" (D&C 68:1-4). Thus, Latter-day Saints have the advantage of over 150 years' worth of the teachings of modern prophets and apostles who have expounded the scriptures and have given new scripture unto the world.

Furthermore, the Prophet Joseph Smith was divinely called to declare God's word to this generation, and his writings and teachings should be considered scripture (see D&C 5:10). The book *Teachings of the Prophet Joseph Smith*, a compilation of many of the doctrinal teachings of Joseph Smith, contains at least thirty-five quotations, paraphrases, and commentaries on the text of Isaiah. These come from twenty-one different chapters in the biblical text, and many are very helpful in understanding these ancient writings (see Appendix F). Other references could be cited, but suffice it to say that we should also study the words which holy men of God have given us in modern times as we try to come to an understanding of the words of Isaiah. Again, it should be emphasized that each individual has the responsibility, as well as the opportunity, to learn for himself through the spirit of prophecy. The Prophet Joseph declared that "the least Saint may know all things as fast as he is able to bear them" (*TPJS*, p. 149).

Know of a Surety When They Come to Pass

The third part of Nephi's formula for understanding the words of Isaiah is an important one, and one which is sometimes overlooked when we read Nephi's admonition. He declared that "in the days that the prophecies of Isaiah shall be fulfilled men shall know of a surety, at the times when they shall come to pass" (2 Nephi 25:7). One evidence of this is the fulfillment of a prophecy in chapter 29 of Isaiah concerning a sealed book being taken to a learned man. Who would ever have known the interpretation of this passage before Martin Harris took a copy of a few characters from the Book of Mormon plates, and the interpretation thereof, to Professor Charles Anthon (see JS-H 1:63-65)? Non-LDS scholars are still pondering the meaning of this chapter. There are many other such prophecies of Isaiah which are understood today, but were not understood in the days of Nephi or at any time since until the events themselves came to pass. Further, there are yet many passages in Isaiah which are not wholly understood, because the events foreseen have not yet happened. It is helpful, therefore, to know which of the events that he spoke of have taken place, and which are yet to come.

The words of Isaiah are hard to be understood, but one can come to an understanding by knowing the manner of prophesying among the Jews, by being filled with the spirit of prophecy, and by living in the day when the prophecies of Isaiah are fulfilled. Applying this formula given by Nephi will bring the modern reader to proclaim with the Savior, "Great are the words of Isaiah."

The Preface 3

Isaiah 1

In writing upon the plates which were later translated into the Book of Mormon, Nephi recorded thirteen consecutive chapters of Isaiah. He commenced with chapter 2 of Isaiah and not chapter 1. The reason for his exclusion of chapter 1 is not given, but an analysis of the whole book of Isaiah seems to suggest a very plausible reason.

Scholars consider the first chapter an introduction to the compilation of the prophecies of Isaiah and other later writings. That the book of Isaiah is a compilation of various prophecies given at different times is quite obvious. However, chapter 1 seems to be much more than an introduction; it is apparently a *preface* given by revelation specifically for that purpose. Thus it is closely akin to section 1 of the Doctrine and Covenants.

On November 1, 1831, during a special conference of elders held at Hiram, Ohio, the Lord gave the revelation now known as section 1. It was to be a preface to a compilation of some of Joseph Smith's revelations which the conference participants had decided to publish. This revelation placed the Lord's sanction upon that publication, and it gave the conference a guide for selecting the revelations to be included. A preface is a preliminary statement about a book or article which outlines its subject, plan, and purpose. Thus, those revelations which met the conditions of the preface statement could rightfully be selected for inclusion. If Isaiah chapter 1 is a preface given by the Lord, as suggested above, it too would have served as a guide for which prophecies of Isaiah were included in the compilation of his writings. Chapter 1 of Isaiah fits the definition of a preface, as will be shown later. The book as a whole also has many other striking similarities to the Doctrine and Covenants; we will briefly examine these to help us understand the book of Isaiah.

The book of Isaiah cannot be followed as a narrative, but is more easily understood if it is broken into sections, as is the Doctrine and Covenants. The first half of the book breaks readily into separate divisions or sections. However, these do not necessarily follow the present chapter divisions of the book of Isaiah. A sectional breakdown of the first thirty-five chapters of Isaiah is suggested below; the next several chapters of the present study will be organized on the basis of this breakdown; occasionally more than one section of Isaiah will be included in a single chapter of this book.

1. Isaiah 1
2. Isaiah 2-4
3. Isaiah 5
4. Isaiah 6
5. Isaiah 7
6. Isaiah 8-12
7. Isaiah 13-14
8. Isaiah 15-16
9. Isaiah 17
10. Isaiah 18
11. Isaiah 19-20
12. Isaiah 21:1-10[1]
13. Isaiah 21:11-12[1]
14. Isaiah 21:13-17[1]
15. Isaiah 22
16. Isaiah 23
17. Isaiah 24-27
18. Isaiah 28-35

In 2 Chronicles 32:32, Isaiah's writings are referred to as "the vision of Isaiah the prophet." It is the opinion of this writer that the original material from which the present-day chapters 40 through 66 of Isaiah have come down to us may have been the original "vision of Isaiah the prophet." This suggests that there may have been two different texts or books of Isaiah—the first a compilation of Isaiah's revelations comprising the present-day chapters 1 through 35, and

1. These three sections, and possibly others, may have been included in a single revelation similar to section 23 of the Doctrine and Covenants, wherein, in the same revelation, instructions are given to Oliver Cowdery, Hyrum Smith, Samuel Smith, Joseph Smith, Sr., and Joseph Knight.

the second the "vision of Isaiah" (consisting of chapters 40 through 66, as previously suggested). The two books may then have been brought together, with the historical account now constituting chapters 36 through 39 being inserted between them. These four historical chapters, apparently lifted out of the abridged records of the kings of Israel and Judah, contain several prophecies which were made by Isaiah, which would account for their being included with his writings.

Just as some of the revelations given to Joseph Smith have not been included in the Doctrine and Covenants, some of Isaiah's prophecies were not included in the compilation of his writings. At least this is the case in our present-day book of Isaiah; there is evidence that Isaiah wrote some prophecies of which we have no record today. For instance, 2 Chronicles 26:22 tells us that Isaiah wrote "the rest of the acts of Uzziah," which we do not have, and 2 Chronicles 32:32 says that "the rest of the acts of Hezekiah" were written in "the vision of Isaiah." Chapters 36 through 39 of Isaiah are basically the same as certain chapters in 2 Kings and 2 Chronicles, so the "rest of the acts" of these kings must be found in other writings. The acts of Hezekiah in 2 Chronicles are limited to the first and fourteenth years of his reign. Hezekiah reigned for twenty-nine years, so the "rest of [his] acts" probably refers to the last fifteen years of his reign. The acts of Hezekiah may once have been included in the book of Isaiah, as it is said that they were recorded in the "vision of Isaiah." Therefore, Isaiah apparently wrote accounts additional to those which were compiled into a book under his name.

Another similarity between the book of Isaiah and the Doctrine and Covenants is the pattern of their makeup. The early sections of the Doctrine and Covenants deal with the early period of Church history. Similarly, the early chapters of Isaiah deal with the early part of his ministry. This is particularly true if Jotham (the second king who was contemporary with Isaiah) reigned while his father, Uzziah, was "cut off from the house of the Lord" because of his leprosy (2 Chronicles 26:21). Since Isaiah's ministry is believed to have begun in the last year of Uzziah's life (Isaiah 6:1), and if Jotham had regency with his father, the early revelations would pertain to the third king, Ahaz. Such seems to be the case. The first stated time period in the book of Isaiah is "the year that king Uzziah died" (Isaiah 6:1), which was the year Isaiah received a vision wherein he was called to the ministry. Chapter 7 then records a prophecy given to King Ahaz by Isaiah. Chapters 1 through 5 refer to no designated time period but are general, long-range prophecies; chapters 2 through 4 form a prophecy of the future of Judah and Israel in the latter days; and chapter 5 is a little parable about the house of Israel and Judah. These prophecies could fit into any of the reigns of Uzziah, Jotham, or Ahaz. Nor were chapters 2 through 5 necessarily written before chapter 6. Similarly, some of the early revelations of the Doctrine and Covenants were not placed in chronological order, section 10 being dated before sections 4 through 9. (The exact dating of section 10 is unknown, however, and there are different opinions regarding when it was given.) The account of Joseph Smith's calling to the ministry was not included in the first compilation of revelations, but was published later in the Pearl of Great Price. In this same pattern, as we noted before, if chapter 1 of Isaiah was given as a preface to the compilation of his writings, it could easily have been written sometime later than the other chapters of Isaiah.

There is still another similarity between Isaiah and the Doctrine and Covenants. Some of the early revelations in the Doctrine and Covenants were given to various individuals concerning the Lord's commandments for them in the work of the Restoration (see sections 6 through 19). Similarly, chapters 13 through 23 of Isaiah are prophecies concerning the nations surrounding Judah. Most of these are short revelations, as are most of the comparable revelations in the Doctrine and Covenants.

The preface to the Doctrine and Covenants, section 1, identifies the subject of the book as the voice of warning (the message of the gospel) to all men (verses 1-3). The plan is for that warning to go forth by the mouth of the Lord's disciples, by publication, and by the arm of the Lord being revealed in power (verses 4-16). And the purpose of the book is to fulfill various promises and blessings given by the prophets (verses 17-33). The first chapter of Isaiah also identifies the subject, the plan, and the purpose of the book of Isaiah, as shown in the following outline.

The opening verse of Isaiah is the early title of the book. It is comparable to the superscriptions which appear at the beginning of several books in the Book of Mormon and which are typical of Hebrew writing. But in the Bible these superscriptions have been incorporated into the first verse of the text.

1. The Subject: The Lord witnesses to all the earth that Israel has rebelled against him (1:2-4).
   a. They are not as responsive as are the animals (1:3).
   b. They are corrupted with iniquity (1:4).
   c. They have provoked the Lord to anger (1:4).
2. The Plan: Israel will be stricken and left desolate except for a small remnant (1:5-24).
   a. They will continue to revolt because the whole head (the leadership) is sick and the whole heart (the people) faint (1:5).
   b. They have done nothing to cure their all-encompassing wounds and bruises (1:6).
   c. Because their sacrifices are a mockery before God, he will not hearken to their prayers (1:10-15; compare D&C 101:6-7).
   d. The penitent are invited to reason with the Lord, who presents them with alternatives (1:16-20).
   e. Their sins have brought God's judgments upon them (1:21-24).
3. The Purpose: Israel will be purged and restored as a city of righteousness (1:25-31).
   a. Judges will be restored as at first (1:26).
   b. The converts will be redeemed with righteousness (1:27).
   c. The transgressors and sinners will be consumed with fire (1:28-31).

Notes and Commentary

According to Oliver Cowdery's account, when the angel Moroni appeared to Joseph Smith on 22 September 1823, he quoted five verses from Isaiah 1 which he said were about to be fulfilled. In speaking of the angel's explanation, Oliver said, "Isaiah, who was on the earth at the time the ten tribes of Israel were led away captive from the land of Canaan, was shown not only their calamity and affliction, but the time when they were to be delivered" (*MA*, Apr. 1835, pp. 109-10). There are also references in the New Testament and the Doctrine and Covenants which help us understand this chapter of Isaiah, as noted below.

Isaiah 1:7. According to Oliver Cowdery, Moroni quoted this verse as a prophecy of the scattering of the ten tribes of Israel. Oliver further stated that this prophecy followed a reproof of the corruption and blindness of Israel. (*MA*, Apr. 1835, p. 110).

Isaiah 1:8. The "cottage in the vineyard" or the "lodge in a garden of cucumbers" is generally thought to be a temporary shelter of branches and leaves for workers during the heat of the day or for watchmen during the night. After the harvest, the shelter falls into decay. The comparison of the "daughter of Zion" with this cottage or lodge indicates that the present harvest of Israel is ended. Her vines are not producing fruit for the Lord, so she is left desolate, a prey to the elements of the world.

Isaiah 1:9. Paul quotes this passage, in conjunction with Isaiah 10:22, as evidence that God would save a remnant of Israel to be his servants at a future time. The Old and New Testament readings of this passage are compared below. (*Note*: In this study, italics will be used to highlight differences between two or more texts, or to emphasize certain words or phrases. The standard biblical use of italics to denote words added by the King James translators has been ignored.)

Except the Lord of *hosts* had left *unto* us a *very small remnant*, we *should* have been as Sodom, and we should have been like unto Gomorrah. (Isaiah 1:9.)

And as Esaias said before, Except the Lord of *Sabaoth* had left us a *seed*, we had been as Sodoma, and been made like unto Gomorrha. (Romans 9:29.)

"The Lord of Sabaoth," as used in Romans, has the same meaning as "the Lord of hosts" used in Isaiah, but it is not the same as "Lord of the Sabbath" (see Mark 2:28). See Doctrine and Covenants 88:2 for a similar use in a modern revelation. The Romans text's "seed" has the same meaning as "a very small remnant."

Isaiah 1:16-17. President Joseph Fielding Smith taught that the word "wash" in verse 16 could well have had reference to baptism (*AQ* 1:51). Verses 16 and 17 are often cross-referenced to 1 Peter 3:11 because the phrases are similar. However, Peter seems only to be using the phraseology and not quoting Isaiah.

. . . cease to do evil; Learn to do well; seek judgment, relieve the oppressed. . . . (Isaiah 1:16-17.)

Let him eschew evil, and do good; let him seek peace, and ensue it. (1 Peter 3:11.)

Isaiah 1:18. Many of the modern Church leaders have referred to verse 18 to show that God invites man to consider his doctrine and reason with him. (See, for example, Bruce R. McConkie and John H. Vandenberg in CR, Apr. 1973, pp. 29, 34.) The same idea is found in D&C 50:10-12. Occasionally verse 18 is used to show that an individual can be cleansed from sin. Although a nation cannot repent unless the individuals within that nation repent, individual repentance is not the context of this passage in Isaiah, as interpreted by President Joseph Fielding Smith:

> This quotation from Isaiah is quite generally misunderstood. It is clear from a careful reading of this first chapter in Isaiah, that this remark had no reference to individuals at all, but to the House of Israel. . . .
>
> . . . So we see that this passage does not apply to individuals and individual sins. (*AQ*, 2:179-80.)

Isaiah 1:19-20. The blessing and cursing in verses 19 and 20 are repeated by the Lord in section 64 of the Doctrine and Covenants, with specific reference to the inhabitants of "the land of Zion in these last days."

If ye be willing and obedient, ye shall eat the good of the land:

But if ye refuse and rebel, ye shall be devoured with the sword: for the mouth of the Lord hath spoken it. (Isaiah 1:19-20.)

Behold, the Lord requireth the heart and a willing mind; and the willing and obedient shall eat the good of the land of Zion in these last days.

And the rebellious shall be cut off out of the land of Zion, and shall be sent away, and shall not inherit the land. (D&C 64:34-35.)

Isaiah 1:23-24. According to Oliver Cowdery, Moroni quoted these verses with reference to the iniquity of the ten tribes of Israel who were led captive from the land of Canaan. (See *MA*, Apr. 1835, p. 110.)

Isaiah 1:25-26. Oliver Cowdery said Moroni used these verses as a prediction of the future restoration of Israel. (See *MA*, Apr. 1835, p. 110.) Joseph Smith quoted the first half of verse 26 as a prophecy of the gathering of Israel in the latter days. (See *TPJS*, pp. 92-93.)

The Vision of Judah and Jerusalem 4

Isaiah 2-4

Before Nephi recorded these chapters of Isaiah upon his plates, he told us he did it so "that whoso of my people shall see these words may lift up their hearts and rejoice for all men" (2 Nephi 11:8). Three chapters of Isaiah are required to present his vision of Judah and Jerusalem. Parts of chapters 2 and 3 paint quite a dismal picture, but chapter 4 describes the final glorious condition of "the branch [or church] of the Lord."

Although Isaiah notes that he saw things concerning Judah and Jerusalem (2:1), his vision includes references to three different peoples and two different lands. He speaks of Judah in the land of Jerusalem, of the "daughters of Zion," and of the "branch of the Lord" in the land of Zion. The prophet Joseph Smith declared, "The prophets have spoken and written upon it [Zion]; but I will make a proclamation that will cover a broader ground. *The whole of America is Zion itself from north to south, and is described by the Prophets, who declare that it is the Zion where the mountain of the Lord should be, and that it should be in the center of the land.* When elders shall take up and examine the old prophecies in the Bible, they will see it." (*TPJS*, p. 362.) Thus, the "daughters of Zion" refer to those who inhabit the Americas.

The "branch of the Lord" spoken of by Isaiah consists of those who are "escaped of Israel" (those of Israel who will have escaped the judgments which are to come upon the world in the last days). He speaks of these as being from the daughters of Zion and from Jerusalem. Therefore, the three peoples include the inhabitants of Jerusalem in general, the inhabitants of Zion in general, and the specific group from Zion and Jerusalem who constitute the beautiful and glorious branch of the Lord. The two lands include the land of Jerusalem and the land of the Americas.

Justification for Isaiah's including people not of Judah and not living in Jerusalem in a vision of Judah and Jerusalem is shown in the Savior's words regarding Isaiah: "For surely he spake as touching all things concerning my people which are of the house of Israel; therefore it must needs be that he must speak also to the Gentiles" (3 Nephi 23:2). Just as it was necessary to speak to or about the Gentiles to show all things concerning the house of Israel, it was also necessary to speak to or about Zion to show the ultimate destiny of Judah. An understanding of that ultimate destiny of both branches of Israel will cause all of Israel to "lift up their hearts and rejoice for all men," fulfilling Nephi's purpose for including Isaiah's words in his writings.

The vision centers around the restoration of the gospel, the second coming of Christ, and the ushering in of his Millennial reign, but it also includes prophecies concerning Judah in Isaiah's own day. Since it is a vision of Judah and Jerusalem, this would be expected. Perhaps a detailed outline of the vision will help us see it as a unit.

1. The Lord will judge among nations and bring peace (2:2-5).
   a. The mountain of the Lord's house will be established in the tops of the mountains, and all nations will flow to it (2:2).
   b. Many people will go to the house of the God of Jacob to be taught (2:3).
   c. Out of Zion will go forth the law (2:3).
   d. The word of the Lord will go forth from Jerusalem (2:3).
   e. All nations will cease making weapons of war and will be at peace (2:4).
   f. The house of Jacob is invited to come and walk in the light of the Lord (2:5).

2. The Lord has forsaken his people, the house of Jacob, and they will be brought down (2:6-22).
   a. They seek after the philosophies and learning of men (2:6).
   b. Their hearts have turned to material things (2:7).
   c. They worship idols, the works of their own hands (2:8).
   d. They are lifted up in pride (2:9).
   e. The wicked hide because of their fear of the Lord (2:10-11).
   f. The day of the Lord will come upon all people everywhere and cause them to forsake their idols (2:12-18).
   g. The wicked will flee to the caves and the mountains because of fear (2:19-21).
   h. The people are admonished to stop following after man (2:22).
3. Jerusalem will fall because its inhabitants have rebelled against God (3:1-15).
   a. The Lord will take away their economic prosperity (3:1).
   b. He will take away their great leadership (3:2-3).
   c. Children, babes, and women will rule over Judah and oppress them (3:3-4, 12).
   d. Judah will resort to family leadership, but men will refrain from leading (3:6-7).
   e. Immorality even as in Sodom will cause their destruction, but the righteous will be saved (3:9-11).
   f. Because their leaders will cause them to err, the Lord will bring judgment upon their leaders (3:12-15).
4. Zion will also be smitten (3:16-4:1).
   a. Social conditions will bring the Lord's judgments (3:16-17).
   b. Religious conditions will bring the Lord's judgments (3:18-24).
   c. A great war will kill off the men, leaving seven women to one man (3:25-4:1).
5. The branch of the Lord will be beautiful and glorious in that day (4:2-6).

a. The Lord will cleanse Zion and Jerusalem (4:2-4).
b. He will protect every dwelling place and assembly of Zion (4:5-6).

NOTES AND COMMENTARY

All three of these chapters are quoted in their entirety in the Book of Mormon, and there are several significant retentions in the text preserved in Nephi's quoting from the plates of brass. There are also several passages from the Doctrine and Covenants and the New Testament and commentaries by modern Church authorities which help us better understand this vision.

Isaiah 2:2-3. The word "that" in verse 2, italicized by the King James scholars because they were unsure of the correct translation, is rendered "when" in the Book of Mormon and in the JST.

And it shall come to pass in the last days, *that* the mountain of the Lord's house shall be established in the top of the mountains, and shall be exalted above the hills; and all nations shall flow unto it. (Isaiah 2:2.)	And it shall come to pass in the last days, *when* the mountain of the Lord's house shall be established in the top of the mountains, and shall be exalted above the hills, and all nations shall flow unto it. (2 Nephi 12:2.)

This is a very significant retention from the plates of brass, as it specifies the time when the Lord would commence to establish the two nations of Israel in Zion and Jerusalem, which would lead to the ushering in of the Millennium.

While many Latter-day Saints believe that the establishment of "the mountain of the Lord's house" in the tops of the mountains represents the Salt Lake Temple, verse 2 has a broader application. The Zion of North and South America was labeled by some Old Testament prophets as the "everlasting hills" or the "ancient mountains" (see Genesis 49:26; Deuteronomy 33:15). This would suggest that Isaiah's prophecy relates to the whole continent, not just Salt Lake City. The first temple built in the "everlasting hills" in this dispensation was the Kirtland Temple in 1836, and the Lord appeared to the Prophet Joseph Smith and Oliver Cowdery in that temple on 3 April 1836 (see D&C 110).

President Charles Penrose taught that the Savior's second coming will occur in three phases: (1) his appearances in the temples of Zion, unbeknown to the rest of mankind; (2) his appearance to the distressed and nearly vanquished sons of Judah; and (3) his appearance in glory to the world (see *MS*, 10 Sept. 1859; as reprinted in *IE*, May 1957, pp. 326-27). Actually, there have already been several appearances of the Lord in his temples, since a temple is his holy house. Elder Harold B. Lee once stated: "I know that this is the Lord's work, I know that Jesus Christ lives, and that he's closer to this Church and appears more often in holy places than any of us realize excepting sometimes to those to whom he makes personal appearance. I know it and the time is hastening when he shall come again to reign as Lord of Lords and King of Kings." (Talk delivered at MIA June Conference, 29 June 1969, as printed in *Living Prophets for a Living Church* [Salt Lake City: The Church of Jesus Christ of Latter-day Saints, 1973], p. 119.)

Further, in answer to the Prophet Joseph Smith's yearning prayer—"When will Zion be built up in her glory, and where will thy Temple stand, unto which all nations shall come in the last days?" (see section heading for D&C 57)—the Lord designated the land of Missouri as the place of the city of Zion, and Independence, Missouri, as the center place for the temple unto which all nations should come (see D&C 57:1-3). Since the building of the New Jerusalem is to mark the gathering of all the tribes of Israel and the work of the Father in gathering his people from all the nations of the earth (see 3 Nephi 21:22-29), the building of the temple in Jackson County, Missouri, seems to be the final fulfillment of the prophecy of Isaiah that the mountain of the Lord's house would be established in the tops of the mountains. Thus Isaiah's prophecy commences with the building of the Kirtland Temple and extends to the future building of the temple in Independence, Jackson County, Missouri.

In a broader sense, the establishment of the kingdom of God occurred earlier, on 6 April 1830, and was the commencement of the fulfillment of the prophecy in Isaiah 2:2-3. The temple could not be built until the kingdom was established. According to Oliver Cowdery, the angel Moroni quoted Isaiah 2:1-4 to Joseph Smith in September 1823 as one of the prophecies which was about to be fulfilled (*MA*, Apr. 1835, p. 110). President Harold B. Lee once quoted Doctrine and Covenants 115:4-5 and said this clearly implied that the coming forth of the Church in this dispensation was the beginning of the fulfillment of Isaiah's prophecy (see CR, Apr. 1973, p. 5). Similarly, Elder Theodore M. Burton stated that the prophecy in Isaiah 2:2-3 was related to Daniel's prophecy of the establishment of the indestructible kingdom of God in the last days (see CR, Apr. 1971, p. 108).

However, the temple in Salt Lake City is the major forerunner of the temple in Independence, Missouri, and is the ensign lifted unto the nations until the time of the temple in Missouri. According to President Harold B. Lee, Elder Orson Pratt declared that the coming of the pioneers to the tops of the mountains was the beginning of the fulfillment of the prophecy in Isaiah 2:2-3: "With the coming of the pioneers to establish the Church in the tops of the mountains, our early leaders declared this to be the beginning of the fulfillment of that prophecy. Orson Pratt, one of the members of the Twelve, delivered an oration on that occasion, in which he declared that this was the beginning of the fulfillment of the prophecy that out of Zion should go forth the law and the word of the Lord from Jerusalem." (*Ensign*, Nov. 1971, p. 15; President Lee quoted Micah 4:1-2, which is virtually identical with Isaiah 2:2-3.) Elder S. Dilworth Young declared that Joseph Smith's prophecy about the Saints going to the Rocky Mountains was a fulfillment of Isaiah 2:2 (CR, Apr. 1974, pp. 88-89). And Elder LeGrand Richards has repeatedly taught that the Salt Lake Temple was the very one which Isaiah saw (see CR, Apr. 1967, p. 22; CR, Oct. 1970, pp. 61-62; CR, Apr. 1971, p. 143).

Isaiah's prophecy clearly designates two headquarters for the righteous children of Israel in the latter days: Zion and Jerusalem (see *DS*, 1:176). While the establishment of the Church in 1830 commenced the fulfillment of this prophecy, as shown above, the building of the temple in Salt Lake City was also a sign for the beginning of the Jerusalem headquarters. This was to be a slow process, but its commencement did closely parallel the movement of the Mormon pioneers to the West. The Salt Lake Temple was completed in 1893, after forty years of labor which was periodically interrupted. The Zionist Federation, an organization established to motivate the return of the Jews to Palestine, began in 1896, and its first conference was held in Basel, Switzerland, in 1897 (see *ST*, pp. 6-7). Just as the temple had been many years in the building, so had this movement of the Jews been under way for many years. In fact, the journey of Elder Orson Hyde (under the direction of the Prophet Joseph Smith) to dedicate Palestine for the return of the Jews was undoubtedly one of the early beginnings. It is of interest to note that Elder Hyde was sent a short time after the Kirtland Temple was completed. (The dedication took place on the Mount of Olives on 24 October 1841; see *HC*, 4:454-59.) With the establishment of both headquarters, the Church members were to gather to Zion and the Jews to Jerusalem: "Let them, therefore, who are among the Gentiles flee unto Zion. And let them who be of Judah flee unto Jerusalem, unto the mountains of the Lord's house." (D&C 133:12-13.) In the early days of the Church, however, Jews who were converted to the gospel were to gather in Zion rather than Jerusalem (see *TPJS*, p. 180).

Isaiah 2:3. While verses 2 and 3 are usually treated as one prophecy, there are some unique aspects of verse 3 which may be related to a later time than the establishment of the temple. Of course, the settlement of the Saints in the valleys of the Rocky Mountains brought people from many nations, but subsequent converts to the Church brought thousands more to those valleys from all over the world to "walk in his paths," as Elder LeGrand Richards has taught (see CR, Oct. 1962, p. 109). Elder Mark E. Petersen has also written of the influx of immigrants to the Rocky Mountains as a fulfillment of this prophecy. He also refers to the tourists who visit Salt Lake Temple Square and the Church general conferences as further fulfillment of Isaiah's prophecy that many people would say, "Let us go up to the mountain of the Lord." (See *Why the Religious Life* [Salt Lake City: Deseret Book Company, 1966], pp. 200-201.)

In verse 2, Isaiah says that "the Lord's house shall . . . be exalted above the hills." Elder Petersen has pointed out that all of the various translations of the Bible emphasize the "temple hill," and that most temples are built on eminent sites (see *Why the Religious Life*, pp. 305-7). Isaiah also said people would come to the house of the Lord to learn of his ways and "walk in his paths." Elder Gordon B. Hinckley has taught that as Latter-day Saints live the standards of the gospel, others will find the strength to follow their example and will do as Isaiah says (see CR, Oct. 1974, pp. 144-45). Elder Harold B. Lee once asked that the Lord continue to pour out his knowledge upon the Church and its members and all honorable people of the earth, that Christ might be the ensign to the world as prophesied by Isaiah (see CR, Apr. 1966, p. 68).

Elder Mark E. Petersen has identified the general conferences of the Church as a fulfillment of Isaiah's prophecy that "out of Zion shall go forth the law," especially as these conferences are broadcast to the world by radio and television (see *Why the Religious Life*, pp. 200-201, 305-7). However, President George Albert Smith taught a broader concept as he dedicated the Idaho Falls Temple. He taught that the "going forth" of the "law" is the establishment in the world of governments similar to "our constitutional form of government." In referring to this dedicatory prayer, President Harold B. Lee later said:

> I have often wondered what that expression meant, that out of Zion shall go forth the law. Years ago I went with the brethren to the Idaho Falls Temple, and I heard in that inspired prayer of the First Presidency a definition of the meaning of that term "out of Zion shall go forth the law." Note what they said: "We thank thee that thou hast revealed to us that those who gave us our constitutional form of government were men wise in thy sight and that thou didst raise them up for the very purpose of putting forth that sacred document [as revealed in Doctrine and Covenants, section 101]. . . .
>
> "We pray that kings and rulers and the peoples of all nations under heaven may be persuaded of the blessings enjoyed by the people of this land by reason of their freedom and under thy guidance and be constrained to adopt similar governmental systems, thus to fulfill the ancient prophecy of Isaiah and Micah that '. . . out of Zion shall go forth the law and the word of the Lord from Jerusalem.' " (*IE*, Oct. 1945, p. 564; *Ensign*, Nov. 1971, p. 15.)

The Prophet Joseph Smith also equated the "law" with the theocracy of God which will rule during the Millennium, as described in verse 4 (see *TPJS*, pp. 248-52). This great principle was alluded to by President Joseph Fielding Smith when he said that the word of the Lord would go forth from Zion and Jerusalem, not only to the members of the Church, but to all nations when the kingdom of God is fully established (see *DS*, 1:176). Elder Orson Pratt interpreted Isaiah's reference to "the law" as follows: " 'Out of Zion shall go forth the law,' says the prophet. What law? A law to regulate the nations, a law teaching them how to be saved, a law informing the kings and emperors and the nobles of the earth how they can save themselves, and how they can save their dead." (*JD*, 14:350.) These interpretations combine the political and spiritual aspects of the law.

Isaiah 2:4. This verse clearly depicts the judgments of God which will usher in the millennial reign (see Elder Bruce R. McConkie, CR, Oct. 1967, p. 43).

Isaiah 2:5. The Book of Mormon supplies the second half of the original verse, which has been lost from the Bible translations.

O house of Jacob, come ye, and let us walk in the light of the Lord. (Isaiah 2:5.)

O house of Jacob, come ye and let us walk in the light of the Lord; *yea, come, for ye have all gone astray, every one to his wicked ways.* (2 Nephi 12:5.)

This retention shows that there would be a complete apostasy upon the earth before the time of the establishment of the mountain of the Lord's house. Therefore, the people of Jacob are invited to walk in the light of the Lord which would be taught in his holy house.

Isaiah 2:9. The Book of Mormon retention of the word "not" in two different places in this verse makes it read sensibly.

And the mean man boweth down, and the great man humbleth himself: therefore forgive them not. (Isaiah 2:9.)

And the mean man boweth *not* down, and the great man humbleth himself *not*, therefore, forgive him not. (2 Nephi 12:9.)

There are some interesting apologies offered by various commentators in the Christian world, trying to justify the present-day Bible readings.

Isaiah 2:10.

Enter into the rock, and hide thee in the dust, for fear of the Lord, and *for* the glory of his majesty. (Isaiah 2:10.)

O ye wicked ones, enter into the rock, and hide thee in the dust, for the fear of the Lord and the glory of his majesty *shall smite thee*. (2 Nephi 12:10.)

The Book of Mormon phrase "O ye wicked ones" clearly identifies those who will be seeking to hide in the rocks and the dust for fear of the Lord and his glory. Both Paul (see 2 Thessalonians 1:7-9) and John the Revelator (see Revelation 6:15-16) foretold this same event. A similar situation existed following the Savior's ministry among the Jews, as he had prophesied (see Luke 23:22-30), but in that case the Jews hid for fear of the Romans during their conquest of Jerusalem in A.D. 70.

Isaiah 2:12.

For the day of the Lord of hosts *shall be* upon every one *that is* proud and lofty, and upon every one *that* is lifted up; and he shall be brought low: (Isaiah 2:12.)

For the day of the Lord of Hosts *soon cometh upon all nations, yea*, upon every one; *yea, upon the* proud and lofty, and upon every one *who* is lifted up, and he shall be brought low. (2 Nephi 12:12.)

In the Book of Mormon, retention of the phrase "soon cometh upon all nations, yea" replaces the italicized "shall be" in the KJV. This phrase establishes the time when this prophecy will be fulfilled—the day the Lord will appear in glory to the entire world.

Isaiah 2:13.

And upon all the cedars of Lebanon, *that* are high and lifted up, and upon all the oaks of Bashan, (Isaiah 2:13.)

Yea, and the day of the Lord shall come upon all the cedars of Lebanon, *for they* are high and lifted up; and upon all the oaks of Bashan; (2 Nephi 12:13.)

The Book of Mormon retention of the phrase "Yea, and the day of the Lord shall come" replaces the introductory "and" in the KJV, further verifying the time period.

Isaiah 2:14.

And upon all the high mountains, and upon all the hills that are lifted up, (Isaiah 2:14.)

And upon all the high mountains, and upon all the hills, *and upon all the nations which* are lifted up, *and upon every people*; (2 Nephi 12:14.)

The 2 Nephi reading retains two phrases, "upon all the nations" and "upon every people," more clearly showing the universal nature of the Lord's coming in glory.

Isaiah 2:16. The late Dr. Sidney B. Sperry, who should be credited for helping members of the Church understand Isaiah, made the following comment about this verse:

> In 2 Nephi 12:16 (cf. Isaiah 2:16) the Book of Mormon has a reading of remarkable interest. It prefixes a phrase of eight words not found in the Hebrew or King James versions. Since the ancient Septuagint (Greek) Version concurs with the added phrase in the Book of Mormon, let us exhibit the readings of the Book of Mormon (B.M.), the King James Version (K.J.), and the Septuagint (LXX) as follows:
>
> B.M. And upon all the ships of the sea,
> K.J.
> LXX And upon every ship of the sea,
>
> and upon all the ships of Tarshish
> And upon all the ships of Tarshish
>
> and upon all pleasant pictures.
> and upon all pleasant pictures.
> and upon every display of fine ships.
>
> The Book of Mormon suggests that the original text of this verse contained three phrases, all of which commenced with the same opening words, "and upon all." By a common accident, the original Hebrew (and hence the King James) text lost the first phrase, which was, however, preserved by the Septuagint. The latter lost the second phrase and seems to have corrupted the third phrase. The Book of Mormon preserved all three phrases. Scholars may suggest that Joseph Smith took the first phrase from the Septuagint. The prophet did not know Greek, and there is no evidence that he had access to a copy of the Septuagint in 1829-30 when he translated the Book of Mormon. (*The Voice of Israel's Prophets* [Salt Lake City: Deseret Book Company, 1965], pp. 90-91.)

Isaiah 2:19, 21. The Book of Mormon retains two phrases, "shall come upon them" and "shall smite them," in each of these verses.

And they shall go into the holes of the rocks, and into the caves of the earth, for fear of the Lord, and *for* the glory of his majesty, when he ariseth to shake terribly the earth. . . .	And they shall go into the holes of the rocks, and into the caves of the earth, for the fear of the Lord *shall come upon them* and the glory of his majesty *shall smite them*, when he ariseth to shake terribly the earth. . . .
To go into the clefts of the rocks, and into the tops of the ragged rocks, for fear of the Lord, and *for* the *glory* of his *majesty*, when he ariseth to shake terribly the earth. (Isaiah 2:19, 21.)	To go into the clefts of the rocks, and into the tops of the ragged rocks, for the fear of the Lord *shall come upon them* and the *majesty* of his *glory shall smite them*, when he ariseth to shake terribly the earth. (2 Nephi 12:19, 21.)

The first retention seems insignificant, but the last shows that all attempts to hide will be fruitless. The reversal of majesty and glory seems insignificant. The previous commentary on 2:10 is also applicable here, since the phrase "for the fear of the Lord and the glory of his majesty" is used in all three verses.

Isaiah 3:4. A possible identification of the "children" who were to rule over the house of Judah is drawn from the Prophet Joseph Smith's explanation of John the Baptist's scathing pronouncement to the Pharisees and Sadducees that "God is able of these stones to raise up children unto Abraham" (Matthew 3:9). Joseph Smith identified the "stones" as the Gentiles (see *TPJS*, p. 319). Perhaps the same designation could be applied here; historically, the Jews have been scattered among the Gentiles, who have ruled over them.

With regard to the "babes" who would rule over them, it should be remembered that Jacob had blessed Judah with the political leadership of all the house of Israel until the birth of Christ (see Genesis 49:8, 10). This leadership, of course, should have been exercised through the priesthood, as shown by the Prophet Joseph Smith in commenting upon the dominion given to Adam (see *TPJS*, p. 157). For "babes" (or "children," if the word does not refer to the Gentiles) to rule over Judah, they would rule without the priesthood. The fulfillment of this prophecy can be seen in the following tabulation of the reign of the seven kings who ruled from the death of Isaiah to the destruction of Jerusalem by Babylon in 589 B.C. (Book of Mormon dating):

King	*Age When Appointed*	*Years of Reign*	*Biblical Label of Character*
Manasseh	12	55	Evil (2 Kgs. 21:1-2)
Amon	22	2	Evil (2 Kgs. 21:19-20)
Josiah	8	31	Right (2 Kgs. 22:1-2)
Jehoahaz	23	3 mos.	Evil (2 Kgs. 23:31-32)
Jehoiakim	25	11 (3 yrs. as puppet king in Babylon)	Evil (2 Kgs. 23:36-37)
Jehoiachin	18 (2 Chr. 36:9 says 8 yrs)	3 mos. (under Babylon)	Evil (2 Kgs. 24:8-9)
Zedekiah	21	11	Evil (2 Kgs. 24:17-19)

Note that these kings were appointed between the ages of eight and twenty-five, and all but one were labeled "evil" in the Bible. The priesthood was not conferred until age thirty (see Numbers 4:3); Numbers 8:24 lists the age as twenty-five, but this may have referred to a preparatory five-year period). Numbers 3:1-13 says the priesthood was reserved for the Levites, but Joseph Smith taught that King David held it (*TPJS*, p. 339).

Isaiah 3:5-7. The only retention of significance in the Book of Mormon is in verse 6, the last phrase of which states "and let *not* this ruin *come* under thy hand."

When a man shall take hold of his brother of the house of his father, *saying*, Thou hast clothing, be thou our ruler, and let this ruin *be* under thy hand: (Isaiah 3:6.)	When a man shall take hold of his brother of the house of his father, *and shall say:* Thou hast clothing, be thou our ruler, and let *not* this ruin *come* under thy hand— (2 Nephi 13:6.)

The KJV has lost the word "not," which points to a desire to escape the coming ruin. This is apparently similar to the situation which came upon the wicked Nephites four years before the Savior visited them. The people divided one against the other and separated into tribes according to families, kindreds, and friends, not as a righteous patriarchal division but as an attempt for survival. (See 3 Nephi 7:1-14.)

Isaiah 3:9. People reflect what they are in their countenances, and the people of Judah could not hide their sins of immorality, which were even as the sins of Sodom. People also reflect their positive spiritual conditions; Alma described the born-again person as one who has received the image of Christ in his countenance (see Alma 5:14). Elder Marion D. Hanks used this passage in Isaiah to show that iniquities separate people from the Spirit (CR, Oct. 1973, p. 16), which would of course leave a countenance of evil upon their faces.

Isaiah 3:11. The Book of Mormon retains the phrase "for they shall perish" in place of "it shall be ill with him," much of which was italicized by the King James translators.

Woe unto the wicked! *it shall be ill with him:* for the reward of *his* hands shall be *given him.* (Isaiah 3:11.)	Wo unto the wicked, *for they shall perish*; for the reward of *their* hands shall be *upon them!* (2 Nephi 13:11.)

The sterner punishment is more consistent with other scriptures regarding the destruction of the wicked at the Second Coming (see, for example, D&C 101:23-24).

Isaiah 3:12. This verse refers to women ruling over Judah. Note that nothing derogatory is said about leadership by women per se, but obviously they would not be ruling with the priesthood. During Judah's dispersion among the Gentiles, there were undoubtedly many women who ruled over them, and in modern times Golda Meir served as modern Israel's prime minister.

Isaiah's statement about "children" oppressing Judah and causing them to err was used by Elder Ezra Taft Benson as a warning to the women of the Church against the sinful practices of birth control and abortion (see CR, Oct. 1970, p. 21).

Isaiah 3:15. President Harold B. Lee cited this passage in explaining the need for strong central authority in the Church to organize means to help the weak and provide for emergencies (see CR, Oct. 1971, p. 58).

Isaiah 3:16-24. The term "daughter of Zion" probably has more than one meaning, and must be interpreted in context each time it occurs in the scriptures. President Joseph Fielding Smith interprets the dress styles of our modern day as a fulfillment of Isaiah's prophecy (*AQ*, 5:172-74). The dictionary definitions of "haughty," "wanton," and "mincing" suggest that Isaiah could easily have been referring to the inhabitants of the Americas, the Zion spoken of by the Old Testament prophets. The haughty are defined as those who are proud of self and scornful of others. Wanton is defined as undisciplined, unmanageable, lewd. Mincing is defined as short, feminine steps or as plain speech. These definitions could apply to the attitudes and practices of many inhabitants of the Americas.

Many of the words in verses 18 through 23 may refer to religious garb of modern-day sectarians. These verses were designated in the chapter outline as a description of the religious conditions of Zion, and verses 16 and 17 as a description of the social conditions. These conclusions are based on the uses of those words according to modern dictionaries.

Isaiah 4:1. The JST and the Hebrew Bible place this verse in the previous chapter, where it fits the context much better. This condition will result from the war described in 3:25-26. While this verse has been interpreted by some as a prophecy of plural marriage in the Church, a close examination will show that it refers to the world, not the Church. The offer of marriage as described by Isaiah is not in keeping with the law of plural marriage as revealed in the Doctrine and Covenants. The proposal to marry (or merely live together) is made here by the woman. Under the Lord's law, the man would initiate the marriage (see D&C 132:58-61). The women described by Isaiah volunteer to remain economically independent rather than make the man responsible for their care while they multiply and replenish the earth, as under the Lord's law (see D&C 132:63 and Jacob 2:30). The innate desire of the woman to be a wife and a mother is noted in the phrase "to take away our reproach." To be childless was considered a reproach in ancient Israel (see Luke 1:25 and Genesis 30:23).

Isaiah 4:2-4. The beautiful and glorious "branch of the Lord" will not become such until after it is cleansed. The Doctrine and Covenants (112:23-26) declares that the Lord will commence his cleansing at his own house. General

Moroni also taught that the Lord had said the "inward vessel" must be cleansed first (see Alma 60:23).

Isaiah 4:5-6. The Book of Mormon retains the words "of Zion" near the end of verse 5:

And the Lord will create upon every dwelling place of mount Zion, and upon her assemblies, a cloud and smoke by day, and the shining of a flaming fire by night: for upon all the glory shall be a defence. (Isaiah 4:5.)	And the Lord will create upon every dwelling-place of mount Zion, and upon her assemblies, a cloud and smoke by day and the shining of a flaming fire by night; for upon all the glory *of Zion* shall be a defence. (2 Nephi 14:5.)

This is consistent with the beginning of the verse, and it suggests the protection of Zion and her stakes in a day when the world is in turmoil. For a fuller description of that time, see Doctrine and Covenants 45:63-75 and 84:2-5; the latter of these passages identifies the cloud as "the glory of the Lord." Note that there is more than one place for the assembly or gathering of the Saints. This is consistent with the Lord's admonition to stand in "holy places" when bloodshed, famine, plague, and other calamities sweep the earth (see D&C 87:6-8). It is also consistent with the following prophecy given by Joseph Smith:

> The time is soon coming, when no man will have any peace but in Zion and her stakes.
>
> I saw men hunting the lives of their own sons, and brother murdering brother, women killing their own daughters, and daughters seeking the lives of their mothers. I saw armies arrayed against armies. I saw blood, desolation, fires. The Son of Man has said that the mother shall be against the daughter, and the daughter against the mother. These things are at our doors. They will follow the Saints of God from city to city. Satan will rage, and the spirit of the devil is now enraged. I know not how soon these things will take place; but with a view of them, shall I cry peace? No; I will lift up my voice and testify of them. How long you will have good crops, and the famine be kept off, I do not know; when the fig tree leaves, know then that the summer is nigh at hand. (*TPJS*, p. 161.)

According to Oliver Cowdery, when the angel Moroni appeared to the Prophet Joseph Smith in September 1823, he quoted Isaiah 4:5-6 as one of the prophecies which was soon to be fulfilled (*MA*, Apr. 1835, p. 110). President Harold B. Lee quoted Doctrine and Covenants 115:4-6 as a prophecy of the time when members of the Church would gather to the stakes of Zion (rather than a specific place in the land of Zion) as a refuge from the storm and wrath which would be poured out upon the whole earth (see CR, Apr. 1973, p. 5).

Elder Orson Pratt taught that the cloud which Isaiah said would protect Zion and her stakes will be literal and will be even as the cloud which watched over Moses and the children of Israel:

> I believe this building is called a Tabernacle, and it will accommodate from twelve thousand to fifteen thousand persons, and it is a tolerably cool place for the people in the heat of summer, especially to be a shade in the day time from the heat, and for a place of refuge and a covert from storm and from rain and tempest. I do not think that storms or tempests would affect a congregation that might be assembled in the Lord's Tabernacle; but I wish particularly to call your attention to the preceding verse—"The Lord shall create upon every dwelling-place of Mount Zion, and upon all her assemblies, a cloud and smoke by day, and the shining of a flame or pillar of fire by night."
>
> I do not see any cloud covering this house, or the congregation that is before me. What is the reason? The time has not yet come. The time is to come when God will meet with all the congregation of his Saints, and to show his approval, and that he does love them, he will work a miracle by covering them in the cloud of his glory. I do not mean something that is invisible, but I mean that same order of things which once existed on the earth so far as the tabernacle of Moses was concerned, which was carried in the midst of the children of Israel as they journeyed in the wilderness.
>
> Did God manifest himself in that tabernacle that was built according to the pattern which he gave unto his servant Moses? He did. In what way? In the day time a cloud filled that tabernacle. The Lord intended his people to be covered with the cloud continually, and he intended to reveal himself unto them, and to show forth his glory more fully amongst them; but they sinned so much in his sight that he declared—"My presence shall not go up with this people, lest I should break forth upon them in my fury and consume them in a moment." Because of their wickedness he withdrew his

presence, and his glory in a great measure was taken from them; but still Moses was permitted to enter the tabernacle, and to behold the glory of God, and it is said that he talked with the Lord face to face—a blessing which God did intend to bestow upon all Israel had they kept his law and had not hardened their hearts against him.

But in the latter days there will be a people so pure in Mount Zion, with a house established upon the tops of the mountains, that God will manifest himself, not only in their Temple and upon all their assemblies, with a visible cloud during the day, but when the night shall come, if they shall be assembled for worship, God will meet with them by his pillar of fire; and when they retire to their habitations, behold each habitation will be lighted up by the glory of God,—a pillar of flaming fire by night.

Did you ever hear of any city that was thus favored and blessed since the day that Isaiah delivered this prophecy? No, it is a latter-day work, one that God must consummate in the latter times when he begins to reveal himself, and show forth his power among the nations. (*JD*, 16:82.)

The Parable of the Vineyard

5

Isaiah 5

This chapter appears to be a continuation of chapters 2 through 4, but is treated separately here because it can be read as an independent unit. It is one of the few parables in the Old Testament and uses imagery similar to that which Jesus used in several parables during his ministry among the Jews. The interpretation of the parable, also given by Isaiah, definitely identifies the vineyard as the house of Israel and the pleasant plant as the men of Judah. Such parables as the laborers in the vineyard (Matthew 20:1-16), the two sons (Matthew 21:28-32), the wicked husbandman (Matthew 21:33-44; Mark 12:1-11; Luke 20:9-18), the barren fig tree (Luke 13:6-9), and the true vine (John 15:1-8) all use the same imagery.

There is also a resemblance to the allegory of Zenos, which is recorded in the Book of Mormon (Jacob 5) and probably was once in the Old Testament record (see Romans 11:17-24). Both concern the whole house of Israel.

Isaiah's parable is followed by six warnings which seem related to the downfall of northern Israel, apparently given as a warning to Judah so she would be left without excuse. However, the warnings are also extended to the latter days, when the Lord will gather the righteous from the wicked unto Zion and Jerusalem. Following is a brief outline of the chapter:

1. The parable and the interpretation are given (5:1-7).

   a. The parable likens Israel to a vineyard (5:1-6).
   b. The interpretation is explained (5:7).
2. The six warnings are given (5:8-25).
   a. A warning is given against socialism (5:8-10).
   b. A warning is given against alcoholism (5:11-17).
   c. Israel is warned against gross dishonesty and a distorted value system (5:18-19).
   d. She is warned against a perverted moral code (5:20).
   e. There is a warning against pseudo-intellectualism (5:21).
   f. A warning is given against false and misleading advertising (5:22-23).
3. The Lord's hand is stretched out in judgment upon his people (5:24-25).
4. The ensign (Book of Mormon) is lifted to the nations (5:26-30).
   a. The messengers will come with speed (5:26-28).
   b. The prey will be carried away safely (5:29).
   c. Darkness will remain upon the land deserted by the righteous of Israel (5:30).

Notes and Commentary

The entire chapter is quoted in the Book of Mormon with several retentions in the text, only a few of which are significant. There is only one reference in the Doctrine and Covenants which relates to Isaiah chapter 5. There are several enlightenments upon the text given by modern-day Church authorities.

Isaiah 5:1. The Book of Mormon introduces the parable with the words "and then" in place of the KJV "now." This modification identifies the time period of chapter 5 as the same period spoken of in chapters 2 through 4. Both of these sections of Isaiah use the current situation in Isaiah's day as a basis for prophesying of the future.

Isaiah 5:2. The tower built in the midst of the vineyard could have been the temple built by Solomon. This inference is drawn from the latter-day parable concerning another tower (temple) which was to be built upon a "very choice piece of land" (Jackson County, Missouri) but has not yet been built (see D&C 101:43-62). (For this interpretation of the tower-temple, see Hyrum M. Smith and Janne M. Sjodahl, *Doctrine and Covenants Commentary*, rev. ed. [Salt Lake City: Deseret Book Company, 1967], p. 647.)

Isaiah 5:3-4. The declaration "what could have been done more to my vineyard" is the same phrase used by the master of the vineyard in the allegory of Zenos (see Jacob 5:47). Although Zenos refers to the whole vineyard, and not just the "pleasant plant" of Judah as designated by Isaiah, both conditions show that the Lord gives full opportunity within the framework of man's agency, wherein man must choose and do his part.

(*Note:* The commentary for 5:8-23 is offered in light of Nephi's admonition to liken the scriptures unto ourselves [see 1 Nephi 19:23]. These warnings refer to conditions similar to those which caused the destruction of Judah and Israel, and which will likewise bring the destruction of the wicked at the Second Coming.)

Isaiah 5:8-10. Most commentators say this warning was given against the land grabbers of Isaiah's day. However, a careful analysis of the text, especially as translated in the Book of Mormon, implies a much broader concept than the obtaining of land by a few rich or aspiring individuals.

Woe unto them that join house to house, *that lay field to field*, till there be no place, that they may be placed alone in the midst of the earth!	Wo unto them that join house to house, till there *can* be no place, that they may be placed alone in the midst of the earth!
In mine ears said the Lord of hosts, Of a truth many houses shall be desolate, *even* great and fair, without inhabitant.	In mine ears, said the Lord of Hosts, of a truth many houses shall be desolate, *and* great and fair *cities* without inhabitant.
Yea, ten acres of vineyard shall yield one bath, and the seed of an homer shall yield an ephah. (Isaiah 5:8-10.)	Yea, ten acres of vineyard shall yield one bath, and the seed of a homer shall yield an ephah. (2 Nephi 15:8-10.)

In the Book of Mormon text, the joining of "house to house" was a situation which would block the establishment of

Judah or the house of Israel, for "there *can* be no place, that they may be placed alone in the midst of the earth." This phrase and the joining of house to house both imply a form of central control. Referring to Isaiah's day and also as a warning to our own day, it appears that Judah was forfeiting her individual freedoms to a central government which was controlling the property. The result would be that Judah could not be "placed alone" but was to be scattered among the nations of the earth, which happened. (The Book of Mormon, for some unknown reason, leaves out the KJV phrase "that lay field to field".)

The Lord has always sought to gather his people, but when they have not hearkened to his commandments he has scattered them and left them desolate instead (see Helaman 7:17-19; 3 Nephi 10:4-7; Matthew 23:37-38). The result of the scattering of ancient Israel was that many "great and fair cities" were left desolate, "without inhabitant" (verse 9). Furthermore, the agricultural production of the area almost ceased, as Isaiah warned (verse 10). The yield of "ten acres of vineyard" was prophesied to be only "one bath" (8¼ gallons) and that of "the seed of an homer" (the equivalent of ten baths) only "an ephah" (the dry-measure equivalent of a bath). Thus the established vineyards would not be productive, as they would yield only one-tenth of the seed planted.

There is still a greater warning in these verses, however. In every dispensation the Lord has given the same commandment revealed to the Saints of this dispensation, to "seek to bring forth and establish the cause of Zion" (D&C 6:6). As Zion can be established only upon the law of consecration and stewardship (see D&C 78:1-7), and as consecration and stewardship must be based upon private ownership and individual initiative (see D&C 42:30-32; 51:1-5; 78:14), individual freedoms and the private ownership of property must be carefully protected. The land of America was preserved for these very purposes (see 3 Nephi 21:4). Zion cannot be established in a socialistic society where individuals own nothing.

Isaiah 5:11-17. The alcoholic is often identified as one who begins to drink "early in the morning," while the so-called social drinker has a drink in the evening before dinner or with a gathering of friends. The music which is usually associated with the alcoholic beverages is not that which invites the Spirit of the Lord, nor do those who operate drinking establishments regard the Lord's work or even his presence in the universe. Verse 13 notes the universal effect alcohol has in bringing captivity upon a nation. Both the honorable men (the leaders) and the multitude (the constituents) lose the knowledge of God and his work. Famine and thirst for the word of God (also described in Amos 8:11-12) come upon the land, causing those who depart this life for the next to swell the numbers in hell. However, God's judgments will destroy these iniquitous places and leave the isolated cities to become grazing lands for sheep.

Isaiah 5:18-19. The gross dishonesty and distorted value system accepted by some in our day labels a man a thief for petty stealing, but regards unscrupulous business deals involving thousands or millions of dollars as just good business. Such people justify their actions by asking for empirical evidence of the Lord's coming or of the validity of his teachings which condemn their actions.

Isaiah 5:20. Proponents of the so-called new morality teach that marriage is unnecessary and that premarital sex is not only allowable but desirable. Such teachers declare that those who would keep the law of chastity are under a disadvantage in marriage, thus calling evil good and good evil. In addition to chastity, many other standards of morality are also questioned. Elder Spencer W. Kimball once said that the infidelity of our day, and the movies, books, and magazines which glamorize the unfaithful husbands and wives and make them heroes and heroines, reminded him of this verse in Isaiah (see CR, Oct. 1962, p. 56).

Isaiah 5:21. This verse seems to refer to the pseudo-intellectualism of our day, wherein people rely solely upon their own wisdom instead of the Lord's (compare 2 Nephi 9:28-29). President N. Eldon Tanner cited this verse as a warning to the present day (see CR, Oct. 1968, p. 49).

Isaiah 5:22-23. The false and misleading advertising of our day fits Isaiah's description. Famous athletes, movie stars, and other celebrities are paid large sums of money to endorse products which may well be harmful. Such advertising leads people away from righteousness.

Isaiah 5:26. An ensign is a standard or a pennant to be seen by others. In 2 Nephi 29:2, the latter-day ensign is identified as the words of Nephi's seed, the Book of Mormon (compare D&C 115:5, 45:9). The word "hiss" has a connotation somewhat different from the present-day meaning. In the Book of Mormon, it is used to identify the going forth of the gospel to the ends of the earth (see 2 Nephi 29:2).

Isaiah 5:27-28. Elder LeGrand Richards has identified these verses as a description of the modern means of transportation which would carry the Lord's messengers to every nation:

> Since there were no such things as trains and airplanes in that day, Isaiah could hardly have mentioned them by name, but he seems to have described them in unmistakable words. How better could "their horses' hoofs be counted like flint, and their wheels like a whirlwind" than in the modern train? How better could "Their roaring . . . be like a lion" than in the roar of the airplane? Trains and airplanes do not stop for night. Therefore, was not Isaiah justified in saying: "none shall slumber nor sleep; neither shall the girdle of their loins be loosed, nor the latchet of their shoes be broken"? With this manner of transportation the Lord can really "hiss unto them from the end of the earth," that "they shall come with speed swiftly." (*A Marvelous Work and a Wonder* [Salt Lake City: Deseret Book Company, 1967], p. 236.)

Elder Richards later used these verses to show that Israel would be gathered with speed (CR, Oct. 1975, pp. 77-78). President Joseph Fielding Smith interpreted these verses the same way (see *DS*, 1:146). Elder Orson Pratt referred to the immigrants' coming to Salt Lake by railroad in two or three days, instead of the ninety or one hundred days it took before the railroad, as an example of Isaiah's prophecy being fulfilled (see *JD*, 16:84).

Isaiah 5:29-30. While verses 26 through 28 seem to describe the messengers sent to the nations, verses 29 and 30 describe the "prey" leaving these lands. The prey are those of Israel, missionaries or members, who, because of the persecution and tribulation which come against them and the turmoil in the land, will be fleeing to Zion for safety. This seems to be describing the fulfilling of the times of the Gentiles, when the gentile nations will completely reject the gospel. The gospel may be taken from these nations on an individual basis rather than from all of them at once (see Bruce R. McConkie, *Mormon Doctrine*, 2nd ed. rev. [Salt Lake City: Bookcraft, Inc., 1967], p. 722).

Isaiah's Call to the Ministry 6

Isaiah 6

This chapter is generally considered to be the first revelation given to Isaiah, although it is not the first chapter. This opinion is based on Isaiah's recounting in this chapter of his call to the ministry through a personal vision of the Lord. This being true, verse 1 also dates the beginning of Isaiah's ministry in the year that King Uzziah died (758 or 740 B.C.; see chapter 14 for a discussion of chronological differences). A symbolic description of the Lord, Isaiah's calling and his mission, and a prophecy of the future are outlined in the overview below.

1. The vision of the Lord is described (6:1-4).
   a. The seraphim are above the throne of the Lord (6:2-3).
   b. The posts of the door and the house are described (6:4).
2. Isaiah is cleansed and called of the Lord (6:5-8).
   a. Isaiah recognizes his need to be cleansed (6:5).
   b. The seraphim pronounce him cleansed (6:6-7).
   c. The Lord calls and Isaiah responds (6:8).
3. Isaiah is called to the ministry (6:9-12).
   a. He is to proclaim truth to "this people" (6:9-10).
   b. He is to go forth until the land is desolate (6:11-12).
4. Isaiah is told that a tenth will return (6:13).

Notes and Commentary

This chapter is quoted in its entirety in the Book of Mormon, with several slight differences but only two significant retentions. Several New Testament and Doctrine and Covenants references help us see the meaning of this chapter. Verses 9 and 10 are referred to six times in the New Testament. Surprisingly, chapter 6 has seldom been quoted or commented on by modern-day Church leaders.

Isaiah 6:1-4. John the Revelator, whose mission was similar to Isaiah's, described his vision in the same figurative terms (see Revelation 4:2, 8). In describing John's revelation, the Prophet Joseph Smith told us that the eyes and the wings represent the light and knowledge of God and his power to move and act (see D&C 77:2-4). Isaiah 6:2 and Doctrine and Covenants 38:1 undoubtedly refer to the angelic hosts of heaven (the suffix *im* is plural masculine in the Hebrew). Revelation 15:8 identifies the smoke which filled the house as being from the glory of God.

Isaiah 6:5. Isaiah's awareness of his uncleanness or unworthiness to be in the presence of God is not a unique experience. Peter felt this unworthiness when he recognized the divinity of the Savior, even when the Lord was not attended by glory (see Luke 5:4-9). Moses acknowledged his nothingness following his vision of the earth and its inhabitants (see Moses 1:9-10). The subjects of King Benjamin fell to the earth and pleaded for the atoning blood of Christ to cleanse them from their carnal state when the king taught them of the Savior's atonement (see Mosiah 4:1-2).

Isaiah 6:6-7. The live coal would be analogous to the cleansing of the Holy Ghost referred to by Moroni in the Book of Mormon (see Moroni 6:4).

Isaiah 6:8. Isaiah's volunteering exemplifies the great desire one feels to serve the Lord when one comes under the influence of his Spirit. Peter was determined to follow Christ wherever he went, even to the laying down of his own life (see John 13:36-37). It is true that he later denied the Savior, as Christ had prophesied; but after the Holy Ghost came upon Peter, he did lay down his life for Christ.

Isaiah 6:9-10. The Book of Mormon helps us with these two difficult verses. It indicates that the people to whom Isaiah was sent would fail to understand his message of their own accord.

And he said, Go, and tell this people, Hear ye indeed, but *understand* not; and see ye indeed, but *perceive* not. (Isaiah 6:9.)	And he said: Go and tell this people—Hear ye indeed, but *they understood* not; and see ye indeed, but *they perceived* not. (2 Nephi 16:9.)

The "making fat" of thc hearts of the people seems to refer to Isaiah's being called to make the truth so plain that they would have to accept it or harden their hearts against it. This was how the Lord hardened Pharaoh's heart in Egypt, according to Brigham Young and Willard Richards:

> God has promised to bring the house of Israel up out of the land of Egypt at his own appointed time; and with a mighty hand and an outstretched arm, and great terribleness (Deut. xxvi, 8.) He chose to do this thing that His power might be known and his name declared throughout all the earth, so that all nations might have the God of heaven in remembrance, and reverence his holy name; and to accomplish this it was needful that He should meet with opposition to give Him an opportunity to manifest His power; therefore He raised up a man, even Pharaoh, who, He foreknew, would harden his heart against God of his own free will and choice, and would withstand the Almighty in His attempt to deliver His chosen people, and that to the utmost of his ability; and he proved himself worthy of the choice, for he left no means unimproved which his wicked heart could devise to vex the sons of Abraham, and defeat the purposes of the Most High, which gave the God of Abraham an opportunity to magnify his name in the ears of the nations, and in sight of this wicked king, by many mighty signs and wonders, sometimes even to the convincing of the wicked king of his wickedness, and of the power of God, (Exod. viii: 28, etc.) and yet he would continue to rebel and hold the Israelites in bondage; and this is what it meant by God's hardening Pharaoh's heart. He manifested Himself in so many glorious and mighty ways, that Pharaoh could not resist the truth without becoming harder; so that at last, in his madness, to stay the people of God, he rushed his hosts into the Red Sea and they were covered with the floods. (*HC*, 4:263-64.)

The Prophet Joseph Smith changed the verses in Exodus which state that the Lord hardened Pharaoh's heart to read that Pharaoh hardened his own heart, but here we see that Pharaoh did it against the obvious truth of the Lord. The last half of Isaiah 6:10 may be misread that the Lord does not want the people to be converted and healed. The real meaning of the last part of the verse, as it is fully quoted in the New Testament, is a declaration that the people did not *want* to understand, lest they should be converted so that the Lord could heal them.

And he said, Go, and tell this people, Hear ye indeed, but understand not; and see ye indeed, but perceive not.	Saying, Go unto this people, and say, Hearing ye shall hear, and shall not understand; and seeing ye shall see, and not perceive:	And in them is fulfilled the prophecy of Esaias, which saith, By hearing ye shall hear, and shall not understand; and seeing ye shall see, and shall not perceive:
Make the heart of this people fat, and make their ears heavy, and shut their eyes; lest they see with their eyes, and hear with their ears, and understand with their heart, and convert, and be healed. (Isaiah 6:9-10.)	*For* the heart of this people is waxed gross, and *their ears are dull of hearing*, and *their eyes have they closed*; lest they should see with their eyes, and hear with their ears, and understand with their heart, and should be converted, and *I should heal them.* (Acts 28:26-27.)	*For* this people's heart is waxed gross, and *their ears are dull of hearing*, and *their eyes they have closed*; lest *at any time* they should see with their eyes, and hear with their ears, and *should* understand with their heart, and should be converted, and *I should heal them.* (Matthew 13:14-15.)

In other words, these people did not want to know the truth. They enjoyed living in sin and did not want to be converted and to change their life-style. Paul further verifies this by stating "that the salvation of God is sent unto the Gentiles, *and that they will hear it*" (Acts 28:28).

Isaiah 6:13. The Book of Mormon retains two words which give a more complete understanding of this verse:

But yet *in it* shall be a tenth, and it shall return, and shall be eaten: as a teil tree, and as an oak, whose substance is in them, when they cast their leaves: so the holy seed shall be the substance thereof. (Isaiah 6:13.)	*But yet there* shall be a tenth, and *they* shall return, and shall be eaten, as a teil-tree, and as an oak whose substance is in them when they cast their leaves; so the holy seed shall be the substance thereof. (2 Nephi 16:13.)

This is clearly a prophecy that, although the cities of Judah will be destroyed and the inhabitants scattered, a remnant of that "holy seed" will return to inhabit the land. Further light is shed upon the phrase "shall be eaten" by a marginal reading in the KJV: "when it is returned, and hath been broused." This has reference to a purging of those who are to be scattered. Isaiah's analogy of a tree's being pruned by animals eating the leaves, and by the natural casting off of the dead leaves, indicates that the tenth to return will be of a new generation.

The Immanuel Prophecy

7

Isaiah 7

Probably the most widely known prophecy of Isaiah is found in chapter 7, but very few people understand its historical setting. From the viewpoint of biblical criticism, this lack of understanding has resulted in several problems associated with the prophecy of a virgin conceiving and giving birth to Immanuel. This prophecy and the problems related to it will be discussed later in the notes and commentary.

Isaiah 7 is one of the few chapters which can be assigned a definite chronological setting. The setting is Judah's threatened wars with Syria and Ephraim (the northern kingdom of Israel) about 734 B.C. or 742 B.C., depending on which chronology is followed. King Ahaz is counseled by Isaiah against seeking help from foreign powers and is given the famous Immanuel prophecy. Chapter 7 also contains several other prophecies, shown in the following outline.

1. Syria and Ephraim threaten to war against Judah (7:1-2).
   a. The enemy has not prevailed against Judah (7:1).
   b. The king and the people are greatly concerned (7:2).
2. The Lord sends Isaiah to Ahaz with a message not to fear (7:3-9).
   a. The threatened conquest will not come to pass (7:3-7).
   b. Ephraim shall not be a people within sixty-five years (7:8).
3. The Lord gives Ahaz a sign (7:10-17).
   a. Ahaz rejects the offer of a sign (7:10-12).

   b. The Lord gives him a sign anyway (7:13-15).
   c. The lands of Ephraim and Syria will both be forsaken of their kings before eight years pass (7:16).
4. The kings of Assyria and Egypt will punish Ahaz and Judah (7:17-25).
   a. A simpler life will replace the agricultural emphasis (7:21-23).
   b. The land will become briers and thorns; hunters will roam and animals will graze where there once was cultivated land (7:24-25).

Notes and Commentary

The entire chapter is quoted in the Book of Mormon with several slight differences, none of which are significant. The famous Immanuel prophecy is quoted by Matthew, but there are no other references to this chapter in the Doctrine and Covenants or the New Testament. There are many references made by General Authorities to the Immanuel prophecy (but not to other verses in this chapter). Most of these are simply the quoting of the prophecy as evidence that Isaiah had foretold the birth of the Savior.

Isaiah 7:3. The Lord's commandment for Isaiah to take his son Shearjashub with him to meet Ahaz is apparently purposeful. A marginal note in the KJV shows the meaning of his son's name to be "The remnant shall return." This meaning comes from the prophecy given by the Lord to Isaiah at the time of his call (6:13). The son's presence may have served either of two purposes. It may have been to remind Ahaz of the prophecy that Judah would not be utterly destroyed, or it may have been a reminder that the Lord had prophesied concerning Judah in order to prepare Ahaz for the prophecy which Isaiah was to deliver.

Their meeting at the "upper pool" may have not been coincidental either. Many biblical scholars have suggested that Ahaz was there inspecting the water supply and deciding how to protect it from the two invading forces. If this was the case, Ahaz's thinking on these matters would also prepare him to receive the prophecy Isaiah had been sent to deliver.

Isaiah 7:4. The designation of the two kings as "the two tails of these smoking firebrands" also carries meaning. A firebrand was a torch. The description of these two kings as tails which are smoking indicates that their strength had been spent, as a torch smokes only when it is burned out.

Isaiah 7:8-9. Here is the first prophecy uttered by Isaiah, and the reason for which Ahaz is not to fear. While Syria is to continue as a country with Damascus as its capital and King Rezin as its ruler, Judah's other enemy, Ephraim (the northern ten tribes of Israel), will not even be a people within sixty-five years. A KJV marginal note renders verse 9 somewhat more clearly: "Do ye not believe? It is because ye are not stable."

This prophecy was fulfilled, but exactly when is not certain. Several cities of the Northern Kingdom were captured by Tiglathpileser shortly following this prophecy, and the inhabitants were carried captive into Assyria (see 2 Kings 15:29). Ahaz did not begin his reign until the seventeenth year of Pekah, king of Israel (see 2 Kings 16:1). Since Pekah's reign was only twenty years long, this conquest would have occurred shortly after Isaiah's prophecy. Hoshea succeeded Pekah as king of Israel, and in the sixth year of his reign, Shalmaneser, king of Assyria, captured Samaria, the capital of Israel. Three years later Shalmaneser carried many more of the children of Israel captive into Assyria (see 2 Kings 17:3-6, 23). This happened following the death of Ahaz, but at least within twelve years of the time of Isaiah's prophecy. At this time, Shalmaneser brought in men from Babylon and Syria and placed them in the city of Samaria (see 2 Kings 17:24).

This marks the end of the occupancy of Samaria by the northern tribes of Israel. But did they exist longer as "a people"? Some writers refer to still another conquest by Assyria wherein King Manasseh was captured by the king of Assyria and carried captive into Babylon (see 2 Chronicles 33:11). This last conquest is very close to the precise sixty-five-year prophecy. However, the capture of King Manasseh has to do with Judah, not northern Israel, and consequently does not apply to the prophecy. Other writers acknowledge this and explain that Isaiah was just using a broad number of years to pronounce the end of the northern kingdom of Israel. There is yet another consideration. The ten northern tribes remained in Assyria for an undetermined number of years and then were led farther into the north (see 2 Esdras 13:39-48; compare D&C 133:26-34). These people have since been known as the lost tribes of Israel and are still not identified. The time of their being led into the north may also figure into the sixty-five-year period spoken of by Isaiah. While the chronology may be uncertain, there is no uncertainty that the prophecy was fulfilled.

Isaiah 7:10-12. Obviously Ahaz was not a believer, because he sent to the king of Assyria for help (see 2 Kings 16:7). Ahaz's disbelief is indicated in Isaiah 7:9, and verse 11 is further evidence of his reluctance to follow the admonition of the Lord. The Lord challenges him to ask for a sign "either in the depth, or in the height above." The RSV renders this phrase "let it be deep as Sheol or high as heaven." In other words, let it be from the spirit world or from God in heaven. Ahaz gives an interesting rationalization for his refusal, quoting Deuteronomy 6:16 to justify his actions. The irony of quoting a scripture out of context in refusing to follow the prophet of the Lord further exemplifies his disbelief.

Isaiah 7:13-16. Bible critics have questioned, explained away, and apologized for the Immanuel prophecy. Many even argue that this is not a messianic prophecy, but relates to an event at the time of Isaiah: a young woman (these scholars reject the translation "virgin") was to give birth to a child, and before the child was very old the kings of Syria and Ephraim would be taken away. They suggest further that Matthew was overzealous in using Old Testament prophecies to convince the Jews of the Messiah and should not have used this passage. Others argue that this is a dual prophecy; there was a young woman in Isaiah's day who was to give birth to a child, but the passage was also applicable to the birth of the Son of God. There are still others who have carefully defended the prophecy as a messianic one (see Edward J. Young, *The New International Commentary on the Old Testament. The Book of Isaiah* [Grand Rapids, Mi.: William B. Eerdmans, 1965], pp. 277-95).

As Latter-day Saints, we have a great advantage in addition to the work of the scholars. Not only is this passage quoted in the Book of Mormon, but we have the record of Nephi's vision of a beautiful virgin, exceedingly fair and white, who was carried away in the Spirit and who returned bearing the Son of God in her arms (see 1 Nephi 11:13-21). We also have the prophecy of Alma that a virgin in the land of Jerusalem was to be the mother of the Son of God (Alma 7:10). Elder Hugh B. Brown considered Matthew's quoting of Isaiah 7:14 an evidence that Isaiah was prophesying of the Savior's birth (see CR, Oct. 1960, p. 93), which refutes the theory of Matthew's overzealousness presented by some scholars. Elder Mark E. Petersen pointed to the recognition of Christ by the shepherds and the wise men from the east, the heralding of this birth by the angelic host, and King Herod's decree to kill the male children of Bethlehem as evidence of the fulfillment of Isaiah's prophecy (see CR, Oct. 1965, p. 60). In spite of the advantage of modern revelation, however, we still need to be able to understand and explain the famous Immanuel prophecy of Isaiah.

Only one verse of the prophecy is usually cited—verse 14—and that out of context. The prophecy is explainable and is shown to be messianic when quoted in its entirety and in context. Ahaz had refused to listen to Isaiah and had refused a sign from the Lord. Therefore, the prophecy uttered by Isaiah was directed, not to Ahaz, but to all the house of David. Whether there were others present at the time is immaterial. Ahaz, as the king of Judah, had rejected the prophecy. In so doing he had "wearied" Isaiah, a man, but was also wearying God, who had promised David that "thy kingdom shall be established for ever" (2 Samuel 7:16). The King of kings was to come through Judah and David's lineage (see Genesis 49:10), so any appointed king who would believe and live righteously would be supported and sustained by the Lord himself. The second prophecy uttered by Isaiah in this chapter, then, is both a reminder of this promise to Judah and David and a declaration of how the Lord would bring about its fulfillment in spite of a wicked king or a wicked generation. The Lord would bring this about through the miraculous conception of a God (Immanuel means "God with us") and the birth of that God unto a virgin. The coming of Christ was a well-known prophecy. All of the ancient prophets (in both the Old Testament and the Book of Mormon) knew and foretold of Christ's coming (see Jacob 4:4;

7:11; Luke 24:27, 44). It may even be that Isaiah was quoting here a prophecy that had been previously given. The point was that, even if Ahaz rejected the counsel and advice of Jehovah through his prophet, and even if Ahaz led his people into captivity, the Lord Immanuel would still come as had been prophesied.

Verse 15 indicates that Immanuel's diet was to be curd and honey. Some commentators regard this diet as that of the caravan, representing the plain and simple life of the Savior, who was not obligated to the aristocracy of his day. Others interpret the "curd and honey" to be symbolic of the royal diet. Perhaps there is a dual prophecy here. The diet of the inhabitants of the land was to become curd and honey (see note on Isaiah 7:17-25). Jesus' birth into the poorer class of people would make this his diet; this suggests a temporal meaning of the passage. A spiritual interpretation would be that Jesus was royalty, the Son of God, through the lineage of King David, and was thus entitled to the revelation from his Father to "know to refuse the evil, and choose the good," to be tempted in all things and yet be without sin (see Hebrews 4:15; D&C 20:22).

Isaiah then gives a further prophecy which may be considered a continuation of the second one. "For before the child shall know to refuse the evil, and choose the good, the land that thou abhorrest shall be forsaken of both her kings." While this has been the problem verse to many critics in relating the Immanuel prophecy to the life of Christ, the problem is resolved in the context of the historical situation. Isaiah had given a prophecy to all of Judah concerning the house of David. He now comes back to the situation at hand, the problem of Syria and Ephraim. Most of the critics have assumed that the child spoken of in verse 16 is the same child spoken of in verses 14 and 15. Could not the child in verse 16 be *any* child? A child is accountable at age eight in the eyes of the Lord (see D&C 68:25). In his first eight years he is to learn to distinguish between good and evil. Therefore, Isaiah could be prophesying that the kings of Syria and Ephraim are both going to be forsaken of their kings in less than eight years. This prophecy was also fulfilled: Pekah was killed by the conspiracy of Hoshea about three years after Ahaz was appointed king (see 2 Kings 15:30), and Rezin, the king of Syria, was killed by the Assyrians in response to Ahaz's plea for help as they went up and took Damascus (see 2 Kings 16:9). Thus within three years both the kings Ahaz feared were removed, and the third prophecy of Isaiah was fulfilled.

As the Brethren have spoken in general conferences, their references to this chapter have been limited to verse 14, which is almost always quoted to show that Isaiah foresaw or foretold the day of the Savior's birth. There is one exception to this: Elder Henry D. Taylor once referred to the missionary slogan which the late Elder B. H. Roberts adopted when he served as mission president. The slogan was "Immanuel," which of course means "God be with us." President Roberts also used this slogan in his discourses, in his correspondence, in autographing books and photos, and on numerous other occasions, according to Elder Taylor's report (see CR, Oct. 1975, p. 93).

Isaiah 7:17-25. The prophet Isaiah now utters a fourth prophecy. King Ahaz wants to ask the king of Assyria to come and help him. Isaiah prophesies that the Lord is going to bring the king of Assyria upon Ahaz and all of Judah. The king's coming against them would be the worst devastation they had experienced since the twelve tribes had divided into the two nations of Ephraim and Judah (approximately 975 B.C.). The prophecy states that the land which has been cultivated for agricultural purposes will be left uncultivated following the Assyrian conquest. The fly and the bee are usually interpreted to be the armies of Egypt and Assyria, which would come upon Judah as a swarm. However, the invasion by Egypt is historically questionable. The prophecy therefore seems to refer to literal swarms of flies and bees inhabiting the land. The fly was and still is notorious in Egypt, and the honeybee was apparently notorious in Assyria. When the land remains uncultivated, the Lord will bring the insects from these lands, where they will find a permanent home in the desolate valleys. The Lord's "shaving with a razor that is hired" symbolizes the comfort of having someone else perform a tedious or unpleasant task, such as shaving every morning, and the Lord's using the king of Assyria to do the unpleasant task of punishing the wickedness of Judah. This punishment will be very thorough, as the whole body (land of Judah) will be shaved. Following the devastating "shaving" of the agricultural land, it will be used to graze a few animals. The cow will produce milk, which will be used for making butter, and the honey gathered from the bees will supplement the diet. The main diet for the few nomadic people who remain upon the land will then be milk, or butter, and honey. Thus the land will become a land of milk and honey. The vineyards will be left unpruned or uncared for and will quickly turn into briers and thorns, and only the hunters shall go among them seeking wild animals for food. Small areas will be digged with the mattock (the hoe) for a few vegetables, but the formerly cultivated land will be primarily a grazing land for a few cattle. When Assyria came and conquered northern Israel, she also came upon the regions round about Jerusalem and thus fulfilled this prophecy. Isaiah 8 also prophesies of Assyria's coming upon Judah during the conquest of Israel.

The Lord Shall Recover His People

8

Isaiah 8-12

Chapters 8 through 11 are one continuous revelation, and chapter 12 is a concluding song of praise unto Jehovah. Chapter 11 should be of special significance to Latter-day Saints because the angel Moroni quoted it to Joseph Smith in September 1823 and said it was about to be fulfilled. The historical setting for the beginning of the revelation is the same as in chapter 7; whereas chapter 7 was given to Ahaz and those few who were with him, chapter 8 appears to say the same thing to a broader audience—all of Judah. It concerns the fate of the kings of Syria and Israel and the coming onslaught of the king of Assyria upon Judah.

Chapter 9 continues from the Assyrian conquest prophesied in chapter 8 to the time period of Christ's personal ministry. Chapter 10 predicts Israel's rejection of Christ in the meridian of time, her dispersion among the Gentiles, the Gentiles' subsequent rejection of Christ and his gospel, and the return of the remnant of Israel from under the yoke of the Gentiles. A more detailed outline of this long revelation follows.

1. Syria and Ephraim will be conquered by Assyria (8:1-4).
    a. The conquest will be written on a great scroll (8:1).
    b. There are two witnesses of the written prophecy (8:2).
    c. Isaiah's son is a sign of the time period (8:3-4).
2. The people of Judah will also be punished by Assyria (8:5-8).

a. They refuse Shiloah and yet rejoice in the defeat of Syria and Ephraim (8:6).
b. The Lord will bring up Assyria like a mighty river overflowing all the land (8:7-8).

3. Those countries which have come against Israel shall also be punished (8:9-10).

4. Isaiah is commanded not to preach to Israel but to stand as a witness (8:11-22).
   a. Isaiah is to trust in the Lord (8:13).
   b. Both houses of Israel will stumble over Christ (8: 14-15).
   c. Isaiah is to seal up the law among the disciples (8:16).
   d. Isaiah has spoken and will wait upon the Lord (8:17-18).
   e. The various sources of spiritualism must be measured against the law and the prophets (8:19-20).
   f. The eventual result will be darkness and anguish (apostasy) (8:21-22).

5. The darkness will not last forever (9:1-7).
   a. A light will come forth in various lands of Israel (9:1-2).
   b. Joy will come as the yoke of the oppressor is broken (9:3-5).
   c. The Son of God will come to the throne of David (9:6-7).

6. Judah is warned of the evils which brought God's destroying judgments upon Ephraim (9:8-10:4).
   a. The Lord warns against pride and stoutness of heart (9:9-12).
   b. Judah's leaders cause the people to err (9:13-17).
   c. Wickedness encompasses as a fire (9:18-21).
   d. The poor and the needy are neglected (10:1-4).

7. The Lord will accomplish his purposes through the Gentiles (10:5-19).
   a. He will send Assyria against Israel (10:5-6).

   b. The king of Assyria will not recognize the Lord but will boast in himself (10:7-11).
   c. The Lord will punish the Assyrians following his judgments upon Israel and Judah (10:12-19).

8. In the times of the Gentiles, the Lord will return a remnant of Israel (10:20-34).
   a. The Lord's people who dwell in Zion will not be afraid of the Assyrian (Gentile) (10:24-26).
   b. The burden of the Gentiles will be broken off (10:27-34).

9. A rod will come out of the stem of Jesse, and a branch shall grow out of his roots (11:1-9).
   a. The Spirit of the Lord will rest upon the rod (the servant of the Lord) (11:2-3).
   b. The earth will be smitten with the word of his mouth (11:4).
   c. Peace and knowledge will be restored to the earth (11:5-9).

10. A root of Jesse will stand as an ensign (11:10-16).
    a. The Gentiles will seek this ensign (the book of Mormon or The Church of Jesus Christ of Latter-day Saints) (11:10).
    b. The Lord will set his hand a second time to recover the dispersed of Judah (11:11-12).
    c. The envy between Judah and Ephraim shall depart, and they will inhabit all the promised land of Abraham. (11:13-14).
    d. The Lord will work miracles in their behalf (11:15).
    e. The remnant which left from Assyria (the ten tribes) will return (11:16).

11. A song of praise will be sung to Jehovah in the day of Israel's restoration (12:1-6).
    a. Jehovah is Israel's strength and salvation (12:2).
    b. Israel will draw water from the well of salvation (12:3).
    c. Israel will praise his name among all the people of the earth (12:4-6).

NOTES AND COMMENTARY

All of these chapters are quoted in their entirety in the Book of Mormon, with parts of chapter 11 quoted twice. Most of the many variations between the Book of Mormon text and the KJV are insignificant. When the angel Moroni quoted the entire eleventh chapter to Joseph Smith, he said it was soon to be fulfilled. There are several quotations from these chapters in the Doctrine and Covenants and the New Testament, and a few quotations from the modern-day prophets and Church leaders.

Isaiah 8:1-3. A marginal note in the KJV gives the meaning of Maher-shalal-hash-baz as "In making speed to the spoil he hasteneth the prey." This name, which Isaiah was to write upon a great roll, was a witness of the speed with which Assyria was to take Syria and Ephraim. The law of witnesses (see Deuteronomy 19:15; Matthew 18:16) is fully exemplified by the prophet Isaiah's saying that two witnesses would observe what he recorded upon the scroll, and by the Lord's giving Isaiah's son a name which would symbolize the Assyrian conquest.

Isaiah 8:4. The Lord says that before the infant can cry "mother" or "father," the prophecy will be fulfilled. That would be two or three years at the most. Assyria's conquest of Israel took place within three years of the beginning of the reign of Ahaz (see note on Isaiah 7:14), so this prophecy was literally fulfilled. Since the longer time period of a child's accountability was used in Isaiah 7:16, it is assumed that the giving of this prophecy followed that one chronologically.

Isaiah 8:6-8. Having foretold the future of Israel, the kingdom to the north, the Lord now prophesies Judah's future. Isaiah uses the metaphor of a calm pool or spring and a strong overflowing river to symbolize the king of Assyria. Since Judah has rejected the still, small voice of the Spirit, the force of Assyria will come upon them and completely devastate the land.

Isaiah 8:9-10. These two verses are acknowledged to be difficult. They seem to be a declaration against the countries coming upon Israel ("all ye of far countries") that they also will be broken in pieces because God is with Israel and will eventually deliver her from all her enemies. This seems acceptable, as God holds "the destinies of all the armies of the nations of the earth" (D&C 117:6).

Isaiah 8:11-18. These are also difficult verses. The Book of Mormon helps, however. Apparently Isaiah was forbidden to preach unto Judah, as Mormon was forbidden to preach to the Nephites and was to stand as an idle witness against her (see Mormon 1:16; 3:16). The Lord had left Judah without excuse by giving her two or three witnesses: the previous testimony of Ahaz, the great roll attested to by two witnesses, and the name of the son of Isaiah. Isaiah was to sanctify the Lord of Hosts and to fear him; the Lord would then be his sanctuary. However, the Lord would be a stumbling block to both the unbelieving houses of Israel.

Both Peter and Paul quoted verse 14 to the Jews as evidence of their stumbling over Christ (see 1 Peter 2:8; Romans 9:33; 1 Corinthians 1:23). Jacob, the Book of Mormon prophet, also foretold that the Jews would stumble over Christ (see Jacob 4:15). To those disciples who would hearken, Isaiah was to "bind up the testimony" and "seal the law." Prophets both ancient and modern are given power to bind and seal something on earth and have it sealed in heaven (see Matt. 16:19; 18:18; D&C 1:8; 68:12). The wording of verse 16 is reversed in D&C 88:84, wherein the Lord sent his disciples among the Gentiles, and in the Appendix to the Doctrine and Covenants, referring to those who refused to believe in the Lord's servants (see D&C 133:71-72). The wording therein is to bind up the law and seal up the testimony instead of binding the testimony and sealing up the law. However, the meaning is the same in either case. While the sealing may be a sealing unto heaven or a sealing against heaven, as shown in the various references cited, Isaiah's charge was to seal up the disciples to heaven. In verses 17 and 18, Isaiah attests that he will follow the Lord and stand as a witness. When Paul uses the first part of Isaiah 8:18 as an evidence of Christ's calling the people his brethren, he is apparently quoting it out of context (see Hebrews 2:13).

Isaiah 8:19-20. When people request revelation from sources not of God, such as the various forms of witchcraft enumerated in verse 19 (compare 1 Samuel 28:7-25), these sources are to be tested according to the law (of Moses) and the testimony (of the prophets). Elder Ezra Taft Benson quoted this scripture as a key for not being deceived and said that this great truth from Isaiah was so important that it was included in the Book of Mormon (see CR, Oct. 1963, p. 16). President Joseph Fielding Smith quoted verse 19 as an example of the Lord's warning Israel not to seek after "familiar spirits" or other "devices prevalent among the heathen nations" (*AQ*, 4:33). The Prophet Joseph Smith used the phrase "to the law and to the testimony" (verse 20) in reference to the scriptures generally (see *TPJS*, pp. 373-74).

Isaiah 9:1-2. Four variations of this passage (those found in the KJV, the RSV, the Book of Mormon, and Matthew 4:15-16) are quoted below to help us understand the message.

Nevertheless the dimness shall not be such as was in her vexation, when at *the* first he lightly afflicted the land of Zebulun and the land of Naphtali, and afterward did more grievously afflict her by the way of the *sea*, beyond Jordan, in Galilee of the nations.

The people that walked in darkness have seen a great light: they that dwell in the land of the shadow of death, upon them hath the light shined. (KJV, Isaiah 9:1-2.)

Nevertheless, the dimness shall not be such as was in her vexation, when at first he lightly afflicted the land of Zebulun, and the land of Naphtali, and afterwards did more grievously afflict by the way of the *Red Sea* beyond Jordan in Galilee of the nations.

The people that walked in darkness have seen a great light; they that dwell in the land of the shadow of death, upon them hath the light shined. (2 Nephi 19:1-2.)

But there will be no gloom for her that was in anguish. *In the former time he brought into contempt* the land of Zebulun and the land of Naphtali, *but in the latter time he will make glorious* the way of the sea, the land beyond the Jordan, Galilee of the nations.

The people who walked in darkness have seen a great light; those who dwelt in a land of deep darkness, on them has light shined. (RSV, Isaiah 9:1-2.)

The land of Zabulon, and the land of Nephthalim, by the way of the sea, beyond Jordan, Galilee of the *Gentiles*;

The people *which sat* in darkness *saw* great light; and *to them which sat in the region and* shadow of death *light is sprung up*. (Matt. 4:15-16.)

Verse 1 in the RSV shows a transition stating that the former anguish or darkness was to be changed to a glorious status. The Matthew account introduces the great Galilean period of the Savior's ministry, which was the first and possibly the most successful of the various periods of his ministry (as usually designated in New Testament studies). When the land of Canaan was divided among the twelve tribes of Israel, the tribes of Zebulun and Naphtali lay to the west of the Sea of Galilee and formed the northern border of Israel next to the gentile nations of the Galilee. The phrase "way of the sea" has puzzled many scholars, but the Book of Mormon has retained the identity of this body of water as the Red Sea. The land of Naphtali and Zebulun was the first area captured by the Assyrians in the time of Isaiah (see 2 Kings 15:29). The phrase "afterwards did more grievously afflict by the way of the Red Sea beyond Jordan in Galilee of the nations," as translated in the Book of Mormon (which is basically the same as Isaiah, with the exception of the identity of the sea), probably has reference to a later captivity by Assyria rather than the promise of "making glorious the way of the sea," as translated in the RSV. The blessing which was to have come to this area, but which had been lost by Israel's wickedness and subsequent subjection by Assyria, would come through the "light" of Christ as he ministered unto Judah in Galilee, as noted in Matthew.

Isaiah 9:3. The Book of Mormon deletes the word "not" (preceding "increased the joy") found in the KJV. The RSV has also dropped the "not."

Thou hast multiplied the nation, and *not* increased the joy: they joy before thee according to the joy in harvest, and as men rejoice when they divide the spoil. (Isaiah 9:3.)	Thou hast multiplied the nation, and increased the joy—they joy before thee according to the joy in harvest, and as men rejoice when they divide the spoil. (2 Nephi 19:3.)

A marginal note in the KJV suggests an alternate reading of "to him increased the joy" instead of "not increased the joy," which would agree with the other versions.

Isaiah 9:4. The Book of Mormon does not have the phrase "as in the day of Midian" at the end of this verse.

This could have been an intentional omission by Nephi, as it did not apply to his people.

Isaiah 9:6-7. The only difference in verse 6 in the Book of Mormon is the capitalization of the words "Mighty" and "Everlasting." Since these further designate the greatness and the Fatherhood of Christ, they seem to be significant. The Book of Mormon does not have the word "his" preceding "government," but the JST does retain the word "his" while following the other slight changes in the Book of Mormon.

The angel who appeared to Mary identified the Son who was to be born to her as He who would occupy the throne of David (see Luke 1:32). The angel who spoke to the shepherds on the night of Christ's birth paraphrased Isaiah 9:6 (see Luke 2:10-11).

The General Authorities often refer to verse 6 as a prophecy of Christ's coming or as a designation of one or more of his titles. But since their comments are not interpretive, they are not quoted here.

Isaiah 9:8. The Book of Mormon retains the identifying "his word" rather than "a word" in the KJV. This retention broadens the meaning to include the gospel rather than just a single prophecy.

The Lord sent *a* word into Jacob, and it hath lighted upon Israel. (Isaiah 9:8.)

The Lord sent *his* word into Jacob and it hath lighted upon Israel. (2 Nephi 19:8.)

This fits the context of the sins or reasons for which the Lord's judgments are to come upon northern Israel or Ephraim. After Isaiah prophesies of a future time when a "light" will come forth in the land which is about to be smitten by the Assyrians, he returns to the reasons for which Israel is going to be smitten. These are listed in the outline at the beginning of this chapter.

Isaiah 9:9-12. The first evil which is to bring the judgments of God upon Ephraim is the pride of their hearts. They have failed to recognize the judgments which have already come, and have rationalized that if their dwellings are destroyed they will build with better materials. Their reliance upon the material things and their own abilities is evidence of that pride which will cause their downfall. The descriptions of this evil and the other three which follow all end with the same pronouncement: God's judgment will not be "turned away."

Isaiah 9:13-17. The second evil to bring the destructive judgments of God upon Israel is her wicked leaders, both the political and the religious leaders. The "head" (government) and the "tail" (false prophets) are identified in verse 15. The phrase "and honourable" is not given in the Book of Mormon as characteristic of the head. Under the government of Israel, the Lord's prophet was to instruct the king or the government leaders (for example, Isaiah taught Ahaz, as Nathan had taught David), but Israel's future prophets will cause her to err. The entire people will be hypocrites. The Book of Mormon phrase "of them" in verse 17, identifying the young men and the fatherless and widows specifically as hypocrites, points up the justice of God in not showing mercy to them.

Isaiah 9:18-21. The third evil to visit Israel is the wickedness which is likened to a forest fire. The fire of wickedness will sweep on, using the people for fuel. All will be consumed in wickedness. This wickedness is so severe that brothers will "consume" brothers, members of their own families, and even themselves—and will still not be satisfied.

Isaiah 10:1-4. The fourth and final evil pronounced by Isaiah is the neglect of the poor and the needy. How we care for the poor and the needy is a high priority with the Lord, and to neglect them is to bring his judgment upon us (see D&C 104:17-18.)

Isaiah 10:5-11. In Mormon 4:5 we read, "But, behold, the judgments of God will overtake the wicked; and it is by the wicked that the wicked are punished." The Book of Mormon renders the ending of verse 5 "and the staff in their hand is *their* indignation" (rather than the KJV "mine indignation").

O Assyrian, the rod of mine anger, and the staff in their hand is *mine* indignation. (Isaiah 10:5.)

O Assyrian, the rod of mine anger, and the staff in their hand is *their* indignation. (2 Nephi 20:5.)

Thus Assyria is a good example of the principle taught in Mormon 4:5. Assyria will punish the wicked nations of Syria and Ephraim in her own wicked indignation. In verse 12 we read that the heart of the king of Assyria is not right.

Isaiah 10:12-19. In the Doctrine and Covenants the Lord says, "And in nothing doth man offend God, or against none is his wrath kindled, save those who confess not his hand in all things, and obey not his commandments" (D&C 59:21). Assyria is a good example of this principle taught by the Prophet Joseph Smith. Although there is nothing said about Assyria's being given the opportunity to keep the commandments of God in these verses, when the full history is known it will undoubtedly show that Assyria did have that opportunity. This conclusion is drawn from the allegory of Zenos in Jacob 5, which outlines the history of the house of Israel. The wild olive branches are the Gentiles, who are to be grafted into the tree of Israel and given the opportunity to bear fruit. That some did bear fruit from this graft is shown by the Savior's declaration to his disciples to harvest the fruit among the Samaritans (see John 4:31-38), who were in part a product of the Assyrian conquest as the Assyrians brought Babylonians and others into Samaria.

Isaiah 10:20-23. Having prophesied the fate of Assyria, Isaiah now comes back again to the promise to a remnant of Israel. Although she will be scattered among the Gentiles and will be dependent upon them, Israel will once again rely upon the Holy One of Israel in truth and will return. Paul quotes Isaiah 10:22 (with other prophecies) to show the Romans, who were Gentiles, that the righteous of Israel will be saved as well as the righteous Gentiles (see Romans 9:27).

Isaiah 10:24-25. These verses are a plea to the people who will dwell in Zion in the future. The Zion spoken of by the Old Testament prophets was identified by the Prophet Joseph Smith as the whole of North and South America (see *TPJS*, p. 362). The "Assyrians" in verse 24 would thus symbolize the Gentiles who were inhabiting that land and were ruling over the blood of Israel scattered among them or living under their rule. The plea is for the Israelites to rely upon the Lord. While they may have trials and tribulations, these will be short-lived and the promised blessings of Israel will be restored.

Isaiah 10:27. An identification of the pronouns in verse 27 will give us a clearer understanding. "His" burden (or yoke) has reference to the Gentile burden of oppression.

"Thy" shoulder refers to the shoulder of Israel under that oppression.

Isaiah 10:28-34. The various towns in these verses are conquered during an Assyrian assault on Jerusalem, but the assault will fail because the Lord will intercede.

Isaiah 11:1. The interpretation of this passage has been given by Joseph Smith in Doctrine and Covenants 113:1-4. The stem of Jesse is Christ. The book of Revelation also identifies Jesus as such (see Rev. 5:5; 22:16). The rod is "a servant in the hands of Christ, who is partly a descendant of Jesse as well as of Ephraim" (D&C 113:4). That the servant is Joseph Smith himself seems evident. President Brigham Young taught that Joseph was a "pure Ephraimite," and this was confirmed by President Joseph Fielding Smith (see *DS*, 3:253-54, for both statements). His being a pure Ephraimite does not necessarily mean he had only the blood of Ephraim; it may mean he had some of the pure blood of Ephraim in his veins. This is also evidenced by the fact that his father was the Patriarch to the Church, which office belongs to "the oldest man of the blood of Joseph or of the seed of Abraham" (*TPJS*, p. 151). Joseph Smith would likely have had the blood of other tribes in his veins as well, since Israel lived among the Gentiles for hundreds of years. Certainly Joseph Smith had "much power" laid upon him, as D&C 113:4 states. All this fits well with the angel Moroni's declaration to Joseph Smith that the eleventh chapter of Isaiah was about to be fulfilled (see JS-H 1:40).

The branch which was to grow out of the roots is Christ (see Bruce R. McConkie, *The Promised Messiah*, [Deseret Book Company, 1978] pp. 192-93). "Branch" is capitalized in the KJV. That a branch of Israel is to come out of the mother tree is mentioned in the allegory of Zenos (see Jacob 5:54-56).

Isaiah 11:2-5. The traditional interpretation of these verses is that they describe Christ. This is supported by passages in the book of Revelation (2:16; 19:15) and the Doctrine and Covenants (19:15; 113:1-2), and by President Joseph Fielding Smith (see *DS*, 1:168). Nephi quotes verses 4 through 9 (see 2 Nephi 30:9-15), clearly indicating that verses 4 and 5 describe "the Lord God." There is one verse inserted between verses 4 and 5 (2 Nephi 30:10) which appears to be

Nephi's comment. There are also three verses following verse 9 which are not in the KJV (2 Nephi 30:16-18).

Isaiah 11:2-5 must be understood within the context established in verse 1, including the "rod" (servant) mentioned there, and verses 2 through 4 especially may refer to Joseph Smith. "The spirit of the Lord shall rest upon *him*." As Doctrine and Covenants 5:6-10 clearly points out, Joseph Smith was chosen to give the Lord's word to this generation. These verses may have a double reference to both Christ and Joseph Smith. (Isaiah uses double references in other passages as well; for example, see note on 52:13-15.) After all, the servant was to be an instrument in the hands of Christ to carry out his work. As the Spirit of the Lord came upon Joseph Smith, he did attain wisdom, understanding, and knowledge; further, Joseph did judge in righteousness through the Spirit of the Lord.

Isaiah 11:6-9. These verses, which describe the millennial reign of Christ for which his servants are preparing, are often quoted in general conferences by modern Church leaders making reference to that future day. The clause "a little child shall lead them" in verse 6 is also quoted occasionally out of context to introduce examples of little children leading today. This is consistent with other scriptures referring to the Lord's speaking "out of the mouth of babes" (see Psalm 8:2; Matthew 21:16; Alma 32:23).

Joseph Smith paraphrased part of verses 6 through 9 in the following two statements:

> Men must become harmless before the brute creation, and when men lose their vicious dispositions and cease to destroy the animal race, the lion and the lamb can dwell together, and the sucking child can play with the serpent in safety. (*TPJS*, p. 71.)
>
> Friendship is one of the grand fundamental principles of "Mormonism"; [it is designed] to revolutionize and civilize the world, and cause wars and contentions to cease and men to become friends and brothers. Even the wolf and the lamb shall dwell together; the leopard shall lie down with the kid, the calf, the young lion and the fatling; and a little child shall lead them; the bear and the cow shall lie down together, and the sucking child shall play on the hole of the asp, and the weaned child shall play on the cockatrice's den; and they

> shall not hurt or destroy in all my holy mountain, saith the Lord of hosts. (*TPJS*, p. 316.)

Joseph Smith also gave a different rendering of the last part of verse 9—"the earth will be filled with *sacred* knowledge, as the waters cover the *great deep*" (*TPJS*, p. 93)—and indicated that this prophecy would be fulfilled after Israel is gathered. President Joseph Fielding Smith has stated, "If the knowledge of the Lord covers the earth as the waters do the sea, then it must be universally received" (*DS*, 3:65). He has quoted Isaiah 11:9 in reference to the millennial conditions and has urged the Saints to study the gospel, exercise faith, and keep the commandments that they might hasten that day, and he has also stated that the wicked will eventually be removed from the earth, which will further allow truths to sweep the earth, although man will still have his agency to accept or reject the gospel (see *AQ*, 1:xvii; 2:xiii-xiv; 2:22; 5:143-144). Elder Orson Pratt taught that this great knowledge which was to cover the earth (spoken of in verse 9) was to include a restoration of all the records which had been kept in former dispensations, and he enumerated many of these records (see *JD*, 16:47ff.; see also Helaman 3:13-15; 3 Nephi 26:8-12; Ether 3:25-4:7). Elder Pratt also taught that

> . . . the earth will be made new, and great knowledge will be imparted to the inhabitants thereof, as predicted in the 11th chapter of the prophecy of Isaiah. The knowledge of God will then cover the earth as the waters cover the mighty deep. There will be no place of ignorance, no place of darkness, no place for those that will not serve God. Why? Because Jesus, the Great Creator, and also the Great Redeemer, will be himself on the earth, and his holy angels will be on the earth, and all the resurrected Saints that have died in former dispensations will all come forth, and they will be on the earth. What a happy earth this creation will be, when this purifying process shall come, and the earth be filled with the knowledge of God as the waters cover the great deep!" (*JD*, 21:324-25.)

Isaiah 11:10. The root of Jesse is identified in Doctrine and Covenants 113:5-6 as "a descendant of Jesse, as well as of Joseph, unto whom rightly belongs the priesthood, and the keys of the kingdom, for an ensign, and for the gathering of my people in the last days." The fact that these keys of the kingdom were given to Joseph Smith for time and eternity (see D&C 90:2-4) helps us identify the servant. Paul quoted this passage with slightly different wording as evidence that the Gentiles were to receive the gospel. This wording also helps to identify the servant as Joseph Smith: "And again, Esaias saith, There shall be a root of Jesse, and *he that shall rise to reign over the Gentiles*; in him shall the Gentiles trust" (Romans 15:12).

Isaiah 11:11-12. The Prophet Joseph Smith provided this enlightening comment on verse 11:

> The time has at last arrived when the God of Abraham, of Isaac, and of Jacob, has set his hand again the second time to recover the remnants of his people, which have been left from Assyria, and from Egypt, and from Pathros, and from Cush, and from Elam, and from Shinar, and from Hamath, and from the islands of the sea, and with them to bring in the fulness of the Gentiles, and establish that covenant with them, which was promised when their sins should be taken away. See Isaiah xi; Romans xi:25, 26 and 27, and also Jeremiah xxxi:31, 32 and 33. This covenant has never been established with the house of Israel, nor with the house of Judah, for it requires two parties to make a covenant, and those two parties must be agreed, or no covenant can be made.
>
> Christ, in days of His flesh, proposed to make a covenant with them, but they rejected Him and His proposals, and in consequence therof, they were broken off, and no covenant was made with them at that time. But their unbelief has not rendered the promise of God of none effect: no, for there was another day limited in David, which was the day of His power; and then His people, Israel, should be a willing people; —and He would write His law in their hearts, and print it in their thoughts; their sins and their iniquities He would remember no more. (*TPJS*, pp. 14-15.)

Elder Orson Pratt identified the outcasts of Israel spoken of in verse 12 as the ten tribes: "Here is a declaration that the two great kingdoms of Israel—its 'outcasts,' the ten tribes, scattered seven hundred and twenty years before Christ, and the 'dispersed of Judah,' dispersed among all nations, shall be gathered. But before he gathers them he will set up an ensign—an ensign is to be raised in the latter-days especially for the gathering of Israel." (*JD*, 14:66.) Thus there are three separate phases of the gathering spoken of in verse

12. President Joseph Fielding Smith also identified Ephraim as the ten tribes, Judah as the two tribes, and the Philistines (in verse 14) as the Gentiles (see *AQ*, 2:181).

The Lord's setting his hand the second time to recover his people is associated with the "marvellous work and a wonder" prophesied in Isaiah 29:14 and in 2 Nephi 25:17 and 29:1. The standard or "ensign" spoken of in Isaiah 11:12 is identified in 2 Nephi 29:2 as the words of Nephi's seed (the Book of Mormon). This has also been more broadly interpreted by the General Authorities as The Church of Jesus Christ of Latter-day Saints. Typical of such statements is one by Elder LeGrand Richards which adds the notation that no other church is accomplishing what this Church is doing for its members and that people come to the Church to learn how it accomplishes what it does (see CR, Oct. 1975, p. 77). This certainly fits the concept of an ensign. Jacob, the Book of Mormon prophet, said that the day the Lord set his hand the second time to recover his people would be the day the Lord would send his servants to prune his vineyard for "the last time," as foretold in the allegory of Zenos (see Jacob 6:2).

Isaiah 11:13-14. These verses describe a return to a united kingdom of Israel as it was before the division following the reign of Solomon. Ephraim was the name by which the northern 10½ tribes were called, and Judah consisted of the southern 1½ tribes. Ephraim will at the time of this reuniting occupy the promised land of Joseph, the Americas (see 3 Nephi 15:12-13). This prophecy speaks of more than a geographical uniting; it is a spiritual and political reuniting. Abraham was promised the land "from the river of Egypt unto the great river, the river Euphrates" (Genesis 15:18), which has never as yet been completely occupied by Abraham's children under one head. In Isaiah's time the Philistines occupied the area of the present-day Gaza Strip on the Mediterranean coast, which falls within the geography of Abraham's promised land; and Edom, the descendants of Esau, occupied the area of Mt. Seir to the south and the east. Moab, the descendants of Lot and his eldest daughter, occupied the territory directly north of Edom on the east side of the Jordan. Together, the Edomites and the Moabites represented the expansion of the land of Abraham on the east. The children of Ammon, the descendants of Lot and his younger daughter, occupied the land directly north of Moab on the east side of the Jordan. Today these all constitute the modern nation of Jordan. That this prophecy is yet to be fulfilled is shown by the declaration that the children of Ammon will obey the house of Israel. None of this land east of the Jordan is under the rule of the house of Israel, nor has the envy yet departed from between Ephraim and Judah to bring about a united rule.

Isaiah 11:15. Nephi said that "in the days that the prophecies of Isaiah shall be fulfilled men shall know of a surety, at the times when they shall come to pass" (2 Nephi 25:7). This prophecy in verse 15 is one of those which will probably not be understood until it comes to pass, but when it does there will be no doubt as to its fulfillment. The identification of "the tongue of the Egyptian sea" and "the river," which today is uncertain in the minds of biblical scholars, will become certain when the Lord delivers his people. According to Oliver Cowdery, the events in this verse and those in verse 16 would need to occur so that the gathering could be fully accomplished (see *MA*, Apr. 1835, p. 111). Elder Orson Pratt referred to this prophecy as a "literal transaction":

> The same thing, not a spiritual, but a literal transaction, as the Lord smote the tongue of the Egyptian sea in ancient days, and caused his people to go through on a highway in the midst of those mighty waters which stood like walls on each side of the assembly of Israel. So in the latter days he will not only cut off the tongue of the Egyptian sea, but the river in its seven streams will also be divided and men will go through dryshod. This is the testimony of the prophets concerning the events that are to take place when the times of the Gentiles are fulfilled. (*JD*, 14:66.)

Isaiah 11:16. The remnant which left from Assyria are, of course, the ten tribes who were taken into the north. The apocryphal book of 2 Esdras tells of miracles which will attend their return like those that attended their departure: "Then they dwelt there until the last times; and now, when they are about to come again, the Most High will stop the channels of the river again, so that they may be able to pass over. Therefore you saw the multitude gathered together in peace." (2 Esdras 13:46-47.) And the Doctrine and Covenants gives an even more sure prophecy of the event spoken of in Isaiah (see D&C 133:26-33). President Joseph Fielding Smith refers to the entire eleventh chapter of Isaiah in speaking of the lost tribes coming to their brother Ephraim, the firstborn in Israel, to receive their crowning blessings (see *DS*, 3:252).

Isaiah 12:1-6. This song of praise unto Jehovah will be sung in the day of Israel's great restoration. Paul, in writing to the Hebrews, may have been quoting a part of verse 2 to show a brotherhood between Christ and his people (see Hebrews 2:13). The water which is drawn "out of the wells of salvation" is similarly promised by John the Revelator (see Revelation 21:6); the "water" which is promised and given through Christ is identified by John as the Holy Ghost (see John 7:38-39).

The Warning to Babylon 9

Isaiah 13-14

Chapters 13 and 14 are the beginning of a series of revelations (chapters 13 through 23) given to nine different nations. Most of these messages of warning begin with the introductory phrase "The burden of," which is usually interpreted to mean a message of doom. Chapters 13 and 14 both concern Babylon and are by far the longest of the series. They are also the only two chapters of this series which are quoted in the Book of Mormon. There is undoubtedly a dual message within them. The basic message is against the old Babylon, which existed before Isaiah's time and became a world power under King Nebuchadnezzar after Assyria's downfall and after the ministry of Isaiah. Babylon became the epitome of wickedness in the ancient world, and was used in both the New Testament and the Doctrine and Covenants as the symbol of the wicked world (see Revelation 14:8; D&C 133:14). Thus a greater message is to modern-day Babylon, the wickedness of our world. It is often difficult to know which Babylon the text is referring to, and it may be that sometimes it refers to both at the same time. Because Nephi included these two chapters in the Book of Mormon record, it would appear that the majority of the text refers to the latter days.

Chapter 14 is an interesting proverb against the king of Babylon. Babylon represents the wicked world, and the king of that wickedness is none other than Satan himself. The graphic description in this chapter of Satan's *fall* is most interesting.

A detailed outline of the two chapters will give the reader insight regarding what to expect as they are studied.

1. "The burden of Babylon" is the introduction or superscription (13:1).
2. The ensign is to be lifted up on a mountain to the world (13:2-5).
   a. Those who respond to this call are invited into the gates of the nobles (13:2).
   b. The whole land of Babylon will be destroyed (13:5).
3. Destruction will come at the day of the Lord (the Second Coming) (13:6-18).
   a. Fear, pain, and amazement will come upon men (13:7-8).
   b. The land will be laid desolate and sinners destroyed (13:9).
   c. Wonders will appear in the heavens (13:10).
   d. The destruction of the wicked will leave but few men (13:11-12).
   e. The earth will remove from her place (13:13).
   f. Men will be chased, children killed, goods spoiled, wives ravished (13:14-18).
4. Ancient Babylon will be overthrown as was Sodom and Gomorrah (13:19-22).
   a. It will never be inhabited by man (13:20).
   b. Wild beasts will have the land (13:21-22).
5. The house of Israel will be established in its own land (14:1-3).
   a. Strangers (Gentiles) will be joined with them (14:1).
   b. Israel will rule over the Gentiles (14:2).
   c. Israel will rest from her sorrow and bondage (14:3).
6. A proverb will be taken up against the king of Babylon in the day of Israel's restoration (14:4-21).
   a. Satan will be cast from the earth (14:4-8).
   b. He will be received in hell (where he is cast) (14:9-11).
   c. Though he fell from heaven, he aspires to be God (14:12-14).
   d. He will fall into hell (spirit prison) and be scorned (14:15-17).

   e. He will eventually be cast out of hell (into outer darkness) (14:18-21).
7. As the Lord has said, so it will happen (14:22-27).
   a. The Lord will rise up against Babylon (14:22-23).
   b. He will tread down the king of Assyria (the Gentiles) (14:25).
   c. His hand will be upon all nations (14:26-27).
8. This revelation was given in the year King Ahaz died (14:28).
9. The Lord will establish Zion (14:29-32).
   a. Palestine will not rejoice over Assyria's fall (14:29-30).
   b. Another devastation will come from the north to make Palestine cry (14:31).
   c. A reason to rejoice is given: Zion will be established, and the poor of the Lord will trust in Zion (14:32).

Notes and Commentary

As stated previously, these two chapters are quoted in their entirety in the Book of Mormon. There are several significant retentions in the Book of Mormon text which aid in understanding the message. The New Testament and the Doctrine and Covenants also provide some important helps in identifying the time period and meaning of the prophecy. Modern Church leaders have spoken about only three subject areas in these two chapters, and only one of them extensively.

Isaiah 13:1. That the Babylon spoken of in this verse includes more than ancient Babylon is obvious from the rest of the chapter, which clearly speaks of the time of the second coming of Christ. Another Babylon is identified in the Doctrine and Covenants as "spiritual Babylon" and is defined as wickedness (see D&C 133:14). Various other sections in the Doctrine and Covenants use Babylon in this context (see D&C 1:16; 35:11; 64:24; 86:3). The book of Revelation also speaks repeatedly of the fall of Babylon in the last days, which has reference to the fall of the kingdom of the devil (see Revelation 14:8; 16:19; 17:5; 18:2-4, 10, 21). Jeremiah chapters 50 and 51 contain the words of the Lord against Babylon by Jeremiah the prophet; these sayings are more detailed than Isaiah's and seem directed toward ancient Babylon.

Isaiah 13:2. The word "banner" may better be translated "ensign," as in Isaiah 5:26. The King James translators rendered the same Hebrew word in three different ways: ensign (Isaiah 11:10), banner (Isaiah 13:2), and standard (Isaiah 62:10). The Book of Mormon uses the word "banner," but the Joseph Smith Translation reads "my banner," which clarifies that it was the Lord's banner which was to be raised. The banner or ensign being lifted up upon the high mountain may also be the establishment of the kingdom of God, as in Isaiah 2:2. The exalted voice in 13:2 could be the "voice of the Lord" crying, "Go ye out of Babylon" (D&C 133:4-8). "That they may go into the gates of the noble" is an invitation for all who will gather to Zion from the gentile countries, and for Judah to flee to Jerusalem (see D&C 133:9-13; compare Revelation 18:4).

Isaiah 13:3-5. These verses, along with verse 2, have the same basic message as the parable of the wheat and tares (see Matthew 13:24-30; D&C 86:1-7). Note the following comparison of the King James and Book of Mormon translations of this passage:

I have commanded my sanctified ones, I have also called my mighty ones for mine anger, *even* them that rejoice in my highness.	I have commanded my sanctified ones, I have also called my mighty ones, for mine anger *is not upon* them that rejoice in my highness.
The noise of *a* multitude in the mountains, like as of a great people; a tumultuous noise of the kingdoms of nations gathered together: the Lord of hosts mustereth the host of the battle.	The noise of *the* multitude in the mountains like as of a great people, a tumultuous noise of the kingdoms of nations gathered together, the Lord of Hosts mustereth the hosts of the battle.
They come from a far country, from the end of heaven, *even* the Lord, and the weapons of his indignation, to destroy the whole land. (Isaiah 13:3-5.)	They come from a far country, from the end of heaven, *yea*, the Lord, and the weapons of his indignation, to destroy the whole land. (2 Nephi 23:3-5.)

Verse 3 has reference to those messengers who are gathered and are to be sent out to warn of the coming destruction of Babylon (the tares) and to invite the righteous (the wheat) to gather out. With the Book of Mormon retention, verse 3 fits much better the context of the entire passage. This gathering may also be correlated with Isaiah 2:2, but includes the forces of heaven (the destroying angels) who will follow those messengers and will literally destroy the nation of wickedness, spiritual Babylon (see D&C 86:1-7).

Isaiah 13:8. The KJV "they shall be in pain as a woman that travaileth" is not in the Book of Mormon, but this deletion does not alter the meaning or the context of the verse.

Isaiah 13:10. This verse is closely akin to a sign given by the Savior on the Mount of Olives which was to precede his second coming (see Matthew 24:29). There are also several references in the Doctrine and Covenants which are very similar to this verse, referring to the period of the Second Coming (see D&C 29:14; 34:9; 45:42; 88:87; 133:49). Oliver Cowdery apparently was quoting or paraphrasing this verse, along with Isaiah 13:13, when he reported what scriptures the angel Moroni quoted to Joseph Smith in September 1823 and noted that they were soon to be fulfilled (see *MA*, Apr. 1835, pp. 111-12). There is one interesting difference in the Book of Mormon rendition: it uses the pronoun "her" to refer to both the sun and the moon, whereas the KJV uses the traditional pronoun "his" in reference to the sun. There is no known reason for this change.

Isaiah 13:11. In the April 1974 general conference, President Spencer W. Kimball stated that it seemed hard for many members of the Church to live *in* the world and yet not be *of* the world. He then quoted this verse as a warning to those who were following worldly ways. (See CR, Apr. 1974, p. 6.)

Isaiah 13:13. This verse, which notes cosmological changes that will affect the earth at the time of Christ's second coming, is partially quoted or paraphrased in Doctrine and Covenants 21:6 and 35:24. It was also quoted by Oliver Cowdery (see note on Isaiah 13:10).

Isaiah 13:14-15. The Book of Mormon translation of verse 15 contains some significant retentions:

And it shall be as the chased roe, and as a sheep that no man taketh up: they shall every man turn to his own people, and flee every one into his own land.	And it shall be as the chased roe, and as a sheep that no man taketh up; *and* they shall every man turn to his own people, and flee every one into his own land.

Every one that is *found* shall be thrust through; and every one that is joined *unto them* shall fall by the sword. (Isaiah 13:14-15.)

Every one that is *proud* shall be thrust through; *yea,* and every one that is joined *to the wicked* shall fall by the sword. (2 Nephi 23:14-15.)

Beginning with verse 14, Isaiah seems to describe the literal conquest of Babylon by the Medes, although this also appears to be a dual prophecy including spiritual Babylon.

Isaiah 13:19-22. The Book of Mormon retains a complete sentence at the end of verse 22 regarding the destruction of the wicked and the Lord's mercy to his people—those who will accept him as their God.

And the wild beasts of the islands shall cry in their desolate houses, and dragons in their pleasant palaces: and her time is near to come, and her days shall not be prolonged. (Isaiah 13:22.)

And the wild beasts of the islands shall cry in their desolate houses, and dragons in their pleasant palaces; and her time is near to come, and her day shall not be prolonged. *For I will destroy her speedily; yea, for I will be merciful unto my people, but the wicked shall perish.* (2 Nephi 23:22.)

This ending is a good transition into the next chapter. In commenting on Isaiah's words, Nephi declared that ancient Babylon would be destroyed and that the Jews would therefore be "scattered by other nations" (2 Nephi 25:15). Elder LeGrand Richards quoted this passage as Isaiah's prophecy of the destruction of ancient Babylon, noting that Elders Spencer W. Kimball and Howard W. Hunter had visited the sites in 1961 and had seen the destruction (see CR, Oct. 1966, p. 42).

Isaiah 14:1-3. These three verses are an extension of the final thought in the Book of Mormon rendition of 13:22. The Lord's mercy will be shown by his gathering his people back to their own land. The strangers who will be joined with them are most probably the Gentiles who will have accepted the gospel while the house of Israel is being gathered. The second verse in the Book of Mormon contains an eighteen-word retention which emphasizes the extent of the gathering of Israel—from "the ends of the earth"—and establishes that there will be more than one land for the gathering.

For the Lord will have mercy on Jacob, and will yet choose Israel, and set them in their own land: and the strangers shall be joined with them, and they shall cleave to the house of Jacob.

For the Lord will have mercy on Jacob, and will yet choose Israel, and set them in their own land; and the strangers shall be joined with them, and they shall cleave to the house of Jacob.

And the people shall take them, and bring them to their place: and the house of Israel shall possess them *in* the land of the Lord for servants and handmaids: and they shall take them captives, *whose* captives they were; and they shall rule over their oppressors.

And the people shall take them and bring them to their place; *yea, from far unto the ends of the earth; and they shall return to their lands of promise.* And the house of Israel shall possess them, *and* the land of the Lord *shall be* for servants and handmaids; and they shall take them captives *unto whom* they were captives; and they shall rule over their oppressors.

And it shall come to pass in *the* day that the Lord shall give thee rest from thy sorrow, and from thy fear, and from the hard bondage wherein thou wast made to serve. (Isaiah 14:1-3.)

And it shall come to pass in *that* day that the Lord shall give thee rest, from thy sorrow, and from thy fear, and from the hard bondage wherein thou wast made to serve. (2 Nephi 24:1-3.)

Verse 2 also shows a reversal of the ruling class: whereas Israel had been captive and in bondage to the Gentiles, the Israelites will now rule (in righteousness) over their former oppressors. Verse 3 retains the wording "*that* day" instead of the KJV "the day," clearly designating the time when Israel will be gathered and freed from bondage.

Isaiah 14:4. The Book of Mormon again retains a designation of the time spoken of: "*And it shall come to pass in that day*, that thou shalt take up this proverb against the king of Babylon" (2 Nephi 24:4).

Verses 4b through 21 are generally considered to be a poem, which Dr. Sidney B. Sperry called "one of the finest examples of Hebrew poetry in the Bible" (*The Voice of Israel's Prophets* [Salt Lake City: Deseret Book Company, 1965], p. 44). While the poem contains a description of Satan as the ruler of spiritual Babylon, the message is a dual one;

Satan, of course, is described under the guise of the ancient king of Babylon, Nebuchadnezzar.

Isaiah 14:4-8. This section of the poem describes the beginning of the Millennium, when Satan will be bound and the earth will rest. The reference is to rulers who have come under the influence of Satan and not solely to Nebuchadnezzar or one of his successors. The binding of Satan at the beginning of the thousand years is also prophesied in the New Testament (see Revelation 20:1-3), the Book of Mormon (see 1 Nephi 22:26), and the Doctrine and Covenants (see 43:31; 88:110; 101:28). First Nephi 22:15 suggests that the prophecy of the binding of Satan used by Nephi may have been taken from Isaiah.

Isaiah 14:9-11. This section of the poem predicts Satan's being restricted to the spirit world of hell during the millennial years of peace on earth, and describes the reaction of hell's inhabitants when it is announced that he is assigned there. That he will have influence there is shown by the Prophet Joseph Smith's statement that "when we have power to put all enemies under our feet in this world, and a knowledge *to triumph over all evil spirits in the world to come*, then we are saved" (*TPJS*, p. 297). Alma 34:34-35 also shows that the spirit of the devil will have power to possess the unrepentant in the spirit world. When he is bound in the spirit world, "the chief ones of the earth"—those leaders who were influential in the devil's kingdom while they lived upon the earth—will assemble to greet him. When they see him, they will be amazed at his having lost his power.

Isaiah 14:12-14. Isaiah here describes Lucifer's fall from heaven in the premortal existence. The same event is described by John in the book of Revelation (12:7-9) and by both Moses and Abraham in the Pearl of Great Price (see Moses 4:1-4; Abraham 3:27-28). Many of the General Authorities quote these verses in this context (e.g., see Marion G. Romney, CR, Apr. 1971, p. 23). Isaiah's reference to Satan as a "son of the morning" is usually interpreted to mean that he was one of the early spirits born of our Father in Heaven; Doctrine and Covenants 76:25-27 also refers to him by that name. His objective—to become God—is echoed by his followers, who are collectively described as "that which . . . seeketh to become a law unto itself" (D&C 88:35). The Book of

Mormon further describes Satan's objective: having been cast out and doomed to a miserable state forever, he seeks to make all men miserable like he is (see 2 Nephi 2:17-18). These verses in Isaiah are often quoted by modern Church leaders in reference to Satan's being cast out of heaven. Joseph Smith taught that Satan's punishment was being forbidden to have a body, and thus he and his followers go throughout the earth seeking to obtain the tabernacles of others (see *TPJS*, pp. 297-98).

Isaiah 14:15-17. Isaiah now prophesies the devil's fall from earth to the spirit prison, and notes that those who inhabit the spirit prison will be astonished. Satan, who had had such a great influence upon the kingdoms of the earth, is now powerless and unable to do anything for those who are prisoners. As Mormon abridged the records of the Nephites, he warned against the outcome of those who perverted the ways of the Lord and followed the devil (see Alma 30:60). The state of such individuals is described in this passage of Isaiah.

Isaiah 14:18-21. The concluding section of the poem describes still a further fall of Satan. "All the kings of the nations, even all of them," will be given some degree of glory in the houses or mansions which they have prepared themselves to receive. Satan will not receive any glory, however, but will be cast into outer darkness. This doctrine is enlarged upon in Doctrine and Covenants 88:21-35 (see also D&C 77:8; 133:73).

Isaiah 14:22-23. These two verses are inserted between the proverb of the king of Babylon and what many scholars consider a second poem, which concerns the Lord's judgments upon all nations. These verses appear to be directed to ancient Babylon.

Isaiah 14:24-27. Verse 25 in the Book of Mormon (2 Nephi 24) is rendered "I will *bring* the Assyrian in my land" instead of "*break* the Assyrian," as in the KJV. The Assyrian represents the Gentiles, and the purpose of the Lord is to give all the gentile nations an opportunity to be numbered with Israel (see 3 Nephi 30:1-2). The judgments of God will be poured out upon those who reject this opportunity.

Isaiah 14:28. This verse identifies the time when the prophecy was given, not the time of its fulfillment. Whether it refers to the whole prophecy concerning Babylon or the verses which follow is unclear, but it does not really matter, since both have reference to a future and not an immediate time.

Isaiah 14:29-32. Compare Doctrine and Covenants 97:21.

The Warnings to the Nations

10

Isaiah 15-23

Chapters 15 through 23 contain the messages of the Lord to the nations surrounding Judah. Most of these chapters will be touched upon here only lightly, since they deal primarily with the destiny of those surrounding nations, much of which is now history. Those elements which are messianic or which deal with the future will be commented on more fully. A briefer outline than usual is given, with some cross-references to other sources for further study.

1. A message of warning is given to Moab (15:1-16:14; compare Genesis 19:30-38; Jeremiah 48; Ezekiel 25:8-11).
2. A message is given to Syria (17:1-14; compare Jeremiah 49:23-27).
3. A message is given to the land of America (18:1-7).
   a. Messengers are sent out to the nations (18:1-6).
   b. The people are gathered back to Zion (18:7).
4. A message of warning is given to Egypt (19:1-20:6; compare Jeremiah 46; Ezekiel 29-32).
   a. It foretells the fall of Egypt as a mighty nation (19:1-15).
   b. Judah will be a terror to Egypt (19:16-17).
   c. The Hebrew language will be taught in Egypt (19:18).
   d. An altar of the Lord will be in the midst of Egypt, and Egypt will be healed (19:19-22).
   e. Egypt will be blessed along with Assyria and Israel (19:23-25).

   f. Isaiah gives an object lesson of Egypt's captivity by Assyria (20:1-6).
5. A message of warning is given to the "desert of the sea" (Babylon?) (21:1-10; compare Jeremiah 50-51).
6. A message is given to Dumah (Edom) (21:11-12; compare Jeremiah 49:7-22; Ezekiel 25:12-14).
7. A message comes to Arabia (21:13-17; compare Jeremiah 49:28-33).
8. The Lord speaks to the "valley of vision" (Jerusalem) (22:1-25).
   a. He foretells of a siege against Jerusalem (22:1-7).
   b. He calls, but they continue in the law of Moses (22:8-14).
   c. A second siege will come against Jerusalem (22:15-19).
   d. The throne of David will be established forever (22:20-25).
9. A message of warning comes to Tyre (23:1-18; compare Ezekiel 26-28).

Notes and Commentary

There is little help given in the other standard works for understanding these chapters, but several significant comments have been made by modern Church leaders. The New Testament contains a few paraphrases or partial quotes, but these could be challenged because they may even refer to other passages of Isaiah or to other Old Testament passages. These prophecies will be better understood, as Nephi said, by those who live in the day when they are fulfilled (see 2 Nephi 25:7). Our understanding is further limited by the fact that these prophecies are applicable to other countries than those explicitly named.

Isaiah 16:5. The "tabernacle of David" referred to in this verse is not the "throne of David" in Luke 1:32. Isaiah appears to be referring to "another by the name of David in the last days" (*TPJS*, p. 339). This is a messianic prophecy.

Isaiah 18:1-7. The KJV "Woe to the land" is translated "Ah land of" in the RSV. Commentators also suggest that Lo, Alas, Hark, or Hail could be accurate, and they are almost unanimous in thinking that this is not a message of doom but of hope. Hyrum Smith said in April 1844, "The gathering will continue here [Nauvoo, Illinois] until the Temple is so far finished that the Elders can get their endowments; and after that the gathering will be from the nations to North and South America, which is the land of Zion. *North and South America, are the symbols of the wings.*" (*HC*, 6:322; italics added.) Elder Orson Pratt also identified the land of North and South America as the land spoken of in this verse, and he emphasized that the ensign mentioned in verse 3 was to go to all the world (see *JD*, 16:84-85). President Joseph Fielding Smith confirmed that "the land shadowing with wings" was America (see CR, Apr. 1966, p. 14); on another occasion he stated that the term "vessels of bulrushes" in verse 2 should read "vessels of speed," and that the "nation scattered and peeled" is Palestine. The *land* of Palestine was denuded or "peeled" of its forests under Turkish misrule. The ensign's being lifted up refers to the restoration of the gospel in America; ambassadors would then go from America to the nations of the earth to gather those *people* who are "scattered and peeled." (See *ST*, pp. 51-55.)

Isaiah 19:1-25. While most commentators believe that this chapter refers to the history of Egypt, there seem to be many prophetic utterances of the latter days in verses 16 through 25. These will be further understood as the day of their fulfillment arrives (see 2 Nephi 25:7). Elder Bruce R. McConkie indicated that this chapter deals with local affairs and that it prophesies salvation for Egypt in the day of restoration (see *Ensign*, Oct. 1973, p. 82).

Isaiah 21:9. This verse is partially quoted in the book of Revelation by an angel announcing that "Babylon is fallen" (Revelation 14:8). This has led some scholars to identify the "desert of the sea" (21:1) as Babylon, while others have suggested the Negev desert. Whether the term refers to either place is questionable.

Isaiah 22:13. Paul paraphrases part of this verse in 1 Corinthians 15:32, but he may have been using a standard scriptural phrase rather than intentionally referring to the prophecy in Isaiah.

Isaiah 22:22. John paraphrases this verse in Revelation 3:7. Again, this is not a fulfillment of the prophecy of Isaiah, but an identification of the personage who holds the "key of the house of David" as Christ.

Isaiah 22:23-25. These verses obviously refer to Christ's being lifted up upon the cross. The "nail that is fastened in the sure place" may have reference to the prints in his hands which he will show to the Jews when he appears upon the Mount of Olives at this second coming (see Zechariah 12:10; 13:6; 14:4; D&C 45:48-53).

Isaiah 23:8. John seems to be paraphrasing part of this verse in Revelation 18:23, but there is no evidence that the two verses are related in time or interpretation.

The Blessings of the House of Israel

11

Isaiah 24-27

These four chapters follow the messages of doom pronounced upon the surrounding nations and are closely associated with them. They were probably given about the same time and represent the message of hope which Isaiah seems always to hold out in contrast to the message of doom previously announced. They appear to be one continuous revelation, probably divided into chapters some time after Isaiah's day. The judgments of God which are to come upon the defiled earth are described in 24:1-12. This is followed by a description of the Lord's people in the isles of the sea (Zion; see 24:13-25:12) and a description of the Lord's people Judah (see chapter 26); chapter 27 is a summation of those descriptions. Nephi, in commenting upon Isaiah, follows a similar pattern: he speaks of separate peoples, then gives a summation chapter about these groups (see 2 Nephi 25-30). A more detailed outline follows.

1. The whole earth is defiled and will be burned (24:1-12).
    a. The earth (land) will become waste and desolate and the people scattered (24:1).
    b. The priest and the people are alike (24:2).
    c. The laws are transgressed, the ordinances changed, the everlasting covenant broken (24:5).
    d. Confusion and desolation are left in the city (24:7-12).
2. The Lord will be glorified only in the isles of the sea (Zion) and in Jerusalem (24:13-23).

a. Praise will be sung elsewhere, but treacherously (24:16-17).
b. The pits and the snares will engulf many (24:18).
c. The earth will reel to and fro as a drunken man (24:19-20).
d. The telestial beings will be shut up in spirit prison (24:21-22).
e. The moon will be confounded and the sun ashamed (24:23).

3. The Lord will be exalted in Mt. Zion (25:1-12).
   a. He will break down the strong and strengthen the weak (25:1-5).
   b. He will make a feast in this mountain (25:6).
   c. He will destroy the veil of darkness and pour out knowledge (25:7).
   d. He will overcome death, sin, and affliction (25:8).
   e. He will be accepted as God by the people (25:9).
   f. He will tread down the oppressors of Israel (25:10-12).

4. A song will be sung in the land of Judah (26:1-21).
   a. Jerusalem will trust in Jehovah and be a strong and peaceful city (26:1-4).
   b. The proud will be brought low and the just led in righteousness (26:5-11).
   c. Jehovah will be recognized as the only Messiah (26:12-15).
   d. The Jews will be delivered and their dead resurrected (26:16-19).
   e. The Lord's people (the Jews) will gather while the earth is punished (26:20-21).

5. Jacob will take root, and Israel will blossom and bud (27:1-13).
   a. The devil will be slain and the wicked burned (27:1-6).
   b. Jacob will be smitten and purged of iniquity (27:7-11).
   c. The land given to Abraham will be occupied by Israel as she gathers and worships in the holy mount at Jerusalem (27:12-13).

Notes and Commentary

There are about a dozen passages from the other standard works which help us understand these chapters, half of them related to chapter 24. There are also several comments by the General Authorities, but again almost all of them concern chapter 24. While much of the interpretation must be left to the "spirit of prophecy" (see 2 Nephi 25:4), there are enough guidelines given in the scriptures to show the overall message.

Isaiah 24:1-6. Following the messages of doom in chapters 13 through 23, Isaiah announces what the Lord's judgments will be upon the whole earth as a result of the wickedness of the nations. The earth will undergo catastrophic changes, and its inhabitants will be scattered.

In the April 1971 general conference, President Spencer W. Kimball identified the "priest" spoken of in verse 2 as "all religious leaders of any faith," and he decried the "many priests who encourage the defilement of men and wink at the eroding trends and who deny the omniscience of God" (CR, Apr. 1971, p. 9). Three years earlier, Elder Marion G. Romney quoted verse 3 as evidence that Isaiah envisioned our day and foresaw the burning of the earth described in verse 6 (see CR, Apr. 1968, p. 113). President Joseph Fielding Smith noted that our generation is heading for the destruction spoken of in verses 4 and 6 (see *DS*, 3:316). The Prophet Joseph Smith said that verse 5 refers to the Gentiles' breaking the covenant:

> Thus after this chosen family had rejected Christ and His proposals, the heralds of salvation said to them, "Lo we turn unto the Gentiles"; and the Gentiles received the covenant, and were grafted in from whence the chosen family were broken off; but the Gentiles have not continued in the goodness of God, but have departed from the faith that was once delivered to the Saints, and have broken the covenant in which their fathers were established (see Isaiah xxiv:5); and have become high-minded, and have not feared; therefore, but few of them will be gathered with the chosen family. Have not the pride, high-mindedness, and unbelief of the Gentiles, provoked the Holy One of Israel to withdraw His Holy Spirit from them, and send forth His judgments to scourge them for their wickedness? This is certainly the case. (*TPJS*, p. 15.)

The Lord repeated the message of verse 5 in Doctrine and Covenants 1:15. Elder Rudger Clawson quoted verse 5 as a warning against administering in the priesthood without authority (see CR, Apr. 1914, pp. 22-23.) Elder George F. Richards stated that the unauthorized changing of the ordinance of baptism from immersion to sprinkling was a fulfillment of Isaiah 24:5 (see CR, Apr. 1930, p. 76). President Joseph Fielding Smith pointed to the need for a restoration of the everlasting covenant which Isaiah said was broken (see *DS*, 1:168); he also used verse 6 as evidence that only telestial beings will be burned at the second coming of Christ (see *DS*, 3:62). Elder LeGrand Richards cited verses 5 and 6 as a prophecy of the nearly one thousand churches in modern America who are following their own wisdom and not the precepts of God (see CR, Oct. 1977, p. 30).

Isaiah 24:8. John uses similar phraseology in Revelation 18:22 in describing the downfall of Babylon, referring to the same time period as Isaiah.

Isaiah 24:13-15. Having described the judgments which were to come upon the wicked world, Isaiah turns to the message of hope. There is to be a group in the midst of the land (the earth) who shall sing unto the Lord and glorify him. He further identifies the place as "in the fires . . . in the isles of the sea." A marginal note in the KJV suggests the word "valleys" instead of "fires." Isaiah consistently uses the term "isles of the sea," undoubtedly with reference to America. Similarly, the Book of Mormon prophet Jacob spoke of the Nephites' being on "an isle of the sea" (2 Nephi 10:20). Thus Isaiah seems to be describing the Latter-day Saints, who will be singing and glorifying God in the day of the earth's turmoils and devastation.

Isaiah 24:19-20. These two verses describe the catastrophic events associated with the Lord's second coming. The Savior quoted part of verse 20 in two revelations given to Joseph Smith (see D&C 49:23; 88:87). Oliver Cowdery paraphrased the same verse in noting which scriptures the angel Moroni said were soon to be fulfilled (see *MA*, Apr. 1835, pp. 111-12). The Prophet Joseph Smith taught that the events spoken of in verse 20 were soon to occur as the Second Coming rapidly approached (*TPJS*, pp. 29, 71).

Isaiah 24:21-23. The "high ones" and the "kings of the earth" have been identified by President Joseph Fielding Smith as some of those who live in the latter days but do not keep the law, and who will therefore be shut up in the spirit prison (see *DS*, 2:155). Elder Theodore M. Burton also referred to these verses as evidence of a spirit prison which Christ visited, noting that it is not a reference to political prisoners on the earth (see CR, Oct. 1964, p. 33). Revelation 21:23 seems to describe a condition similar to the one in Isaiah 24:23. According to Elder Orson Pratt, the moon will be confounded and the sun ashamed "because of the superior light that will attend the presence of the being who is to reign in Zion and Jerusalem" (*JD*, 20:12).

Isaiah 25:6. In Doctrine and Covenants 58:3-4, the Saints were told that even though Zion would not be established in all her glory until "after much tribulation," there were still reasons for their going into Jackson County at that time. One of these reasons was to fulfill the words of the prophets, and Isaiah 25:6 was quoted as an example. The following verses shed much light on Isaiah's message:

> And also that a feast of fat things might be prepared for the poor; yea, a feast of fat things, of wine on the lees well refined, that the earth may know that the mouths of the prophets shall not fail;
>
> Yea, a supper of the house of the Lord, well prepared, unto which all nations shall be invited.
>
> First, the rich and the learned, the wise and the noble;
>
> And after that cometh the day of my power; then shall the poor, the lame, and the blind, and the deaf, come in unto the marriage of the Lamb, and partake of the supper of the Lord, prepared for the great day to come.
>
> Behold, I, the Lord, have spoken it. (D&C 58:8-12.)

The Saints who went into Jackson County in 1831 were to invite the rich and the learned, the wise and the noble (the Gentiles) to participate in the establishment of Zion. Since the Gentiles rejected this opportunity, the work would be accomplished later by the poor, the lame, the blind, and the deaf (the house of Israel) through the Lord's power. This is the time spoken of by Isaiah in verse 6. The law of consecration was to do away with poverty, and the feast would be physical as well as spiritual.

Isaiah 25:7. The "vail that is spread over all nations" is undoubtedly the veil of darkness and ignorance. It will be destroyed by the Lord's pouring out knowledge upon the heads of the Latter-day Saints, and all others who will hearken in the dispensation of the fulness of times, as spoken of in Doctrine and Covenants 121:26-33 (see also Isaiah 11:9).

Isaiah 25:8. Paul quotes this passage to the Corinthians and says that when the resurrection takes place, this saying will be brought to pass (see 1 Corinthians 15:54). The wiping away of the tears refers to the effects of the Atonement; this metaphor is used twice by John (see Revelation 7:17; 21:4). The "rebuke of his people" represents the continual trials and afflictions which the Savior will cause to cease among Israel. Thus this verse is clearly a messianic prophecy, or a testimony of what Christ will do for the world, and especially for Israel.

Isaiah 26:3. This verse was quoted by Elder Howard W. Hunter as an example of the "perfect peace" which is not understood by the world, but which comes through a belief in God (see CR, Oct. 1966, p. 15). The context of this verse is the time when Judah in Jerusalem will trust in Jehovah and thus experience this perfect peace. Consequently, it describes the day of Judah's restoration.

Isaiah 26:17. The Savior used the same analogy of a woman delivering a child, but did not relate it to the text of Isaiah (see John 16:21). Isaiah spoke of the delivery of Judah as a nation, while the Savior referred to the sorrow the disciples would experience over his death, which sorrow would be replaced with joy when he was resurrected.

Isaiah 26:19. Elder B. H. Roberts, in correspondence with a Jewish rabbi, used this verse as evidence of the Messiah's being Jesus Christ, noting that his resurrection was foretold in the Old Testament (see *Rasha the Jew*, pp. 48-49).

Isaiah 26:20-21. President Charles W. Penrose applied these verses to the Latter-day Saints living in seclusion in the mountains of Zion (see CR, Oct. 1918, pp. 17-18). Joseph Smith used this passage to show that Judah would obtain deliverance at Jerusalem (see *TPJS*, p. 17). The context shows that the verses refer to the time when Judah will be secluded in Jerusalem and the arm of the Lord will fall upon the nations, as foretold by the Savior and repeated to the Prophet Joseph Smith (see D&C 45:16, 43-47).

Isaiah 27:1. The "serpent" may be identified as Satan (see Revelation 20:2), who is referred to also as the "dragon" (see Revelation 12:9).

Warnings to the House of Israel

12

Isaiah 28-29

Chapters 28 through 35 of Isaiah may have been one revelation concerning the relations between Israel and her surrounding nations. Chapters 28 through 33 present various warnings about different situations that Israel faces and identify promises made by the Lord to correct those situations; chapters 34 and 35 give a general warning of the day of vengeance to all nations, with a promise that Israel will blossom as a rose in her glory. Because of the length of this revelation, and the relationship between the direct fulfillment of chapter 29 and the restoration of the gospel, we will divide our discussion into two chapters. A detailed outline will clarify the overall message of chapters 28 and 29.

1. A prophecy is given of the fall of the northern kingdom of Israel (28:1-13).
   a. Pride and drunkenness will cause the fall (28:1-4).
   b. There will be a future glory for the saved remnant (28:5-6).
   c. "The priest and the prophet" have led them astray (28:7-8).
   d. They have rejected the revelation of the Lord (28:9-13).
2. The leaders of Judah should have learned from Israel's fall (28:14-29).
   a. Her leaders have covenanted with death and are in agreement with hell (28:14-15).

b. The Lord will lay in Zion a sure foundation (28:16-17).
c. Their covenant of death will be disannulled through the Restoration (28:18-22).
d. The Lord will plow and sow and harvest to bring about his purposes (28:23-29).

3. Jerusalem will continue in the law of Moses, and the Nephites will also be destroyed (29:1-10).
a. Jerusalem will have heaviness and sorrow (29:1-2).
b. The Lord will camp also against the Nephites and bring them down to the dust (29:3-4).
c. The Nephites will speak out of the ground (29:4).
d. Those who are not destroyed (the Lamanites) will be smitten by the Gentiles (29:5-6).
e. Those nations who fight against Zion will suffer a spiritual famine (29:7-8).
f. The Lord will take away their rulers and seers because they have rejected the prophets (29:9-10).

4. The Lord God will bring forth a book from those who slumbered (29:11-12 and 2 Nephi 27:7-23).
a. The book will be sealed (29:11).
b. It will contain a revelation of God from the beginning to the end of the world (2 Nephi 27:7).
c. The sealed part will not be delivered in the day of wickedness (2 Nephi 27:8).
d. The words of those who have slumbered will be delivered to an unlearned man (2 Nephi 27:9).
e. The sealed part will be revealed later from the housetops by the power of Christ (2 Nephi 27:10-11).
f. Three witnesses will behold the book by the power of God, and a few others will view it according to the will of God (2 Nephi 27:12-14).
g. A learned man will be shown the words which are not sealed, but he will not read them (2 Nephi 27:15-18).
h. They will be returned to the unlearned man to bring forth the work of the Lord (2 Nephi 27:19-21).
i. After the work is completed, the unlearned man will seal the record up again until the Lord sees fit to reveal all things (2 Nephi 27:22-23).

5. A marvelous work and a wonder (the Book of Mormon) is to come forth (29:13-24).
   a. The people give lip service to the Lord, but their hearts are far from him (29:13).
   b. The wise and the learned will perish, and their understanding will be hid (29:14).
   c. Those who seek to hide their counsel from the Lord will be known (29:15-16).
   d. Lebanon will be turned into a fruitful field and the fruitful field into a forest following this marvelous work (29:17).
   e. The deaf will hear and the blind will see the words of the book (29:18-19).
   f. The scorner, the iniquitious, and the contender will be cut off (29:20-21).
   g. The house of Jacob will sanctify and fear the God of Israel (29:22-23).
   h. Those who erred and murmured will learn from the book (29:24).

Notes and Commentary

Chapter 29 is undoubtedly the most widely quoted and understood chapter of Isaiah among the Latter-day Saints, but it would not be so if Nephi had not included it in the Book of Mormon. By doing so, he retained important truths in many of the verses, plus at least eighteen complete verses which undoubtedly are some of the "plain and precious things" that were taken away from the record of the Jews by the "great and abominable church" (see 1 Nephi 13:23-29). Quotations from Isaiah 28 and 29 in the Doctrine and Covenants and the New Testament also provide some added insights into these two chapters. Chapter 29 is quoted more often by the Brethren in general conferences than any other chapter of Isaiah. Elder LeGrand Richards in particular has seemingly made this chapter his theme and has quoted from it in almost every conference in which he has spoken.

Isaiah 28:9. The principle of revelation taught here through the analogy of a baby's being fed on milk before taking solid foods was also taught by Paul (see 1 Corinthians

3:1-2; Hebrews 5:11-14), by Peter (see 1 Peter 2:2), and by the Prophet Joseph Smith (see D&C 19:21-22). One must learn basic principles before he is ready to understand the mysteries of God.

Isaiah 28:10.

For precept must be upon precept, precept upon precept; line upon line, line upon line; here a little, and there a little: (Isaiah 28:10.)

For behold, thus saith the Lord God: I will give unto the children of men line upon line, precept upon precept, here a little and there a little; *and blessed are those who hearken unto my precepts, and lend an ear unto my counsel, for they shall learn wisdom; for unto him that receiveth I will give more; and from them that shall say, We have enough, from them shall be taken away even that which they have.*

Cursed is he that putteth his trust in man, or maketh flesh his arm, or shall hearken unto the precepts of men, save their precepts shall be given by the power of the Holy Ghost. (2 Nephi 28:30-31.)

Nephi records (in 2 Nephi 28:30) a fuller rendition of this verse than is presently found in the KJV; 2 Nephi 28:31 may also have been part of the original writings of Isaiah. Although Nephi does not identify this passage as a quotation from Isaiah, he does indicate clearly that it is a statement of the Lord. The principle of revelation taught in Isaiah 28:9 is also amplified in 2 Nephi 28:30-31. The Lord gives us revelation; as we accept and live by that revelation, we are given more revelation, but if we do not accept what is revealed, we lose the knowledge we have already gained.

Isaiah 28:11-13. Taken out of context, verse 11 might be difficult to understand. But in the context provided by the surrounding verses, it becomes clear that the Lord is teaching that revelation is understood only by those who are willing and prepared to listen. Paul, in writing to the Corinthians about speaking in tongues, quotes this verse to show that we must be prepared to understand prophecy, and we prepare by believing (see 1 Corinthians 14:20-22; note that Paul attributed the verse to Moses, not Isaiah—perhaps it was written by both).

Isaiah 28:15, 18-19. The "overflowing scourge" mentioned here is also mentioned several times in the Doctrine and Covenants (see D&C 5:19; 45:31; 97:23); however, these passages may refer to different times. In fact, Isaiah mentions the scourge twice (verses 15 and 18), which may also indicate two different time periods. Of course, the Lord has sent and will yet send many scourges upon the earth. The Prophet Joseph Smith identified one of these: "The servants of God will not have gone over the nations of the Gentiles, with a warning voice, until the destroying angel will commence to waste the inhabitants of the earth, and as the prophet [Isaiah] hath said, 'It shall be a vexation to hear the report' " (*TPJS*, p. 87).

Isaiah 28:16. This verse is quoted both by Peter and Paul in the New Testament, and these references add to our understanding:

Therefore thus saith the Lord God, Behold, I lay in Zion for a foundation a stone, a tried stone, a precious corner stone, a sure foundation: he that believeth shall not *make haste*. (Isaiah 28:16.)	Wherefore also it is contained in the scripture, Behold, I lay in Sion a chief corner stone, elect, precious: and he that believeth *on him* shall not *be confounded*. (1 Peter 2:6.)	As it is written, Behold, I lay in Sion a stumblingstone and rock of offence: and whosoever believeth *on him* shall not *be ashamed*. (Romans 9:33.)

Peter quotes the verse as an incentive to believe in Jesus Christ, saying, "he that believeth on him shall not *be confounded*," whereas the Isaiah reading is "shall not *make haste*." Paul uses it to demonstrate that the Jews had stumbled over Christ and the gospel was therefore taken to the Gentiles. Although he ends with the words "shall not be *ashamed*," a marginal note in the KJV suggests "confounded," as in 1 Peter. The RSV translates both Romans and

1 Peter "ashamed." In any case, either "confounded" or "ashamed" seems to give a plainer meaning than Isaiah's "shall not make haste."

The prophecy that the stone would be rejected by the Jews is also found in Psalm 118:22 and is quoted by the Savior in the New Testament (see Matthew 21:42). In the Book of Mormon, Jacob quoted the allegory of Zenos to show how the rejected stone would become the head of the corner (see Jacob 4:15-18).

Isaiah 28:21. The "strange act" referred to in this verse is identified in the Doctrine and Covenants as the restoration of the gospel in the latter days and its going forth through the Spirit of the Lord (see D&C 95:4; 101:95). Joseph Smith also used the term in relationship to the Book of Mormon's being proven in the eyes of all people (see *TPJS*, p. 267). The Lord probably calls his work a strange event because the world does not usually rely upon the Spirit to prove things. Oliver Cowdery said the angel Moroni told Joseph Smith that this strange act would bring about a marvelous work and a wonder, and that the scripture in Isaiah was about to be fulfilled (see *MA*, Feb. 1835, p. 79). This shows a chronological link between chapters 28 and 29.

Isaiah 28:22. Paul may have been quoting a part of this verse in Romans 9:28 in referring to a "short work" upon the earth. Isaiah uses the word "consumption." Paul was quoting Isaiah 10:22 in Romans 9:27 and seemed to be continuing in verse 28 (compare Isaiah 10:23 and 28:22; the rest of this prophecy concerning the remnant's return may also have been in the original Isaiah chapter 10). Both Paul and Isaiah were speaking within the context of a prophecy concerning latter-day restoration.

Isaiah 29:1-2. These are the only two verses in chapter 29 which are not quoted in the Book of Mormon. Almost all of the biblical commentators recognize some difficulties in the wording and in determining the meaning of these verses. The wording in both the KJV and the RSV suggests that Ariel, the city of David (Jerusalem), is being compared to another place. Although Joseph Smith changed the wording of verse 2 in the JST, he did not clarify it. A study of the early verses of chapter 29 in the JST and the same verses quoted in the Book of Mormon indicates that Joseph Smith probably did not complete his work on this portion of the chapter. Elder Orson Pratt has interpreted verse 1 to mean that the Jews continued to "kill sacrifices" after the day of sacrifices had been done away with, and that they added "year to year" in their futile observance of the law of Moses:

> After the Messiah came and was sacrificed for the sins of the world, the Jews continued to "kill sacrifices," when they should have been done away; they added "year to year" to the law of Moses, until they brought down "heaviness and sorrow," and great "distress" upon their beloved city. The Roman army encompassed the city—cast a trench about it, and, finally, brought it down "even with the ground." The principal part of the Jews perished, and a remnant was scattered among the nations, where they have wandered in darkness unto this day. (*Works*, p. 270.)

He further said that the "it" in "it shall be unto me as Ariel" (verse 2) referred to a place other than Jerusalem: "This cannot have reference to Ariel itself, but it must refer to something which should be "As Ariel." It would be folly to say that Ariel shall be as Ariel. Therefore the word "*it*" must refer to a nation that should suffer similar judgments to those which should befall Jerusalem." (*Works*, p. 270.) Elder LeGrand Richards has interpreted these opening verses as Isaiah's seeing the destruction of Jerusalem and of another great center which was identified when the Book of Mormon came forth (see CR, Apr. 1967, p. 21). The Savior also uses some of Isaiah's phraseology from verses 3 and 4 in prophesying the coming destruction of Jerusalem in his day (see Luke 19:43-44).

Isaiah 29:3-4. Nephi, in prophesying what would happen to his people in the last days, quoted these two verses with some significant additions and retentions. A comparison of the Book of Mormon and the KJV texts illustrates them clearly.

And I will camp against *thee* round about, and will lay siege against *thee* with a mount, and I will raise forts against *thee*.	*After my seed and the seed of my brethren shall have dwindled in unbelief, and shall have been smitten by the Gentiles; yea, after the Lord God shall have* camped against *them* round about, and shall have laid siege against *them* with a mount, and

	raised forts against *them*; and *after they shall have been brought down low in the dust, even that they are not, yet the words of the righteous shall be written, and the prayers of the faithful shall be heard, and all those who have dwindled in unbelief shall not be forgotten.*
And thou shalt be brought down, and shalt speak out of the ground, and thy speech shall be low out of the dust, and thy voice shall be, as of one that hath a familiar spirit, out of the ground, and thy speech shall whisper out of the dust. (Isaiah 29:3-4.)	*For those who shall be destroyed* shall speak *unto them* out of the ground, and *their* speech shall be low out of the dust, and *their* voice shall be as one that hath a familiar spirit; *for the Lord God will give unto him power, that he may whisper concerning them, even as it were out of the* ground; and *their* speech shall whisper out of the dust. (2 Nephi 26:15-16.)

Note that Nephi says these things shall happen before the Book of Mormon comes forth. Furthermore 2 Nephi 26:17 appears to be the Lord speaking to Nephi, but it may indicate a retention of the original text of Isaiah. Its significance is noted by Elder LeGrand Richards who said that Isaiah 29:3-4 could not be explained without 2 Nephi 26:15-17 (see CR, Apr. 1963, p. 118; CR, Apr. 1967, p. 21). President Joseph Fielding Smith has said that Isaiah chapter 29 contains "one of the most important predictions regarding the Book of Mormon" (*DS*, 3:213).

Orson Pratt says verses 3 and 4 describe the conquest of Jerusalem by Rome. However, he says the speech coming "out of the ground" could not refer to Jerusalem, but is a prophecy about the Nephites:

> These predictions of Isaiah could not refer to Ariel, or Jerusalem, because their speech has not been "out of the ground," or "low out of the dust," but it refers to the remnant of Joseph who were destroyed in America upwards of fourteen hundred years ago. The Book of Mormon describes their downfall, and truly it was great and terrible. At the crucifixion of Christ, "the multitude of their terrible ones," as Isaiah predicted "became as chaff that passeth away," and it took place, as he further

> predicts, "at an instant suddenly." Many of their great and magnificent cities were destroyed by fire, others by earthquakes, others by being sunk and buried in the depths of the earth. This sudden destruction came upon them because they had stoned and killed the prophets sent among them. Between three and four hundred years after Christ, they again fell into great wickedness, and the principal nation fell in battle. Forts were raised in all parts of the land, the remains of which may be seen at the present day. Millions of people perished in battle and they suffered just as the Lord foretold by Isaiah. (*Works*, pp. 270-71.)

The voice to be "as of one that hath a familiar spirit" may have two different meanings. Elder Orson Pratt describes the Book of Mormon as speaking "in a most familiar manner." He further shows that there is no way they could "speak out of the ground" except by a record:

> One of the most marvelous things connected with this prediction is, that after the nation should be brought down, they should "speak out of the ground." This is mentioned or repeated four times in the same verse. Never was a prophecy more truly fulfilled than this, in the coming forth of the Book of Mormon. Joseph Smith took that sacred history "out of the ground." It is the voice of the ancient prophets of America speaking "out of the ground"; their speech is "low out of the dust"; it speaks in a most familiar manner of the doings of bygone ages; it is the voice of those who slumber in the dust. It is the voice of prophets speaking from the dead, crying repentance in the ears of the living. In what manner could a nation, after they were brought down and destroyed, "speak out of the ground"? Could their dead bodies or their dust, or their ashes speak? Verily, no: they can only speak by their writings or their books that they wrote while living. Their voice, speech or words, can only "speak out of the ground," or "whisper out of the dust" by their books or writings being discovered. (*Works*, p. 271.)

Elder LeGrand Richards called our attention to a minister of another religion who said that the Book of Mormon read with the same sweet feeling as the New Testament (see CR, Apr. 1976, p. 124). In other words, the message of the Book of Mormon sounds familiar to those who have received the message of the Bible, the gospel, or the Spirit of God. On the other hand, "familiar spirits" in Old Testament times referred to a form of spiritualism wherein spirits from the dead were called back out of the ground through witchcraft or enchantment (see 1 Samuel 28; Isaiah 8:19-20). Some have used this meaning to disclaim the Book of Mormon. However, a careful reading of Isaiah shows that the words of the record would be "as" a familiar spirit. Just as the spirits came "out of the ground," so would the record of a people who had been destroyed. Nephi in 2 Nephi 26:16 shows that the power of God would be given to these people to "whisper . . . even as it were out of the ground."

Isaiah 29:5-6.

Moreover the multitude of thy strangers shall be like small dust, and the multitude of the terrible ones shall be as chaff that passeth away: yea, it shall be at an instant suddenly.

Thou shalt be visited of the Lord of hosts with thunder, and with earthquake, and great noise, with storm and tempest, and the flame of devouring fire. (Isaiah 29:5-6.)

Wherefore, as those who have been destroyed have been destroyed speedily; and the multitude of their terrible ones shall be as chaff that passeth away—yea, thus saith the Lord God: It shall be at an instant, suddenly—

And when that day shall come they shall be visited of the Lord of Hosts, with thunder and with earthquake, and with a great noise, and with storm, and with tempest, and with the flame of devouring fire. (2 Nephi 26:18; 27:2.)

Elder Orson Pratt said that verse 5 is a description of the destruction which came upon the Nephites because they killed the prophets (see note on 29:3-4 for his statement quoted from *Works*, pp. 270-71). Elder Mark E. Petersen has said that, following the sudden destruction referred to in verse 5, the Nephites would speak "literally from the grave" (CR, Oct. 1977, p. 16). Elder LeGrand Richards taught that verse 6 referred to the destruction of the Nephites at the coming of Christ, as described in 3 Nephi chapter 8 (see CR, Apr. 1976, p. 123). A further interpretation of verse 6 was given by Nephi. He said that those who were not destroyed but who dwindled in unbelief would be smitten by the Gentiles (see 2 Nephi 26:19). Nephi then described in great detail the conditions which would exist among the Gentiles in the last days, causing the Lord to visit *them* with thunder, earthquakes, and so forth (see 2 Nephi 26:20-27:2).

Isaiah 29:7-8. These verses, describing the spiritual famine of the latter days (also described in Amos 8:11-12), have several variations, but the most significant is the Book of Mormon's usage of *Zion* in place of the KJV *Ariel*. In the JST, the Prophet Joseph Smith also made some slight changes in verse 8, but none in verse 7. This may indicate either that he did not complete the revision of this section in the JST or that the word "Ariel" may have a broader application than previously supposed. Note that the KJV verse 8 concludes with "mount Zion" and not "Ariel."

Isaiah 29:9-10. Again, the Book of Mormon contains some significant retentions in these verses:

Stay yourselves, and wonder; cry ye out, and cry: *they* are drunken, but not with wine; *they* stagger, but not with strong drink.	*For behold, all ye that doeth iniquity*, stay yourselves and wonder, *for ye shall* cry out, and cry; *yea, ye shall be* drunken but not with wine, *ye shall* stagger but not with strong drink.
For the Lord hath poured out upon you the spirit of deep sleep, and hath closed your eyes: the prophets and your rulers, the seers hath he covered. (Isaiah 29:9-10.)	For *behold*, the Lord hath poured out upon you the spirit of deep sleep. *For behold, ye have* closed your eyes, *and ye have rejected* the prophets; and your rulers, *and* the seers hath he covered *because of your iniquity*. (2 Nephi 27:4-5.)

Second Nephi 27:4 retains an introduction to verse 9—"For behold, all ye that doeth iniquity"—designating that it was the iniquitous people who would "cry out." The 2 Nephi rendition of the next verse shows that these iniquitous people had closed their own eyes and rejected the prophets, and that the Lord had covered their rulers and seers because of their iniquity. The KJV reads as though the Lord were responsible for these problems, but the Book of Mormon shows that it was the people's choices which had brought upon them their conditions. Paul quoted verse 10 to the Romans as evidence that those of Israel who had hardened their hearts had lost their standing as Israelites, although a remnant had, through the grace of Christ, retained their covenant status (see Romans 11:5-8). Orson Pratt said these verses describe the apostate world at the time the Book of Mormon came forth (see *Works*, p. 275).

2 Nephi 27:6-14. All of these verses were once a part of the original text of Isaiah, but were lost (see JST, Isaiah 29:11-19). They contain many great truths, as given in the outline of this chapter, and should be studied as part of the text of Isaiah 29. The opening phrase in verse 11 of the KJV—"And the vision of all"—is an authentication of the contents of the sealed portion of the record, as described in these verses in 2 Nephi 27 (see especially verses 7, 10-11).

Isaiah 29:11-12.

And the vision of all is become unto you as the words of a book that is sealed, which men deliver to one that is learned, saying, Read this, I pray thee: and he saith, I cannot; for it is sealed:

And the book is delivered to him that is not learned, saying, Read this, I pray thee: and he saith, I am not learned. (Isaiah 29:11-12.)

But behold, it shall come to pass that *the Lord God shall say unto him to whom he shall deliver the book: Take these words which are not sealed and deliver them to another, that he may show them* unto the learned, saying: Read this, I pray thee. *And the learned shall say: Bring hither the book, and I will read them.*

And now, because of the glory of the world and to get gain will they say this, and not for the glory of God.

And the man shall say: I cannot bring the book, for it is sealed.

Then shall the learned say: I cannot read it.

Wherefore it shall come to pass, that *the Lord God will deliver again* the book *and the words* thereof to him that is not learned; and the man that is not learned shall say: I am not learned.

Then shall the Lord God say unto him: The learned shall not

> *read them, for they have rejected them, and I am able to do mine own work; wherefore thou shalt read the words which I shall give unto thee.* (2 Nephi 27:15-20.)

The Book of Mormon retains a much more detailed account of this prophecy, which was literally fulfilled when Martin Harris took a copy of some of the translated characters from the plates to the learned linguist Professor Charles Anthon. Words from the unsealed part of the record were to be given to "another" (Martin Harris) by the man to whom the book was delivered (Joseph Smith). The intentions of the learned were also foretold in Isaiah. The arguments regarding the authenticity of Martin Harris' visit will not be treated here; suffice it to say his story has been authenticated. He told one story and maintained it over the years, while Anthon told several contradictory stories (see B. H. Roberts, *A Comprehensive History of the Church* [Provo, Utah: Brigham Young University Press, 1965], 1:99-109). See the brief account given by Martin Harris (as recorded by Joseph Smith) which shows the literal fulfillment of this prophecy (JS-H 1:63-65).

Joseph Smith said that the angel Moroni quoted many scriptures to him which were soon to be fulfilled (see JS-H 1:41). Oliver Cowdery, in relating some of those scriptures, cited Isaiah 29: 11-14 as having been quoted by Moroni (see *MA*, Feb. 1835, p. 80). Moroni probably referred to the whole chapter. President Joseph Fielding Smith, along with many other General Authorities, proclaimed that the Martin Harris incident literally fulfilled the prophecy of Isaiah (see *DS*, 3:213). Elder Mark E. Petersen noted the significance of Isaiah's referring to Joseph Smith as an unlearned man (see CR, Oct. 1977, pp. 16-18).

The Book of Mormon shows the detail of the prophecy when it records that the Lord God would "deliver *again* the book . . . to him that is not learned" (2 Nephi 27:19). It further shows that the Lord was giving an opportunity for the wisdom of the world to reject these words before he showed the world that he was not dependent upon the learned for the accomplishment of his purposes (see 2 Nephi 27:20). That the

2 Nephi reading was once in the original text of Isaiah is attested to by its presence in the JST.

2 Nephi 27:21-23. Joseph Smith also placed these verses, which concern the sealed section of the book (plates), in the JST.

Isaiah 29:13-14. As stated above, Oliver Cowdery said that the angel Moroni told Joseph Smith these verses were soon to be fulfilled. The Book of Mormon retains the fact that the Lord was going to speak these words to the one who would read the unsealed portion of the plates (Joseph Smith):

	And again it shall come to pass that the Lord shall say unto him that shall read the words that shall be delivered him:
Wherefore the Lord said, Forasmuch as this people draw near me with their mouth, and with their lips do honour me, but have removed their heart far from me, and their fear toward me is taught by the precept of men: (Isaiah 29:13.)	Forasmuch as this people draw near *unto* me with their mouth, and with their lips do honor me, but have removed their hearts far from me, and their fear towards me is taught by the precepts of men— (2 Nephi 27:24-25.)

The "marvellous work and a wonder" in verse 14 is associated with the Lord's setting his hand the second time to recover his people (see Isaiah 11:11) in 2 Nephi 25:17 and 29:1. According to 2 Nephi 25:18, this marvelous work would be accomplished through the bringing forth of the Lord's words, specified as the words of Nephi's seed (the Book of Mormon) in 2 Nephi 29:2. This is also confirmed by the Savior's words to the Nephites after his resurrection (see 3 Nephi 21:1-9).

Joseph Smith recorded that in the spring of 1820 two divine Personages appeared to him and told him that he should join no church because "they draw near to me with their lips, but their hearts are far from me, they teach for doctrines the commandments of men, having a form of godliness, but they deny the power thereof" (JS—H 1:17-19).

The Savior called the scribes and Pharisees "hypocrites," saying that Isaiah had prophesied of them and then quoting verse 13 (see Matthew 15:7-9; Mark 7:6-7). This might lead some to believe that the prophecy was limited to the time of the Savior, and that it was fulfilled. But the fact that he quoted only verse 13, and not verse 14 with it, indicates the Savior was saying that the Pharisees were the *kind* of people Isaiah prophesied of—not that they were the fulfillment of his prophecy. Many of the General Authorities have quoted verse 13 in describing the conditions of the world at the time of the restoration of the gospel (see Appendix B under Isaiah 29:13).

The "marvellous work and a wonder" which was to come forth to correct the situation described in verse 13 is referred to repeatedly in the early sections of the Doctrine and Covenants (see 4:1; 6:1; 11:1; 12:1; 14:1). This marvelous work has been identified by the General Authorities as the Church, Mormonism, the restoration of the gospel, the everlasting gospel, the translation of the Book of Mormon, and several other principles of the gospel (see Appendix B under Isaiah 29:14). An examination of every aspect of the Restoration would show it to be a marvelous work performed or inspired by God. The General Authorities have also testified that this marvelous work has caused the wisdom of the "wise men" to perish and their understanding to be hid. Paul used the latter part of verse 14 in writing to the Corinthians to show that the mission of Christ had confounded the wise and made them look foolish (see 1 Corinthians 1:19-20).

Isaiah 29:15-16. The third in a series of six "woes" in Isaiah chapters 28 through 33 is stated here, but it actually begins with verse 13. The Book of Mormon retains the word "and" in introducing the verse, which indicates that it refers back to what has been said. The warning is to those who refuse the message of the "marvellous work and a wonder" —the Book of Mormon—which would come forth to correct the precepts of men and who even try to work against it in secret. The Book of Mormon also retains the declaration that the Lord will show them that he is aware of their doings (see 2 Nephi 27:27). Probably this is partly a reference to those who would take the 116 pages of manuscript with the intent to change them and frustrate the works of God. In his foreknowledge, God had prepared the way to frustrate their work (see D&C sections 3 and 10). Paul quoted part of verse

16 in demonstrating how the Lord brings out his purposes (see Romans 9:20).

Isaiah 29:17. The Book of Mormon retains the introductory "But behold, saith the Lord of Hosts; I will show unto the children of men that. . . ." This helps to confirm the time when this marvelous work was to come forth. "Lebanon" in this verse has been interpreted by at least three General Authorities—Elders Orson Pratt, Joseph Fielding Smith, and Mark E. Petersen—as the whole land of Canaan, which was given to the house of Israel. Elder Mark E. Petersen has pointed out that Isaiah said a sacred book was to come forth before Palestine would become a fertile land, and that Palestine is now a fertile land (see CR, Oct. 1970, p. 142; see also CR, Oct. 1965, p. 61). President Joseph Fielding Smith cited the change which has come upon Palestine, since the coming forth of the Book of Mormon, through irrigation and cultivation of the land (see *DS*, 3:260-61). Elder Orson Pratt gave a further interpretation of this verse:

> The book, therefore, that Isaiah prophesies of, is to come forth just before the great day of the restoration of Israel to their own lands; at which time Lebanon and all the land of Canaan is again to be blessed, while the fruitful field occupied by the nations of the Gentiles, 'will be esteemed as a forest;' the multitude of the nations of the Gentiles are to perish, and their lands which are now like a fruitful field, are to be left desolate of inhabitants and become as Lebanon has been for many generations past; while Lebanon shall again be occupied by Israel, and be turned into a fruitful field. These great events could not take place until the Lord should first bring forth a book out of the ground. (*Works*, pp. 276-77.)

Isaiah 29:18-19. The "deaf" and the "blind" are those who have been deafened or blinded by the precepts of men, as the Lord had described to Isaiah at the time of his call (see Isaiah 6:9). The effects of the book's coming forth are then described by Isaiah: the deaf shall hear, the blind shall see, and the meek and the poor shall rejoice in the Lord. Elder Mark E. Petersen related this to the spiritual force which would attend the book, and its remarkable effect on those who would read it (see CR, Oct. 1965, p. 61). Elder Orson Pratt saw a literal fulfillment of Isaiah's prophecy in the physically deaf being restored to hearing: "Those who were so deaf that they could not hear the loudest sound, have had their ears opened to hear the glorious and most precious words of the Book of Mormon, and it has been done by the power of God and not of man" (*Works*, p. 277). And Elder LeGrand Richards has given a further application of this passage by noting that the Book of Mormon has been printed in braille so that the physically blind would be able to know its message (see CR, Apr. 1976, p. 124).

Isaiah 29:20-21. The Book of Mormon retains an opening phrase in verse 20 which attributes to the Lord the action referred to in these verses. The Book of Mormon also retains a more definite identification of those spoken of in verse 21:

For the terrible one is brought to nought, and the scorner is consumed, and all that watch for iniquity are cut off:	For *assuredly as the Lord liveth they shall see that* the terrible one is brought to naught, and the scorner is consumed, and all that watch for iniquity are cut off;
That make a man an offender for a word, and lay a snare for him that reproveth in the gate, and turn aside the just for a thing of nought. (Isaiah 29:20-21.)	*And they* that make a man an offender for a word, and lay a snare for him that reproveth in the gate, and turn aside the just for a thing of naught. (2 Nephi 27:31-32.)

Joseph Smith, in writing of the persecution he and other Saints had suffered in Missouri, referred to verse 21: "We refer you to Isaiah, who considers those who make a man an offender for a word, and lay a snare for him that reproveth in the gate. We believe that the old Prophet verily told the truth: and we have no retraction to make." (*TPJS*, p. 124.)

Isaiah 29:22-23. Elder Orson Pratt says that this restoration of the house of Jacob will come through the Book of Mormon:

> The house of Jacob has been made ashamed, and his face has waxed pale, ever since he was driven away from Lebanon or Canaan, but the Lord has now brought forth out of the ground a book which shall, accompanied by His power, restore the tribes of Jacob from the four quarters of the globe, and establish them in the land of Palestine and Lebanon forever; and His holy name they shall no more profane, but shall be a righteous

> people throughout all their generations, while the earth shall stand, and they shall possess their promised land again in eternity, never more to pass away; therefore, they shall never again be made ashamed. It is in vain for the Gentiles to seek the conversion of Jacob, and to bring about their great redemption, only in the way that the Lord God of Israel hath predicted and appointed: they may call meetings and conventions to convert the Jews, but let them know assuredly that the book spoken of by Isaiah is to accomplish the salvation of the house of Jacob, and bring about the restoration of all Israel, while the Gentiles who will not receive it and be numbered and identified with the house of Jacob, must surely perish, yea, and they shall be utterly wasted with storm and tempest, with earthquakes and famine, with the flame of devouring fire, and their fruitful lands shall be esteemed as a forest, while Jacob shall dwell in safety for ever. (*Works*, p. 278; see also 2 Nephi 25:17-18; 29:1-2.)

Isaiah 29:24. The purpose of the Book of Mormon specifically, and of the gospel in general, is shown here. As President Ezra Taft Benson has stated, the Book of Mormon is the great standard which we are to use today in measuring truth (see CR, Apr. 1975, p. 96). Elder Orson Pratt also spoke of the precious contents of the Book of Mormon, which was given to deliver mankind from the "precepts of uninspired men":

> Oh, How precious must be the contents of a book which shall deliver us from all the errors taught by the precepts of uninspired men! Oh, how gratifying to poor, ignorant, erring mortals who have murmured because of the multiplicity of contradictory doctrines that have perplexed and distracted their minds, to read the plain, pure and most precious word of God, revealed in the Book of Mormon! It is like bread to the hungry—like the cool refreshing fountain to him that is ready to perish with thirst. Lift up your heads ye meek of the earth; let the poor among men rejoice in the Holy One of Israel; let them that have erred in spirit and stumbled in judgment, drink from the fountain of understanding; let all that have murmured because of the uncertainty of the precepts of men, read the words of the book, and they shall learn doctrine; let the humble and contrite in heart among all nations be exceedingly glad, for the hour of their redemption from Babylon is at hand; let all Israel praise the God of their fathers in songs of everlasting joy; for that which He spake by the mouth of their prophets, concerning their restoration to

their lands is at hand to be fulfilled; already has the book which Isaiah said should accomplish your restoration and turn Lebanon into a fruitful field, made its appearance; and it truly is "a marvelous work—even a marvelous work and a wonder!" (*Works*, pp. 278-79).

Further Warnings 13

Isaiah 30-35

Chapters 30 through 35 present the last three of the six "woes" beginning in Isaiah chapter 28. These three warnings appear to be based on actual historical incidents. They sound very similar to each other, especially the first two, as they refer to seeking help from Egypt, but careful analysis reveals a distinction between them. The first warning speaks against trusting the *wisdom* of man, and the second against trusting the *power* of man, as shown in the following outline.

1. Woe to those who trust in their own wisdom instead of the Lord's counsel (30:1-17).
   a. Their trust will turn to shame and confusion (30:1-7).
   b. A testimony of their rebellion against the seers and prophets will be recorded (30:8-11).
   c. Because of this false trust, they will be purged until only a remnant is left as an ensign on a hill (30:12-17).
2. The Lord will wait to be exalted in Jerusalem (30:18-33).
   a. He will then answer Israel's prayers (30:19).
   b. After adversity, they will see their Messiah (30:20).
   c. The Holy Ghost will be given as their guide (30:21).
   d. Idols will be cast away (30:22).
   e. The land will be productive, and animals will prosper (30:23-25).
   f. The night will be as bright as the sun, and the day seven times as bright (30:26).

   g. The anger of the Lord will remove the corruptible elements from the earth (30:27-33).

3. Woe to those who trust in the arm of flesh (31:1-9).
   a. The Lord will destroy evil in his own time and wisdom (31:2).
   b. The Egyptians and their horses are flesh, not spirit (31:3).
   c. The Lord will defend Jerusalem (31:4-5).
   d. In the future, people will turn to the Lord and cast away their idols (31:6-7).
   e. The Gentiles will fall from the sword of the Lord and will be afraid of the ensign which is in Zion and in Jerusalem (31:8-9).

4. The Lord will reign in righteousness, and his princes will judge righteously (32:1-20).
   a. The righteous man will receive great knowledge (32:2-4).
   b. The wicked man will not prosper (32:5-8).
   c. The women who are at ease are warned of a coming long period of tribulation (32:9-15).
      1) The land will become thorns and briers.
      2) The houses will be left desolate, and animals will inhabit them.
      3) They will remain desolate until the Spirit is poured out from on high.
   d. The work of righteousness will go forth in peace (32:16-17).
   e. The Lord's people will dwell in peaceful habitations, sure dwellings, and quiet resting places (32:18-20).

5. A warning is given to those who take other men's goods rather than labor with their own hands (33:1-12).
   a. As they sowed, so will they reap (33:1).
   b. The Lord will dwell in Zion (33:2-10).
   c. The spoilers will be burned by fire (33:11-12).

6. Zion will be purged, and the righteous will dwell in everlasting fire (33:13-24).
   a. The sinners in Zion will be afraid (33:14).

   b. The righteous will dwell on high with great blessings and understanding (33:15-19).
   c. Zion and Jerusalem will be permanently established (33:20).
   d. The Lord will the the king and lawgiver (33:21-22).
   e. The inhabitants will be forgiven of their sins (33:23-24).
7. A warning is given that destruction will come upon all nations (34:1-15).
   a. The heavens will be rolled together as a scroll (34:4).
   b. The Lord's sword will come down in judgment (34:5-8).
   c. The whole land will burn night and day (34:9-10).
   d. The land will be desolate, and birds and beasts will inhabit it (34:11-15).
8. The names of the righteous will be written in the book of the Lord (34:16-35:10).
   a. None of these will fail (34:16).
   b. They will inherit the land forever (34:17).
   c. The desert will blossom as a rose (35:1-2).
   d. The weak and the afflicted will be strengthened and healed (35:3-6a).
   e. There will be water in the desert (35:6b-7).
   f. The ransomed of the Lord will return on a highway called the "way of holiness" (35:8-10).

Notes and Commentary

Although none of these chapters are quoted in the Book of Mormon, several passages from chapter 35 are cited in the Doctrine and Covenants, and a few verses appear in the New Testament. These passages give insight into an understanding of Isaiah's message. There are also several very enlightening comments by the Brethren, especially on some of the verses in chapters 32 and 35.

Isaiah 30:1-7. The Book of Mormon prophet Jacob admonished his brethren to "seek not to counsel the Lord, but to take counsel from his hand" (Jacob 4:10). The Lord, through Isaiah, taught a similar lesson to Judah, who was seeking help from Egypt and had not consulted with the Lord about it. President Joseph Fielding Smith cited verses 1 through 17 as an example of the Lord's sending the prophets to warn Israel and Judah before the scattering and captivity came upon them (see *DS*, 3:4).

Isaiah 30:8-17. The warning in verses 1 through 7 is here extended to our day by the Lord's commanding Isaiah to record it as a witness for the latter days (verse 8); a marginal note in the KJV specifically identifies "the latter day." Judah had rebelled against the law of the Lord and would listen only to the false prophets who taught what she wanted to hear. This same condition existed among the Nephites at the time Samuel the Lamanite came among them (see Helaman 13:25-28). Because of this rebellion and rejection of the prophets, a purging was going to come until only a small number of them would be left to become as "a beacon upon the top of a mountain" or "an ensign on a hill." Elder Marion D. Hanks quoted verses 9 and 10 as a warning to those who, in pride or arrogance, think they do not need God or his Christ (see CR, Apr. 1972, p. 127). Elder Thomas S. Monson referred to verse 17 when speaking of the name of the new *Ensign* magazine which was to begin publication in 1971; he referred to the significance which Isaiah had given to the term "ensign" (see CR, Oct. 1970, p. 105; see also Isaiah 5:26; 11:10, 12; 31:9).

Isaiah 30:18-21. These verses are the message of hope which Isaiah holds out for the time when Jerusalem shall become a Zion society, when the Lord will hear Israel's prayers and answer them. The Jewish Publication Society Translation capitalizes and singularizes the word "Teacher" in verse 20, showing that they consider the verse to be a messianic prophecy of the time following their affliction among the nations, when they shall see the Messiah among them. But verse 21 shows that the Holy Ghost will also be their guide. Elder Thomas S. Monson cited this verse as a reference to the "still, small voice which testifies of truth" (CR, Apr. 1975, p. 23). Elder Marion D. Hanks said this verse provided an example of the right voice to follow among the world's many existing voices (see CR, Oct. 1965, p. 120), and he cited verse 18 as an example of the Father's waiting until we recognize our need and open the door for him (see CR, Apr. 1972, pp. 126-27; see also CR, Oct. 1977, p. 56). Elder Mark E. Petersen referred to this verse to show that the Lord expects us to walk in his way (see CR, Apr. 1977, p. 110).

Isaiah 30:26. That Isaiah is referring to the latter days is evidenced by the millennial condition he describes. John gives a similar description in Revelation 21:23.

Isaiah 32:1. The king spoken of here is undoubtedly Christ, and the "princes" are the judges in Israel who will rule and judge in Zion under the law of consecration and during the Millennium (see D&C 58:17-22).

Isaiah 32:13-20. These verses were given the following interpretation by Elder Orson Pratt: Verse 13 was the curse seen by Isaiah to come upon the land of Palestine, that instead of productive land to sustain the people, thorns and briers were to come forth, and this desolation was to remain for a long time, until the Spirit was poured out from on high. "What are we to understand by the prediction that the wilderness shall be a fruitful field when the Spirit is poured out from on high? We are to understand the same as is recorded in the thirty-fifth chapter of this prophecy. . . ." (*JD*, 18:144-45). Elder Pratt was undoubtedly acquainted with the Prophet Joseph Smith's changing of a clause in verse 14 in the JST—"the *houses* of the city shall be left *desolate*"—because he cross-referenced verse 15 (on the wilderness becoming a fruitful field) to Isaiah 35:1-2, Isaiah's prophecy of the wilderness blossoming as a rose. It should be noted that 32:15 contains basically the same phrasing as 29:17. Elder Pratt interpreted verses 17 and 18 as a description of the Saints' dwelling in peace and safety in the wilderness of the Rocky Mountains (which were to "blossom as the rose"), in contrast to their troublesome times in Missouri: " 'You shall be persecuted from city to city and from synagogue to synagogue, and but few shall stand to receive their inheritance.' But when the time should come for Zion to go up into the wilderness things would be changed; [']then my people shall dwell in peaceable habitations, in sure dwelling places, and in quietness and assurance.' " (*JD*, 18:149). He also used verse 19 as a description of Salt Lake City, organized at the base of the mountains and enjoying vegetation, while in the mountains surrounding them there were snow and storms in great fury:

> Will they have any capital city when they get up into the mountain desert? O, yes. Isaiah says here—"When it shall hail, coming down on the forest, the city shall be low in a low

> place." How often have I thought of this since we laid out this great city, twenty-eight years ago! How often have this people reflected in their meditations upon the fulfillment of this prophecy! They have seen, on this eastern range of mountains and on the range of mountains to the west of this valley, snow and storms pelting down with great fury, as though winter in all its rigor and ferocity had overtaken the mountain territory, and at the same time, here, "low in a low place," was a city, organized at the very base of these mountains, enjoying all the blessings of a spring temperature, the blessings of a temperature not sufficient to cut off our vegetation. What a contrast! "When it shall hail, coming down on the forest, the city shall be low in a low place." That could not be Jerusalem, no such contrast in the land of Palestine round about Jerusalem! It had reference to the latter-day Zion, the Zion of the mountains. (*JD*, 18:149.)

Finally, Elder Pratt interpreted verse 20 as the Saints' making their settlements along the sides of streams, where they could build canals to send out water over the land. Elder Eldred G. Smith cited verse 17 to describe the assurance one receives when he is living in accordance with God's will (see CR, Apr. 1972, p. 147).

Isaiah 33:14-16. Elder Bruce R. McConkie has given an enlightening explanation of these verses:

> Now for a text I take these words of Isaiah, words which he addressed to us, to the House of Israel, to the members of the Lord's Kingdom. He asked: ". . . Who among us shall dwell with the devouring fire? who among us shall dwell with everlasting burnings?" (Isaiah 33:14.)
>
> That is, who in the Church shall gain an inheritance in the celestial kingdom? Who will go where God and Christ and holy beings are? Who will overcome the world, work the works of righteousness, and enduring in faith and devotion to the end hear the blessed benediction, "Come, and inherit the kingdom of my Father"? Isaiah answers: "He that walketh righteously, and speaketh uprightly; he that despiseth the gain of oppressions, that shaketh his hands from holding of bribes, that stoppeth his ears from hearing of blood, and shutteth his eyes from seeing evil; He shall dwell on high. . . ." (Isaiah 33:15-16.)
>
> Now if I may, I shall take these words of Isaiah, spoken by the power of the Holy Ghost in the first instance, and give

some indication as to how they apply to us and our circumstances.

First, "He that walketh righteously, and speaketh uprightly." That is, building on the atoning sacrifice of the Lord Jesus Christ, we must keep the commandments. We must speak the truth and work the works of righteousness. We shall be judged by our thoughts, our words and our deeds.

Second, ". . . he that despiseth the gain of oppressions." That is, we must act with equity and justice toward our fellowmen. It is the Lord himself who said that he, at the day of his coming, will be a swift witness against those that oppress the hireling in his wages.

Third, ". . . he that shaketh his hands from holding of bribes." That is, we must reject every effort to buy influence, and instead deal fairly and impartially with our fellowmen. God is no respecter of persons. He esteemeth all flesh alike; and those only who keep his commandments find special favor with him. Salvation is free; it cannot be purchased with money; and those only are saved who abide the law upon which its receipt is predicated. Bribery is of the world.

Fourth, he ". . . that stoppeth his ears from hearing of blood, and shutteth his eyes from seeing evil." That is, we must not center our attention on evil and wickedness. We must cease to find fault and look for good in government and in the world. We must take an affirmative, wholesome approach to all things. (CR, Oct. 1973, pp. 55-56.)

Isaiah 33:18. This verse is quoted by Paul, although with some differences, in 1 Corinthians 1:20 to show that God has made the wise of the world foolish.

Isaiah 33:20. The Prophet Joseph Smith reminded the Saints who had been driven out of Jackson County that they should not sell their lands but should hold them until the Lord opened the way for their return (see *TPJS*, p. 33; see also D&C 90:37). Isaiah indicates that it applies to both Zion and Jerusalem.

Isaiah 34:1-10. Elder Joseph Fielding Smith quoted Isaiah 34:1-8 to show that the Old Testament prophets spoke of the conditions of today. He supported his premise by noting that the word "Idumea" means the world, and that the heavenly host's being "dissolved" and the heavens' being "rolled together as a scroll" will take place in the dispensation of the fulness of times. (*ST*, pp. 150-51.) This is also taught in the

Doctrine and Covenants and the Book of Mormon; Doctrine and Covenants 1:36 identifies Idumea as the world, and the Savior, in teaching the Nephites, referred to the time when he would come in his glory and the earth would be "wrapt together as a scroll" (3 Nephi 26:3). The Lord also used the language of verse 5 in the preface to the Doctrine and Covenants in referring to the day of his coming (see D&C 1:12-14). Peter paraphrased verse 4 in his second general epistle as he proclaimed that the day of the Lord's return would come (see 2 Peter 3:10-13). John, on the Isle of Patmos, also saw this future event (see Revelation 6:14), and Joseph Smith referred to the time of Christ's coming as a time when the heavens "are to be unfolded as a scroll when it is rolled up" (*TPJS*, p. 29). The wording of verse 10 is similar to Revelation 14:11.

Isaiah 34:16-17.

Seek ye out of the book of the Lord, and read: no one of these shall fail, none shall want *her* mate: for my mouth it hath commanded, and *his* spirit it hath gathered them.

And *he hath* cast the lot for them, and *his hand hath* divided it unto them by line: they shall possess it for ever, from generation to generation shall they dwell therein. (KJV, Isaiah 34:16-17.)

Seek ye out of the book of the Lord, and read *the names written therein*; no one of these shall fail; none shall want *their* mate; for my mouth it hath commanded, and *my* Spirit it hath gathered them.

And *I have* cast the lot for them, and *I have* divided it unto them by line; they shall possess it forever; from generation to generation they shall dwell therein. (JST, Isaiah 34:16-17.)

The "book of the Lord" is the book containing the names of those who have eternal life (see D&C 85:9, 128:6-7; Revelation 20:12-15). Elder Orson Pratt said verse 16 showed that the Spirit of the Lord should be the instrument used in gathering Israel together (see *JD*, 18:145). These two verses seem to fit better into the context of chapter 35.

Isaiah 35:1-2. These two verses are often mentioned by Latter-day Saints in relationship to the settlement of the Saints in the valleys of the Rockies. President Joseph Fielding Smith (see *DS*, 3:346-47), Elder LeGrand Richards (see CR, Oct. 1966, p. 42), Elder Milton R. Hunter (see CR, Oct. 1965, p. 81), and Elder Orson Pratt (see *JD*, 18:145) have all so interpreted these verses. However, the Doctrine and Covenants gives a broader interpretation: it refers to Jacob's flourishing in the wilderness and the Lamanites' blossoming as a rose, noting also that Zion will flourish upon the hills and be assembled to the place which the Lord has appointed (see D&C 49:24-25). Isaiah 35:1-2 is frequently said to refer to a blossoming taking place in the land of Judah; obviously, the Lord can and will make more than one place blossom as he gathers his people (see D&C 117:6-8).

Isaiah 35:3-7. Elder Orson Pratt quoted verses 3 and 4 to show that the blossoming spoken of in verses 1 and 2 was to be fulfilled before the second coming of Christ and not after. He stated that until the kingdom of God was set up in all its purity and with all its ordinances, the weak could not be strengthened and the blossoming could not take place. But with the restoration of the Church, those assembled should look for the coming of the Great Redeemer. He further spoke of the healings noted in verses 5 and 6 as being fulfilled when Jesus comes (see *JD*, 18:145-46). President Hugh B. Brown also cited verse 4 as a Second Coming prophecy (see CR, Apr. 1966, p. 120). Paul quoted verse 3 as an admonition, but not as a fulfillment of prophecy (see Hebrews 12:12). The Lord, through the Prophet Joseph Smith, used the wording in verse 3 to instruct Frederick G. Williams in his duties as a member of the First Presidency (see D&C 81:5).

Elder Orson Pratt used verses 6 and 7 as a prophecy of the Saints' coming to the wilderness of the Rocky Mountains: "Have you seen anything of the nature of this prediction fulfilled? Latter-day Saints, how was it with this wilderness twenty-eight years ago this summer when the pioneers entered this land, and when several thousands followed them in the autumn of that same year?" (*JD*, 18:147.) Elder Paul H. Dunn quoted verse 7 as a description of the "happy future of Zion" (CR, Oct. 1968, see p. 52). These verses seem to describe more specifically the Saints in the Rockies; this is concluded from the verses which follow.

Isaiah 35:8-10. The events spoken of in these verses are treated more fully in Doctrine and Covenants 133:26-34, where the return of the ten lost tribes is described. They shall come to Ephraim, who will bless them with "the blessing of the everlasting God." This will be preceded, of course, by Ephraim's gathering in preparation for the other tribes to come (see D&C 45:71; 66:11; 101:18). The Prophet Joseph Smith said that verse 10 referred to the Zion on the American continent, unto which the ransomed of the Lord would return (see *TPJS*, pp. 17, 34). President David O. McKay cited verse 8 as evidence that the scriptures are so simple that "wayfaring men, though fools," could understand them (see CR, Oct. 1966, p. 137).

There is a clarifying change in the Joseph Smith Translation which corresponds with Doctrine and Covenants 133:26-34.

And an highway shall be there, and a way, and it shall be called The way of holiness; the unclean shall not pass over it; but it shall be for those: the wayfaring men, though fools, shall not err therein. (KJV Isaiah 35:8.)

And a highway shall be there: *for* a way *shall be cast up*, and it shall be called the way of holiness. The unclean shall not pass over *upon* it; but it shall be *cast up* for those *who are clean, and* the wayfaring men, though *they are accounted* fools, shall not err therein. (JST Isaiah 35:8.)

The Historical Setting

14

Isaiah 36-39

The Prophet Joseph Smith taught, "Every man who has a calling to minister to the inhabitants of the world was ordained to that very purpose in the Grand Council of heaven before this world was" (*TPJS*, p. 365). Isaiah was thus foreordained to come forth in a very crucial period of Israel's history, and was undoubtedly one of the "noble and great" intelligences (spirits) chosen in the premortal life to be rulers in God's kingdom (see Abraham 3:22-23). As a ruler or servant in God's kingdom, Isaiah was sent to the earth to witness against the rulers of men in a period which saw the Assyrian conquest of the ten and one-half tribes who occupied the northern kingdom of Israel. Isaiah was further assigned to warn, testify, and prophesy to the kings and people of the southern kingdom of Judah, the other nation of God's covenant people, as they faced threats and conquests from foreign nations.

Isaiah's ministry was centered in Jerusalem and spanned the reigns of four kings of Judah: Uzziah (or Azariah, as he is named in 2 Kings 15:1), Jotham, Ahaz, and Hezekiah (see Isaiah 1:1). The length of time covered in his ministry is considered to be as long as sixty or as short as forty years, depending upon which chronology one follows. Isaiah's great vision of Christ, given to him in the year that king Uzziah died (see Isaiah 6:1), is considered to be his call to his ministry. According to Jewish tradition his martyrdom came under the hands of Manasseh, the son of (and successor to) Hezekiah, who had him sawn asunder with a wooden saw (thus later artists have often depicted Isaiah holding a saw). Therefore, his ministry included only the last year, or part of the last year, of the reign of King Uzziah, but the full reigns of the two and possibly three succeeding kings. According to the biblical accounts of Kings and Chronicles, this would total about sixty-two years—758 to 697 B.C. However, there is a nearly complete list of the dates of the Assyrian kings. Uzziah's name is thought to be on that list at the date 740 B.C. If Uzziah was still alive in 740 B.C., then Isaiah's ministry would not have commenced before that date and would have lasted about forty-three years—740 to 697 B.C.

The length of his ministry is not as important as is the message of Isaiah. A reading of the available historical accounts in the Bible would help us understand the message of Isaiah. Nephi was able to understand Isaiah because he knew "concerning the regions round about . . . [and] the judgments of God, which hath come to pass among the Jews" (2 Nephi 25:6). Since we cannot live in those regions and times as Nephi did, we will have to read about them to gain insights which will help us understand God's judgments among the Jews. The reigns of the four kings under whom Isaiah prophesied are recorded in 2 Kings, 2 Chronicles, and Isaiah 36-39. We should keep in mind that these accounts are abridgments and not full histories; nevertheless, they are helpful. (An additional source which would be helpful to students of this period is the record of the Jewish historian Josephus.)

One of the problems we face in reading these accounts is keeping the chronology straight. Because each account contributes something unique to the history, we will give a synopsis of the reign of each of the four kings below. For convenience and clarity, we will also provide a parallel reference harmony of the various accounts where it is deemed helpful. Although Isaiah's ministry began at the end of Uzziah's reign, an outline of the full reign of Uzziah is included for background.

1. Uzziah (Azariah), the first king. (2 Kings 15:1-7; 2 Chronicles 26. The account in 2 Chronicles, although an abridgment, is the most detailed.)

a. Uzziah began to reign at age sixteen and reigned fifty-two years in Jerusalem. (2 Kings 15:1-2; 2 Chronicles 26:1-3.)
b. Uzziah did what was right in the sight of the Lord, except he did not destroy the worship of Baal (the pagan god). (2 Kings 15:3-4; 2 Chronicles 26:4.)
c. Uzziah sought God and had understanding in the visions of God; as long as he sought the Lord, God made him to prosper. (2 Chronicles 26:5.)
d. God helped him in wars against the Philistines and the Arabians, and his fame spread. (2 Chronicles 26:6-8.)
e. He built towers in Jerusalem and the desert and dug many wells, for he had many cattle and loved husbandry. (2 Chronicles 26:9-10.)
f. Uzziah had an army of 307,500 men. Uzziah made engines to shoot arrows and stones from the towers and bulwarks. (2 Chronicles 26:11-15.)
g. He was smitten with leprosy because he usurped the authority of the sons of Aaron and attempted to burn incense upon the altar. He thus dwelt in seclusion, and Jotham reigned in his stead. (2 Kings 15:5; 2 Chronicles 26:16-21.)
h. Isaiah had a vision of the Lord and was called to be a prophet in the last year of Uzziah's reign. (Isaiah 6.)
i. A fuller account of Uzziah's acts were written in the "chronicles of the kings of Judah." (2 Kings 15:6-7.)
j. Isaiah the prophet wrote a further account of Uzziah. (2 Chronicles 26:22.)

2. Jotham, the second king. (2 Kings 15:32-38; 2 Chronicles 27.)
   a. Jotham began to reign at age twenty-five and reigned sixteen years. (2 Kings 15:32-33; 2 Chronicles 27:1. Part or all of his reign may have occurred while his father dwelt in seclusion, and thus may have overlapped somewhat with the reign of his father. This would account at least partially for the time discrepancy between the biblical and the Assyrian accounts.)
   b. Jotham did right in the sight of God, but entered not

into the temple. The people were corrupt. (2 Kings 15:34; 2 Chronicles 27:2.)

c. Jotham built the high gate of the house of the Lord. He also built much on the wall of Ophel, and cities, castles, and towers. He did not remove the "high places" (places for the worship of Baal). (2 Kings 15:35; 2 Chronicles 27:3-4.)

d. Jotham defeated the Ammonites and received tribute from them. He became mighty because he "prepared his ways" before the Lord. (2 Chronicles 27:5-6.)

e. Rezin, king of Assyria, and Pekah, king of Israel, began to come against Judah. (2 Kings 15:37.)

3. Ahaz, the third king. (2 Kings 16; 2 Chronicles 28.)

a. Ahaz began to reign at age twenty and reigned sixteen years. He did not do right in the sight of God, but followed the practices of Baalism—pagan worship. (2 Kings 16:1-4; 2 Chronicles 28:1-4.)

b. The Lord delivered Ahaz into the hands of the kings of Syria and Israel, both of whom slew many and took many more captive. (2 Chronicles 28:5-8.)

c. A prophet named Oded appeared in Samaria and informed the house of Israel why they were able to capture Judah and also warned them of their own sins. In response to this warning, Israel repented and took the captives to Jericho, along with their spoils, and freed them to return to Judah. (2 Chronicles 28:9-15.)

d. King Ahaz, following Judah's defeat by the Syrians and Israel, sent to the king of Assyria for help because the Lord had allowed Judah to be smitten again, this time by the hand of Edom and the Philistines. Ahaz gave the king of Assyria riches out of his own house and the house of the Lord, but the king of Assyria did not help him. (2 Chronicles 28:16-21.)

e. The kings of Syria and of Israel came up again against Judah, but did not prevail. The Lord sent Isaiah to prophesy of the breaking up of the Northern Kingdom (the capture of the ten tribes). This was to be accomplished by the Assyrians and Egyptians. (2 Kings 16:5; Isaiah 7:1-3.)

f. The king of Syria captured Elath and drove the Jews out. Ahaz sent silver and gold to the king of Assyria and asked him for help. Assyria responded and took Damascus (Syria). (2 Kings 16:6-9.)

g. King Ahaz sacrificed unto the gods of Damascus because he thought these gods had helped the Syrians. He visited the king of Assyria at Damascus and saw an altar. Upon returning, he had his priest build one like it to offer sacrifices. He also removed sacred vessels from the temple and thus desecrated it further. (2 Kings 16:10-17; 2 Chronicles 28:22-25.)

h. In the twelfth year of the reign of Ahaz, Pekah (king of Israel) died, fulfilling Isaiah's prophecy that both lands would be forsaken of their kings (see Isaiah 7:16). Hoshea was appointed king of Israel. (2 Kings 17:1.)

i. Ahaz died, but was not buried in the sepulchres of the kings of Israel. (2 Kings 16:19-20; 2 Chronicles 28:26-27.)

4. Hezekiah, the fourth king. (2 Kings 18-20; 2 Chronicles 29-32; Isaiah 36-39.[1])

a. Hezekiah began to reign at age twenty-five and reigned twenty-nine years in Judah. (2 Kings 18:1-2; 2 Chronicles 29:1. His reign commenced in the third year of the reign of Hoshea, the last king of Israel before the conquest by Assyria carried the ten tribes into captivity. The conquest of Israel took place six years after Hezekiah commenced his reign in Judah, which shows why Hezekiah was concerned about Assyria.)

b. Hezekiah, according to the authors of both Kings and Chronicles, "did that which was right in the sight of the Lord." (2 Kings 18:3; 2 Chronicles 29:2.) The accomplishments of his first year in office—as recorded in 2 Chronicles 29-31—exemplify why he was so described:

---

1. These chapters in Isaiah are almost identical to part of the account in 2 Kings, and were probably included in the book of Isaiah because they contain four prophecies uttered by Isaiah during this time. The other references in Kings, although covering the time period of Isaiah, do not include any events which mention Isaiah.

1) He reopened the doors of the house of the Lord, which his wicked father Ahaz had closed (see 2 Chronicles 28:24), and he repaired and cleansed the temple. This he accomplished through restoring the stewardship for the temple services to the sons of Levi. Following this cleansing, they offered sacrifices unto God therein. (2 Chronicles 29:3-36.)
2) He invited all of Israel from Dan to Beersheba (the northern and southern boundaries) to come to Jerusalem and observe the Passover. This they had not done for a long time. When invitations were sent out, many scorned the idea, but many of the tribes of Asher, Manasseh, and Zebulun responded. Many of Ephraim and Manasseh participated in the Passover also, though not according to the written instructions. However, Hezekiah prayed for them, asking for their pardon based upon the intentions of their hearts. The Lord hearkened to Hezekiah and "healed the people." (From this we learn that the Lord judges by the heart, and not by outward appearances; compare 1 Samuel 16:7; D&C 46:9.) There was great joy in Jerusalem following the keeping of the Passover. (2 Chronicles 30.)
3) He removed the images and groves of Baal until they were utterly destroyed.[2] He appointed the courses of the priests and Levites, and urged the people to give their tithes and offerings to the priests. They responded, and the priests were to lay up a great store. (2 Chronicles 31.)

The author of 2 Chronicles concluded his record of the events in the first year of Hezekiah's reign with the following two verses:

> And thus did Hezekiah throughout all Judah, and wrought that which was good and right and truth before the Lord his god.
>
> And in every work that he began in the service of the house of God, and in the law, and in the commandments, to seek his

---

2. He also broke in pieces the brazen serpent which Moses had made (see Numbers 21:4-9) because the children of Israel had apparently been worshipping it by burning incense to it. (2 Kings 18:4.)

God, he did it with all his heart, and prospered. (2 Chronicles 31:20-21.)

c. Hezekiah trusted in the Lord and kept his commandments. The Lord was with him, and he prospered wherever he went. (2 Kings 18:5-8.)
   1) He rebelled against the king of Assyria and served him not.
   2) He smote the Philistines.

d. In the fourth year of Hezekiah's reign, 722 B.C., Shalmaneser, king of Assyria, besieged Israel, Judah's sister kingdom to the north. Three years later, Shalmaneser carried the ten and one-half tribes of Israel into captivity in Assyria and replaced them with other captives from Babylon and Syria. These intermarried with those Israelites who remained and thus became the Samaritan nation. (This is a good example of a gentile "graft" [a wild olive branch] into Israel [a tame olive tree], as spoken of by the prophet Zenos in Jacob 5:7-14 in the Book of Mormon.) The record states that the reason these tribes were taken away was that they obeyed not the voice of the Lord, but transgressed his covenant and all the commandments given by Moses. (2 Kings 18:9-12.)

e. The bringing in of these Babylonian captives illustrates one of the customs of the times which brought the judgments of God. The record states that, at the beginning of the Babylonians' dwelling in their new land, the Lord sent lions among them, which slew some of them. These Babylonians attributed their problem to their not knowing "the manner of the God of the land." Each land purportedly had its own god, which was to be worshipped in that land. This belief was a continual nemesis to the Israelites, and explains why Jehovah often proclaimed that "beside me there is no God" (see Isaiah 44:6). The captives sent word of their problem to the king of Assyria, who sent one of the priests of Israel back to Samaria to teach them the manner of the God of the land. This priest taught them to fear the Lord. They did fear the Lord, but they also made gods of their own nations and put them in the places where the Israelites had worshipped Baal, the pagan god. This illustrates again how the Lord gave these people (the gentile "grafts") an opportunity to learn of him, but they rejected him. (2 Kings 17:24-41.)

Isaiah	*2 Kings*	*2 Chronicles*
f. Sennacherib, king of Assyria, came against the cities of Judah, and Hezekiah paid tribute to him.		
36:1	18:13	32:1
	18:14-16	
g. Hezekiah stopped the water, strengthened his defenses, and admonished his people to trust in the Lord.		
		32:2-8
h. Sennacherib's servants brought an army against Jerusalem. Isaiah 36:5 is rendered more plainly in the JST, as noted below.		
36:2	18:17	32:9
36:3	18:18	
36:4	18:19	32:10
36:5	18:20	

I say, *sayest thou, (but they are but vain words)* I have counsel and strength for war: now on whom dost thou trust, that thou rebellest against me? (KJV, Isaiah 36:5.)

I say, *thy words are but vain when thou sayest*, I have counsel and strength for war. Now, on whom dost thou trust that thou rebellest against me? (JST, Isaiah 36:5.)

Isaiah	*2 Kings*	*2 Chronicles*
36:6-14	18:21-29	
36:15	18:30	32:11
		32:12
36:16-18	18:31-33	
36:19-20	18:34-35	32:13-14
		32:15-16
36:21	18:36	
i. The servants of Hezekiah brought the message of the Assyrians.		
36:22	18:37	
37:1	19:1	

Isaiah	*2 Kings*	*2 Chronicles*

j. Hezekiah sent his servants to Isaiah the prophet.

37:2-4	19:2-4	

k. Isaiah prophesied that the king of Assyria would fall by the sword in his own land. This was the first of four prophecies uttered by Isaiah in these historical chapters.

37:5-7	19:5-7	

l. The servants of Sennacherib returned to meet their king.

37:8	19:8	

m. The king of Assyria sent another message to Hezekiah. The JST adds "he" to the last phrase of Isaiah 37:17—"which *he* hath sent to reproach the living God." While this is a plainer reading, it does not affect the meaning of the verse.

37:9-10	19:9-10	32:17
37:11	19:11	
		32:18
37:12	19:12	32:19
37:13	19:13	
37:14	19:14	32:20
37:15-20	19:15-19	

n. Isaiah sent to Hezekiah the answer to his prayer unto the Lord. After chastising Sennacherib, king of Assyria, the Lord (through Isaiah) uttered another prophecy—the second in these historical chapters—and gave a sign (see Isaiah 37:30). This sign seems to be a description of the year of Jubilee, which was celebrated every fifty years among the Israelites. Every seventh year the land was to rest (this was the sabbatical year). After seven sabbatical years (forty-nine years), the land was also to rest the fiftieth year (see Leviticus chapter 25). Thus the Lord, through Isaiah, was assuring the Jews' continuation in the land and his blessings upon the land for an extended period of time. However, he also foretold a future time when a remnant of Judah (the Mulekites in 589 B.C.) would escape and "come up upon mount Zion." This is based on the

Isaiah	*2 Kings*	*2 Chronicles*

JST, as noted below. (See also Ezekiel 17:22-24; *Works*, pp. 280-81.)

37:21-32	19:20-31	

For out of Jerusalem shall go forth a remnant, and they that escape out of mount Zion: the zeal of the Lord of hosts shall do this. (KJV, Isaiah 37:32.)	For out of Jerusalem shall go forth a remnant; and they that escape out of *Jerusalem shall come up upon mount Zion*; the zeal of the Lord of hosts shall do this. (JST, Isaiah 37:32.)

The Lord, through Isaiah, then prophesied further concerning the king of Assyria's returning by the way he came.

37:33-35	19:32-34	

The fulfillment of the prophecy is then recorded (Isaiah 37:36); the JST clarifies a confusing reading in the KJV, as noted below.

37:36	19:35	32:21

Then the angel of the Lord went forth, and smote in the camp of the Assyrians a hundred and fourscore and five thousand: and when they arose early in the morning, behold, they were all dead corpses. (KJV, Isaiah 37:36.)	Then the angel of the Lord went forth, and smote in the camp of the Assyrians a hundred and fourscore and five thousand, and when they *who were left* arose, early in the morning, behold, they were all dead corpses. (JST, Isaiah 37:36.)

		32:22-23

o. Isaiah's first prophecy in these historical chapters was then fulfilled as the king of Assyria returned to Nineveh.

37:37-38	19:36-37	

p. Hezekiah's life was extended fifteen years. Hezekiah reigned for twenty-nine years, so his illness would have been in his fourteenth year as king of Judah. The extension of Hezekiah's life (see Isaiah 38:4-8)

Isaiah	*2 Kings*	*2 Chronicles*

was the third prophecy uttered by Isaiah in these historical chapters. Concerning this event, President Spencer W. Kimball has written: "I believe we may die prematurely but seldom exceed our time very much. One exception was Hezekiah, 25-year-old king of Judah who was far more godly than his successors or predecessors." (*Faith Precedes the Miracle* [Salt Lake City: Deseret Book Company, 1975], p. 104.)

38:1	20:1	32:24
38:2-6	20:2-6	
38:7-8	29:9-11	
		32:25-26
38:9-17		

The following changes in the JST clarify the reading:

What shall I say? he hath both spoken unto me, and himself hath done it: I shall go softly all my years in the bitterness of my soul.	What shall I say? he hath both spoken unto me, and himself hath *healed me.* I shall go softly all my years, *that I may not walk* in the bitterness of my soul.
O Lord, *by these things men live, and in all these things is the life of my spirit:* so wilt thou recover me, and make me to live.	Oh Lord, *thou who art the life of my spirit, in whom I live;* so wilt thou recover me, and make me to live; *and in all these things I will praise thee.*
Behold, *for peace* I had great bitterness: but thou hast in love to my soul delivered it from the pit of corruption: for thou hast cast all my sins behind thy back. (KJV, Isaiah 38:15-17.)	Behold, I had great bitterness *instead of peace,* but thou hast in love to my soul, *saved me* from the pit of corruption, for thou hast cast all my sins behind thy back. (JST, Isaiah 38:15-17.)

38:18-20		
38:21-22	20:7-8	

q. Isaiah prophesied that the king's treasures and the king's sons would be carried into Babylon. This was the fourth prophecy in these historical chapters, and it concluded the historical account recorded in Isaiah.

Isaiah	*2 Kings*	*2 Chronicles*
39:1	20:12	32:31
39:2-8	20:13-19	

r. Hezekiah had great riches and honor. He built large treasures, storehouses, and cities. He had flocks and herds in abundance, for God had given him much substance. (2 Chronicles 32:27-29.)

s. Hezekiah stopped the upper watercourse of Gihon and brought it to the west side of Jerusalem. (2 Chronicles 32:30. This account was highlighted in 1880 when two boys discovered some engravings in the middle of the tunnel leading from the spring of Gihon to the pool of Siloam, telling the history of Hezekiah's excavation. The inscription was removed and is kept today in the Museum of Ancient Orient in Istanbul. Whether this tunnel was the same one referred to in 2 Chronicles 32:2-4 or a separate one is not clear. However, many tourists have waded through "Hezekiah's tunnel" on their visits to Jerusalem. For a fuller account, see *IE*, Aug. 1967, pp. 4-11.)

t. The rest of the acts of Hezekiah were written in "the vision of Isaiah the prophet." (2 Chronicles 32:32.)

Isaiah was thus a prophet raised up in the midst of turmoil in the nations of Israel. He stood before kings and warned them of the consequences of their actions, or gave directions to them as the will of the Lord was revealed to him. He witnessed the downfall of Judah's sister nation to the north, and stood fearless in the face of Judah's threatened overthrow, knowing and testifying that God would deliver that nation. The inspiring prophecies he made to Hezekiah were all fulfilled.

Although Isaiah knew of the eventual downfall of Judah, he stood not merely as a witness against the nation. More importantly, he was a proclaimer of the great blessings which would be restored unto Israel in the latter days, as he had been shown by the Lord. This, in fact, is the primary message of the book of Isaiah.

The Lord's Coming in Glory

15

Isaiah 40

Chapters 40 through 66 are considered by most scholars today to have been written by a different author (or different authors) than the one who wrote the first part of the book (see Appendix A). Without repeating the arguments against multiple authorship, we will simply state here that we do not agree. However, we recognize that these chapters are different in certain aspects from chapters 1 through 35. While the revelations of the first chapters fall into separate sections rather easily, these later chapters may originally have been one continuous vision or series of visions (see chapter 3 of this work). It is therefore somewhat difficult to divide the present-day chapters 40 through 66 into distinct sections for study. Some of the divisions are more easily determined because of the way they are quoted in the Book of Mormon; but those long sections which are not in the Book of Mormon —chapters 40 through 47 and 56 through 65—are placed into rather arbitrary divisions.

Because chapter 40 seems to stand by itself, it may be an introductory chapter to all the remaining ones. Most noted for its prophecy of John the Baptist's preparing the way for the coming of Christ, it reveals a much broader context. The two great capitals of the house of Israel, Zion and Jerusalem (Judah), are both prominent in this chapter. A recurring comparison between the all-powerful Lord God of Israel and the nothingness of the idol-gods of men is introduced here as well. Chapter 40 seems to set the stage for a study of the remaining chapters of Isaiah.

1. A comfort is given Jerusalem by the Lord (40:1-2).
    a. Her iniquity is pardoned (40:2).
    b. She has paid double for her sins (40:2).
2. The glory of the Lord will be revealed to all flesh (40:3-8).
    a. The spirit of Elias will prepare the way before the Lord (40:3).
    b. The earth will be restored as it was before the curse (40:4).
    c. The Spirit of the Lord will consume all corruptible flesh (40:6-8).
3. The Lord will come with a strong hand, and his arm will rule (40:9-11).
    a. Zion will bring good tidings from a high mountain before he comes (40:9).
    b. Jerusalem will lift up its voice and proclaim God before he comes (40:9).
    c. The Lord will feed his flock like a shepherd when he comes (40:11).
4. God has created all things, and has all knowledge and all power (40:12-31).
    a. The nations of the earth are nothing in comparison (40:12-17).
    b. The graven images worshipped by man are nothing (40:18-24).
    c. Even Jacob (Israel) does not recognize the power of God (40:27).
    d. Those who wait upon the Lord will be given power and strength (40:29-31).

Notes and Commentary

A careful study of the New Testament helps us understand the first part of this chapter. The New Testament passages can be misleading, however, if not thoroughly analyzed. The Doctrine and Covenants and modern Church leaders have also given great insight into the first part of the chapter. If we correctly understand the early verses, we can understand the remainder more easily.

Isaiah 40:1-2. The message of comfort to Jerusalem, "that her warfare is accomplished, that her iniquity is pardoned," clearly refers to the latter days. The Anchor Bible translates this line "that her sentence is served, her penalty is paid." Judah was to be sent through the "furnace of affliction" (see 48:10), so the message given here is to be fulfilled after she has been through that furnace. A look at history and at present-day circumstances shows her still to be going through that furnace. The rest of the chapter also supports a Second Coming time period.

Isaiah 40:3-5. Because these verses are quoted in the New Testament in connection with John the Baptist, it is generally assumed that John's mission was their fulfillment. It is true that John was sent to prepare the way of the Lord. Lehi prophesied of a prophet who "should go forth and cry in the wilderness: Prepare ye the way of the Lord, and make his paths straight" (1 Nephi 10:8). He also foretold that this prophet would baptize the Messiah with water (see 1 Nephi 10:9). This clearly identifies the prophet as John the Baptist. His father Zacharias prophesied at the time he named him that John would "go before the face of the Lord to prepare his ways" (Luke 1:76). John himself announced that he was "the voice of one crying in the wilderness . . . as said the prophet Esaias [Isaiah]" (John 1:23). All three of the other gospel writers also identify him as such (see Matthew 3:3; Mark 1:3; Luke 3:4). However, Matthew and Mark quote only verse 3 of Isaiah 40—not verses 4 and 5, which clearly speak of the Lord's second coming. Luke quotes verses 3 through 5, but the JST interrupts this passage with five additional verses which outline the mission of Christ from the meridian of time until his second coming:

As it is written in the book of the words of Esaias the prophet, saying, The voice of one crying in the wilderness, Prepare ye the way of the Lord, make his paths straight.	As it is written in the book of the prophet Esaias; and these are the words, saying, The voice of one crying in the wilderness, Prepare ye the way of the Lord, and make his paths straight.
	For behold, and lo, he shall come, as it is written in the book of the prophets, to take away the sins of the world, and to bring salvation unto the

	heathen nations, to gather together those who are lost, who are of the sheepfold of Israel; Yea, even the dispersed and afflicted; and also to prepare the way, and make possible the preaching of the gospel unto the Gentiles; And to be a light unto all who sit in darkness, unto the uttermost parts of the earth; to bring to pass the resurrection from the dead, and to ascend up on high, to dwell on the right hand of the Father, Until the fullness of time, and the law and the testimony shall be sealed, and the keys of the kingdom shall be delivered up again unto the Father; To administer justice unto all; to come down in judgment upon all, and to convince all the ungodly of their ungodly deeds, which they have committed; and all this in the day that he shall come;
Every valley shall be filled, and every mountain and hill shall be brought low; and the crooked shall be made straight, and the rough ways shall be made smooth;	For it is a day of power; yea, every valley shall be filled, and every mountain and hill shall be brought low; the crooked shall be made straight, and the rough ways made smooth;
And all flesh shall see the salvation of God. (KJV, Luke 3:4-6.)	And all flesh shall see the salvation of God. (JST, Luke 3:4-11.)

John the Baptist was the prophet to prepare the way for the Lord's ministry in the flesh in the meridian of time. He came again on 15 May 1829 to restore the keys of the Aaronic Priesthood and thus commence the preparation for the Lord's second coming (see D&C 13). Joseph Smith taught that John came in the "spirit of Elias" to prepare the way for a greater work:

> There is a difference between the spirit and office of Elias and Elijah. It is the spirit of Elias I wish first to speak of; and in order to come at the subject, I will bring some of the testimony from the Scripture and give my own.
>
> In the first place, suffice it to say, I went into the woods to inquire of the Lord, by prayer, His will concerning me, and I saw an angel, and he laid his hands upon my head, and ordained me to a Priest after the order of Aaron, and to hold the keys of this Priesthood, which office was to preach repentance and baptism for the remission of sins, and also to baptize. But I was informed that this office did not extend to the laying on of hands for the giving of the Holy Ghost; that that office was a greater work, and was to be given afterward; but that my ordination was a preparatory work, or a going before, which was the spirit of Elias; for the spirit of Elias was a going before to prepare the way for the greater, which was the case with John the Baptist. He came crying through the wilderness, "Prepare ye the way of the Lord, make his paths straight." And they were informed, if they could receive it, it was the spirit of Elias; and John was very particular to tell the people, he was not that Light, but was sent to bear witness of that Light. (*TPJS*, p. 335; see also p. 319.)

Ezra Thayre and Northrop Sweet were called by the Lord in October 1830 to go forth in this same spirit to prepare the way of the Lord (see D&C 33:10). Joseph Smith, in a prayer given by revelation, used Isaiah 40:3 as a voice to all men "unto the ends of the earth" (see D&C 65:1, 3). Doctrine and Covenants 133:22 and 101:23 use the phraseology of verses 4 and 5, respectively, in speaking of the Second Coming. Another application of the opening phrase in verse 3 was given through revelation to Joseph Smith in December 1832 (see D&C 88:66). Therein the "voice" in the wilderness is described as the voice of the Spirit, and the "wilderness" is defined as such because one cannot see the Spirit.

Elder Orson Pratt, in expounding on this text of Isaiah, identified the "highway for our God" as "The same as you have made, or assisted in making, the great highway through this desert region, and constructed highways here in the desert called the iron railroad" (*JD*, 18:149; see also *JD*, 18:183).

President Joseph Fielding Smith quoted verse 4 as scriptural evidence that the earth is going to be restored to the same condition it was in before the curse came upon it (see *DS*, 2:316-17).

Isaiah 40:6-8. Peter quoted these verses in his first epistle to show the eternal surety of the word of God, but did not interpret the original meaning of Isaiah. He used the phrase "all the glory of man" instead of Isaiah's phrase "all the goodliness thereof":

> The voice said, Cry. And he said, What shall I cry? All flesh is grass, and *all the goodliness thereof is* as the flower of the field:
>
> The grass withereth, the flower fadeth: *because the spirit of the Lord bloweth upon it:* surely the people is grass.
>
> The grass withereth, the flower fadeth: but the word of our God shall stand for ever. (Isaiah 40:6-8.)

> Being born again, not of corruptible seed, but of incorruptible, by the word of God, which liveth and abideth for ever.
>
> For all flesh is *as* grass, and *all the glory of man* as the flower of grass. The grass withereth, and the flower thereof falleth away:
>
> But the word of the Lord endureth for ever. And this is the word which by the gospel is preached unto you. (1 Peter 1:23-25.)

The flesh is corruptible and therefore temporary, and will burn at the second coming of Christ when his Spirit is poured out on the earth. While flesh is temporary, the word of God declaring these things is definite and will surely come to pass. The Savior taught the same principle, declaring that the word of God would endure even though heaven and earth would pass away (see Mark 13:31). Those who are sanctified to endure the glory of the Lord which shall be poured out (alluded to in verse 7) will not be burned (see D&C 101:24-25; compare 3 Nephi 10:12-14).

Isaiah 40:9-11. Elder Orson Pratt interpreted verse 9 as a prophecy which was fulfilled when the Saints became established in the Rocky Mountains:

> "O Zion"—something about Zion now, before the Lord comes—"O Zion, that bringest good tidings, get thee up into the high mountains." Did you come up into these high moun-

> tains, you people of the latter-day Zion? What did you come here for? Because Isaiah predicted that this was the place you should come to, you should get up into the high mountain. He foretold it, and you have fulfilled it. "O Zion, that bringest good tidings." What good tidings? What tidings have you been declaring the last forty-five years to the nations and kingdoms of the earth? What have you testified to, you missionaries? Your missionaries have gone from nation to nation and from kingdom to kingdom, proclaiming to the people that God has sent his angel from heaven with the everlasting Gospel to be preached unto all people upon the face of the whole earth. This is what you have been proclaiming. Is not the everlasting Gospel glad tidings to the children of men? I think it is, and especially when it is brought by an angel to prepare the way for the great and glorious day of the coming of the King of kings and Lord of lords. It is good tidings that people who receive this everlasting Gospel, are commanded to get up into the high mountain. You have fulfilled it, you have been at it now for twenty-eight years, coming up from the eastern slope, from the great Atlantic seaboard, and gradually rising and ascending until you have located yourselves in a place upwards of four thousand feet above the level of the sea. (*JD*, 18:150; see also *JD*, 18:182-83.)

Elder Pratt further said that verse 10 showed verse 9 to be a latter-day prophecy, and that the coming of the Lord would be after Zion had gone up into the mountains (see *JD*, 18:150, 183). Some of the wording of verse 10 is used in Revelation 22:12 in describing the Second Coming, which is further evidence that these verses concern the Lord's return.

Isaiah 40:12-17. These verses proclaim the power of God in contrast to the nothingness of the nations of the earth. Moses, after being shown the world and the ends thereof, came to the same conclusion (see Moses 1:7-10). And King Benjamin taught his subjects that they should always remember the greatness of God and their own nothingness (see Mosiah 4:11). Paul paraphrased verse 13, and possibly verse 14, in proclaiming the wisdom and knowledge of God:

Who hath directed the Spirit of the Lord, or being his counsellor hath taught him?	O the depth of the riches both of the wisdom and knowledge of God! how unsearchable are his judgments, and his ways past finding out!

With whom took he counsel, and who instructed him, and taught him in the path of judgment, and taught him knowledge, and shewed to him the way of understanding? (Isaiah 40:13-14.)

For who hath known the mind of the Lord? or who hath been his counsellor?

Or who hath first given to him, and it shall be recompensed unto him again? (Romans 11:33-35.)

The wording in Romans is somewhat easier to understand.

Isaiah 40:18-27. These verses declare the power of God in contrast to the graven images which men worship. There are none equal to God; he created all things, knows all things, and has all power. Verse 27 shows that Israel was also lax in recognizing God's greatness.

Isaiah 40:28-31. Those of Israel who wait upon the Lord shall be given power and strength. The same promise is given to those who keep the Word of Wisdom in this dispensation (see D&C 89:20).

The Servant of the Lord

16

Isaiah 41-44

These four chapters constitute a rather long and somewhat repetitious message. Perhaps they could be broken into smaller units, but they all have a central theme—the servant of the Lord. As a matter of fact, this "servant" concept runs through the rest of the book of Isaiah, and identifying the various "servants" Isaiah discusses is vital to an understanding of what he is saying. It must be kept in mind that chapters 40 through 66 are prophetic in nature, not historical. Attempts to explain them historically have led to questions about authorship, as the scholars have tried to tie all the prophecies to historical events. Accepting Isaiah's declaration that the Lord knows the end from the beginning helps us see the prophetic nature of these chapters. They are outlined below to provide an overview.

1. The Lord will bring his judgments by servants from the isles of the sea (41:1-9).
   a. The Lord covenanted with Abraham and supported him in the land of Canaan (41:2-3).
   b. The Lord promises to bless future generations through Abraham (41:4).
   c. The isles (America—see 2 Nephi 10:20) will respond to the Lord's direction and become a mighty nation (41:5-7).
   d. Israel will be the Lord's servant through whom he will fulfill the covenant of Abraham (41:8-9).

2. The servant Israel shall not fear, for the Lord will uphold him (41:10-29).
   a. Those who oppose him will be as nothing (41:11-13).
   b. The servant Israel shall thresh out Israel from the nations (41:14-16).
   c. The Lord will make the wilderness fertile for the sustenance of gathered Israel (41:17-20).
   d. The Lord has declared the end from the beginning, and he challenges those who oppress his servant to show that he is wrong (41:21-24).
   e. No one is able to meet the Lord's challenge (41:26-29).
3. The Lord has a mission for his elect servant (42:1-4).
   a. The servant shall bring forth judgment to the Gentiles (42:1).
   b. He shall not contend with Judah, but shall withdraw from them (42:2).
   c. He shall heal the physically weak and strengthen the spiritually weak (42:3).
   d. He will not complete his work until judgment has come to all the nations of the earth (42:4).
   e. The isles (America) shall await his revelation (42:4).
4. The Lord will restore the covenant of Abraham to those on the isles of the sea (42:5-16).
   a. They shall be a light to the Gentiles (42:6).
   b. They shall open the eyes of the blind (42:7).
   c. They shall open the prison house and free the prisoners (42:7).
   d. They shall sing a new song of praise unto the Lord (42:10-13).
   e. The Lord has waited a long time for this restoration, but it shall be forever (42:14-16).
5. The blind and the deaf are invited to look and to hear (42:17-25).
   a. The Lord's servant will be sent unto them (42:19).
   b. They shall be made perfect if they will hearken (42:20).
   c. They are imprisoned by their enemies because of their not observing (42:20-21).

   d. The judgments of God will come upon those who are not obedient (42:22-25).
6. Israel will be gathered from all the ends of the earth (43:1-28).
   a. Messengers will be sent as witnesses to gather those who will see and hear (43:8-13).
   b. The Lord will send them among the Gentiles to bless them (43:14-17).
   c. Israel's oppression will pass, and the Lord will do a new thing in gathering Israel (43:18-21).
   d. Israel could have been gathered earlier had she sought the Lord (43:22-28).
7. Israel, the Lord's servant, shall not fear, for there is no God beside him (44:1-20).
   a. The Lord will restore the parched ground (44:3).
   b. He will pour out his Spirit upon Israel's seed (44:3-5).
   c. All graven images will profit nothing (44:9-20).
8. The Lord will not forget his servant Israel (44:21-23).
   a. The Lord will blot out her transgressions (44:22).
   b. The heavens, the spirit world, and all the earth will sing (44:23).
9. The Lord does all things (44:24-28).
   a. He created man, the heavens and the earth (44:24).
   b. He confounds the works of men (44:25).
   c. He confirms the words of his servants (44:26).
   d. He commands Jerusalem to be built or to be desolate (44:26-28).
      1) He commands Cyrus to be his shepherd.
      2) He commands that the foundation of the temple be laid.

Notes and Commentary

Very little insight into these chapters is given in the standard works. Only one section is actually quoted elsewhere in the scriptures, and that not fully. The biggest help comes from the last part of chapter 42 in the JST, and from the identification of the servant as Israel in the Doctrine and

Covenants. As noted later, the word "servant" carries dual meanings.

Most of the comments made by General Authorities either identify the time period of which Isaiah speaks, which of course is very helpful, or make timely applications from some of his statements.

Isaiah 41:1. The Bible scholars have long troubled over this verse: Where are the islands to whom the Lord speaks? The answer to this question will lead to an understanding, not only of this verse, but also of the subsequent verses and chapters of Isaiah. The RSV translates the word "coastlands" instead of the KJV "islands." Most commentators feel that the islands or coastlands are the islands and coasts of the Mediterranean—or even the whole Mediterranean basin. However, the Anchor Bible (20:27) notes, "No particular nations are meant, the 'coastlands' for the Israelites meant the limits of the earth." This supports the Book of Mormon teaching that the Nephites were "upon an isle of the sea" (2 Nephi 10:20).

The command to "keep silence before me" may have reference to the Americas' being kept hidden from the world lest they be overrun by other nations (see 2 Nephi 1:8). "Let the people renew their strength" could refer to the establishment of a free nation in the land of America that the Lord might accomplish his purposes (see 3 Nephi 21:4). After the free nation is established, the Lord commands to "let them come near"; this alludes to the restoration of the gospel, whereby Israel now comes to him to be his people. "Then let them speak" refers to the proclaiming of the gospel to the nations of the earth. All these things will bring about the purposes of the Lord (through his servants in the isles of the sea) to "let us come near together to judgment," meaning to commence the work of the last days, to sound a warning to all the nations of the earth so that they may either accept the gospel and be gathered to Israel or suffer the wrath which will follow the testimony of the Lord's servants (see D&C 43:23-28).

Isaiah 41:2-4. A second problem for the scholars has been the identification of the "man from the east." He has been identified as Christ, Abraham, Paul, and Cyrus of Persia. Abraham and Cyrus seem to be the prominent identifications, with older scholars leaning to Abraham and more modern scholars to Cyrus. Since Cyrus is actually named in 44:28 and 45:1, modern scholars feel that chapter 41 begins the passage building up to his being named. This is further enforced by their theory that the so-called second Isaiah (chapters 40 through 55) was written at a later time by someone other than Isaiah the son of Amoz.

The "man from the east" appears to be Abraham, as suggested by many older scholars. The arguments regarding the latter-day restoration in the isles of the sea (see note on 41:1) seem to support this identification. The KJV phrase "called him to his foot" is translated "calls him to follow" in the Anchor Bible (20:26), which also adds a footnote indicating that the Hebrew says "called." Abraham was called by the Lord to leave Ur of the Chaldees and go to the land of Canaan (see Genesis 11:31; 12:1; Abraham 2:1-6). He was given "the nations before him" extending from "the river of Egypt unto the great river, the river Euphrates" (Genesis 15:18). Isaiah 41:2b seems to refer to Abraham's smiting of the kings as he rescued his nephew Lot (see Genesis 14). A more positive identification of Abraham comes from verse 4, wherein the Lord makes reference to "calling the generations from the beginning." Abraham was chosen in the premortal life to be a ruler (see Abraham 3:22-23; Genesis 18:19) and was blessed that through the literal seed of his body the Lord would bless all the nations of the earth (Genesis 12:2-3; Abraham 2:8-11). These verses in Isaiah proclaim that the Lord was the one who had so ordained these things. The Anchor Bible (20:27) suggests, "Yahweh calls the generations from the beginning; he directs history from the origins of man." Verse 4, cross-referenced to the book of Revelation (1:8, 17; 22:13), shows that the same person spoke to both Isaiah and John.

Isaiah 41:5-7. These verses are usually interpreted as a description of the nations of the Mediterranean coastlands, fearing and turning to their idols. In light of verse 1, however, we can see an entirely different meaning. Verse 5 describes the gathering of the nations to the Americas, as prophesied in verse 1. "The isles saw it, and feared," meaning they responded to Jehovah's call and, in the fear (love) of the Lord, "drew near, and came," and built up a mighty

Gentile nation in the land of America (see 1 Nephi 22:7). Verses 6 and 7 describe the cooperation required of the people from many lands who firmly established a nation "that it should not be moved." Actually, this could be a dual prophecy of the establishment of the nation and of the Church upon that land.

Isaiah 41:8-9. These verses identify the servant who is to speak. The Lord promised Abraham that his literal seed would bless the nations of the earth (Abraham 2:11). He now calls Israel, the literal seed of Abraham, whom he has gathered from the nations of the earth to the islands (America), to be his servant in bringing judgment upon all the nations of the earth. The Doctrine and Covenants identifies the Latter-day Saints who had gathered as the literal seed of Abraham (see D&C 103:17; 132:30-31) and as the Lord's servants (see D&C 93:46; 133:30-32). Thus chapter 41 is a prophecy of latter-day Israel, called initially to gather upon the isles of the sea (America) to be servants in the hand of the Lord to fulfill the covenant he made with Abraham to bear the ministry and the priesthood to the nations of the earth.

Isaiah 41:10. "How Firm a Foundation," a favorite hymn among Latter-day Saints, was composed from the words of this verse. The admonition is to the Lord's servant Israel, who is to carry the gospel to the nations of the earth. The following verses treat the various ways in which the Lord will help Israel accomplish this calling. President Joseph Fielding Smith quoted verse 10 along with other scriptural passages to show why the right hand is used in performing ordinances (see *DS*, 3:107-8).

Isaiah 41:11-13. The servant is not to fear those who have oppressed him (probably the Gentiles). He is to "seek them," to go among them and proclaim the gospel, but will "not find them" because very few of the Gentiles will accept it (see D&C 45:28-29). Although the Gentiles war against the servant, they shall be as nothing because the Lord God will uphold Israel.

Isaiah 41:14-16. "Thou worm Jacob" is not a derogatory label, but a recognition of Israel's smallness in comparison to the world's population. (A marginal reading in the KJV gives "few men" as an alternative to "men of Israel.") The Lord is going to make them as a "threshing instrument" to gather Israel out of the Gentiles and leave them as "hills of chaff." "The whirlwind shall scatter them" refers to the judgments which will follow their rejection of the gospel, while Israel, who has been gathered out of those nations, will rejoice in the Lord.

Isaiah 41:17-20. Those of Israel who gather will be blessed by the Lord. Again, the Lord describes the wilderness and the solitary places which he will cause to become fertile for Israel's sustenance that his people may know he is with them.

Isaiah 41:21-24. The Lord has declared what is going to happen, and he now challenges those who will oppose his servants to show differently. He has shown how Abraham was called from the beginning and how his seed will fulfill his covenant in the future. The challenge to the oppressors is to do the same: show us "the former things" and also "the latter end of them." The Lord concludes with a declaration of the oppressors' nothingness. Elder Bruce R. McConkie quoted verse 21 as an example of the divine counsel to reason over the scriptures (see CR, Apr. 1973, p. 35).

Isaiah 41:25-29. Again the Lord declares that he has established his covenant with one from the north and also from the east ("the rising of the sun"). Abraham came to the land of Canaan from Haran, in the north, and he came to Haran from Ur, in the east. The Anchor Bible (20:34) gives an interesting translation of verse 27: "In the beginning I spoke to Zion, and to Jerusalem I will send a messenger." The fact that this prophecy occurs in the context of the future events which Jehovah has declared supports the interpretation of verse 1 outlined earlier in this chapter. There were none who could declare the future, as there had been none who could declare the premortal past. All was vanity and nothing, as were graven images.

Isaiah 42:1. The passage in Isaiah 42:1-4 is the first of four so-called servant songs in the book of Isaiah (see also 49:1-6; 50:4-9; 52:13-53:12). The servant of the songs is usually considered to be Christ, although there are many other interpretations. Some say it is Israel collectively; others cite various historical figures of the past; still others point to an historical figure in the future; and yet others say it is an ideal figure. To those who identify the servant as Israel collectively, the argument is raised that the servant goes far beyond the Israel which was known in Isaiah's day or the days following Isaiah, when most scholars feel these servant songs were written. With this we would heartily agree, because the designation of Israel as the servant in the Isaiah text has reference to the future restored Israel, as already identified and discussed in Isaiah 41:8-9. However, not all four songs necessarily refer to the same servant, nor is the servant in any one song necessarily limited to a single identification. There are possibly dual representations for the servant, with reference either to different time periods or to specific and broader meanings in each situation. Therefore, the servant must be identified within the given context in each case.

Isaiah 42:1-4. The testimony of Matthew identifies the servant spoken of here as Christ. Matthew wrote that the Pharisees plotted to destroy Christ, and that his withdrawing from them fulfilled Isaiah 42:1-3 (see Matthew 12:14-20); he also added another verse which originally may have been a part of the Isaiah text: "And in his name shall the Gentiles trust" (Matthew 12:21).

Behold my servant, whom I uphold; mine elect, in whom my soul delighteth; I have put my spirit upon him: he shall bring forth judgment to the Gentiles.

He shall not cry, nor lift up, nor cause his voice to be heard in the street.

A bruised reed shall he not break, and the smoking flax shall he not quench: he shall bring forth judgment unto truth.

He shall not fail nor be discouraged, till he have set judgment in the earth: and the isles shall wait for his law. (Isaiah 42:1-4.)

Behold my servant, whom I have chosen; my beloved, in whom my soul is well pleased: I will put my spirit upon him, and he shall shew judgment to the Gentiles.

He shall not strive, nor cry; neither shall any man hear his voice in the streets.

A bruised reed shall he not break, and smoking flax shall he not quench, till he send forth judgment unto victory.

And in his name shall the Gentiles trust. (Matthew 12:18-21.)

Jesus' withdrawing from the Pharisees is fulfillment of verse 2; he does not strive or contend with them, but continues his work elsewhere, and his voice is not "heard in the street."

His healing the sick among the multitude which followed him into the solitary places (see Matthew 12:15) seems to fulfill the prophecy, "A bruised reed shall he not break." Rather than denouncing the physically defective as being cursed of God, which was the attitude of the times, he healed their infirmities to show the works of God (see John 9:1-3). Similarly, the "smoking flax" (or the "dimly burning wick," as the RSV translates it) refers to the spiritually weak who will not be put out but will be patiently fanned or encouraged until a later time when he sends for judgment "unto victory," as Matthew renders Isaiah's "unto truth."

The reference to Christ's ultimate victory shows that his mortal ministry did not fulfill Isaiah's prophecy. Verse 1 refers to his bringing forth "judgment to the Gentiles." Christ did not personally go to the Gentiles but only to the "lost sheep" of the house of Israel (see Matthew 15:24). Peter, as President of the Church, was later given revelation to preach to the Gentiles (see Acts 10); this was done, but the "victory" spoken of in Matthew 12:20 was certainly not attained at that time. The fact that Matthew does not quote verse 4, which is a part of the so-called servant song, is significant. Verse 4 gives a broader meaning to the passage by declaring that the work of the servant will not "fail nor be discouraged, till he have set judgment in the earth," meaning that the mission of the servant is not ended until the judgment has ended in victory. The verse concludes with the declaration that "the isles shall wait for his law." The Anchor Bible (20:36) uses the word "instruction" in place of "law" and adds this informative note: "Here the meaning seems to be wider, almost equivalent to revelation." Again, the "isles" have reference to the restoration of Israel in the Americas, where she will become the servant to fulfill the work which was commenced by the Savior in the meridian of time.

Isaiah 42:5-9. The Savior was to be a light to the Gentiles, as foretold here by Isaiah and pronounced by Simeon, the devout temple worker, in a blessing given to the infant Jesus (see Luke 2:32). However, this light was also to be held up by others. Christ told the Nephites that he was the light to be held up by them (see 3 Nephi 18:24). And he may have been quoting part of verse 7 in sending Paul to the Gentiles to hold up that light (see Acts 26:17-18). These verses in Isaiah speak of those servants who were to be called, following Christ's personal ministry, to further the mission which he would begin. The passage also speaks of another aspect of his mission—his preaching to the spirits in prison. Peter bore witness that Christ visited the spirits in prison during the interim between his death and resurrection (see 1 Peter 3:18-19). After quoting Isaiah 42:7, Joseph Smith commented, "It is very evident from this that He not only went to preach to them, but to deliver, or bring them out of the prison house" (*TPJS*, p. 219). This work of liberating the captive spirits in the spirit world, which was begun by Christ, is now being furthered by the latter-day servants, restored Israel, as they perform ordinances vicariously for those who have died and entered into the spirit world. Isaiah 42:5-9 has been cited by modern Church leaders as evidence of restored Israel's responsibility to help save the dead (see Joseph Fielding Smith, *DS*, 2:155; Theodore M. Burton, CR, Oct. 1964, p. 33). Such is the work of the Lord extended to the latter days before his judgments come upon the earth.

Isaiah 42:10-13. A new song is to be sung in the isles when and where Israel is to be restored. Israel will be gathered from the ends of the earth, where she was previously scattered, and will give glory and praise from the tops of the mountains in the islands (America), and the Lord will prevail against his enemies.

Isaiah 42:14-16. The Lord has waited a long time for this restoration, and he now promises to restore Israel and not forsake her. This latter-day restoration will stand forever, as shown to Nebuchadnezzar and interpreted for him by the prophet Daniel (see Daniel chapter 2, especially verse 44).

Isaiah 42:17-25. Those who are deafened and blinded by trusting in false gods are invited by the Lord's servant to hear and see. Joseph Smith made several significant changes in this text in his inspired translation.

Who is blind, but my servant? or deaf, as my messenger that I sent? who is blind as he that is	*For I will send my servant unto you who are blind; yea, a messenger to open the eyes of*

perfect, and blind as the Lord's servant? (KJV, Isaiah 42:19.)

the blind, and unstop the ears of the deaf;

And they shall be made perfect notwithstanding their blindness, if they will hearken unto the messenger, the Lord's servant. (JST, Isaiah 42:19-20.)

The servant is not blind, as the various versions indicate, but the Lord is going to send his servant unto those who are blind and deaf to open their eyes and unstop their ears so they can be made perfect if they will hearken to the Lord's servant.

Seeing many things, but thou observest not; opening the ears, but *he heareth* not.

The Lord is well pleased for his righteousness' sake; he will magnify the law, and make it honourable.

But this is a people robbed and spoiled; *they are* all of them snared in holes, and they *are hid* in prison houses: they *are* for a prey, and none delivereth; for a spoil, and none saith, Restore. (KJV, Isaiah 42:20-22.)

Thou art a people, seeing many things, but thou observest not; opening the ears *to hear*, but *thou hearest* not.

The Lord is *not* well pleased *with such a people, but* for his righteousness' sake he will magnify the law and make it honorable.

Thou art a people robbed and spoiled; *thine enemies*, all of them, *have* snared *thee* in holes, and they *have hid thee* in prison houses; they *have taken thee* for a prey, and none delivereth; for a spoil, and none saith, Restore. (JST, Isaiah 42:21-23.)

Again, the servant is not the one who does not see or listen, but it is the people unto whom the servant is sent. "The Lord is not well pleased with such a people." Their enemies have imprisoned them and kept them for a prey.

Who among *you* will give ear *to this; who will* hearken and hear for the time to come?

Who gave Jacob for a spoil, and Israel to the robbers? did not the Lord, he against whom *we* have sinned? for they would not walk in his ways, neither were they obedient unto his law.

Who among *them* will give ear *unto thee, or* hearken and hear *thee* for the time to come? *and* who gave Jacob for a spoil, and Israel to the robbers? did not the Lord, he against whom *they* have sinned?

Therefore he hath poured upon *him* the fury of his anger, and the strength of battle: and *it* hath set *him* on fire round about, yet *he* knew not; and it burned *him*, yet *he* laid it not to heart. (Isaiah 42:23-25.)

For they would not walk in his ways, neither were they obedient unto his law; therefore he hath poured upon *them* the fury of his anger, and the strength of battle; and *they* have set *them* on fire round about, yet *they* know not, and it burned *them*, yet *they* laid it not to heart. (JST, Isaiah 42:24-25.)

Will their enemies listen to their plight? Did not the Lord scatter Israel among them? But Israel will not walk in the way of the Lord, so his judgments are to come upon them.

Isaiah 43:1-7. The reference in verse 3 to "the Lord thy God, the Holy One of Israel, thy Saviour" is another evidence of Jesus Christ's being the God who administered the affairs of the Old Testament. The Prophet Joseph Smith prefaced verses 5 and 6 with these words: "In addition to all temporal blessings, there is no other way for the Saints to be saved in these last days, [than by the gathering] as the concurrent testimony of all the holy prophets clearly proves" (*TPJS*, p. 183). President Joseph Fielding Smith referred to verses 5 through 7 as one of the predictions of the gathering of Israel (see *DS*, 3:254). Through Isaiah, the Lord here assures Israel that he will be with them as they are gathered. Elder Orson Pratt spoke of verses 6 and 7 and the time when all Christians would be gathered together out of the world: "Will it leave a Christian behind? Not one. Go and search New York, Philadelphia, and all the eastern States, and the middle and southern States, and then all Europe, for a Christian after this prophecy is fulfilled, and you can't find one. Why? Because they are all gathered in one. How? By new revelation." (*JD*, 18:186.) Those who are "called by his name" are those who have taken the name of Christ upon them in the waters of baptism and know his voice, as defined in Mosiah 5:6-15.

Isaiah 43:8-13. These verses seem to be an extension of Isaiah 42:19-20 in the JST, where it states that the Lord will send his servant to gather those who will see and hear. The Lord again identifies himself as the Savior and the messengers as his "witnesses." Elder Bruce R. McConkie has identified verse 12 as a prophecy of this day:

> The power of God unto salvation is found here in the tops of these everlasting hills; and this glorious truth is spreading out to all the nations of the earth as rapidly as people in them accept the testimony and witness that is borne and believe the truths that our fellow representatives proclaim. This is a day of which God has said that all of gathered Israel shall be witnesses of his name. ". . . ye are my witnesses, saith the Lord, that I am god." (CR, Apr. 1972, p. 135; see also CR, Oct. 1969, pp. 82-83; CR, Apr. 1973, p. 36.)

In section 76 of the Doctrine and Covenants, the Lord identified himself in nearly the same words as those given in Isaiah 43:11 (see D&C 76:1).

Isaiah 43:14-17. Most scholars believe that these verses refer to a historical setting, but are uncertain of which setting. It is probably a general reference to the Lord's bringing Israel under the reign of the Gentiles for Israel's own good, and to the fact that he will also bring the Gentiles down because they will not recognize his hand or accept the gospel.

Isaiah 43:18-21. The Lord, through Isaiah, now instructs his people to forget their past oppression under the Gentiles and to see the new things he will do for them in the restoration of Israel.

Isaiah 43:22-28. Israel is now chastised for failing to call upon the Lord and perform his ordinances, but is invited to trust in the Lord. "Thy first father" in verse 27 probably refers to Israel as a nation in former times rather than some specific personage. The Israelites were scattered because they did not follow the Lord.

Isaiah 44:1-8. The Lord again confirms his promise to Israel, his servant whom he has chosen, that he will restore his people and they need not fear. In verse 6 the Lord identifies himself in the same terminology used in the book of Revelation, showing that Jesus Christ is speaking in both passages (see Revelation 1:8, 17; 22:13).

Isaiah 44:9-26. (See chapter outline.)

Isaiah 44:27-28. The naming of Cyrus in this passage has led almost all biblical scholars to reject Isaiah as the author, because Cyrus lived approximately two hundred years after Isaiah. Influenced by the humanistic thinking of the times, they do not comprehend that a prophet can foretell the name and specific activities of a man so far in the future. This is no problem to the believer in the Book of Mormon. Joseph, who was sold into Egypt, prophesied of Moses by name more than two hundred years before he delivered Israel out of Egypt. He further prophesied of a choice seer in the latter days who would be called after his own name—Joseph—and he said that his father's name would be the same (see 2 Nephi 3); this prophecy was fulfilled approximately thirty-five hundred years later. As Isaiah testified, the Lord knows the end from the beginning (see Isaiah 46:10), so he certainly could reveal the name of a person and identify the man's activities to his prophets as he saw fit. The actual prophecy about Cyrus delivering the Jews will be treated in the next chapter.

Cyrus, the Lord's Anointed 17

Isaiah 45-47

The mention of Cyrus in Isaiah 44:28 has led some scholars to suppose that the division between chapters 44 and 45 should have been made elsewhere. However, the earlier chapter is merely referring to the revelation given to Isaiah concerning the future Cyrus who was to be raised up. He tells us in chapter 44 that the Lord has foretold the mission of Cyrus, then in chapter 45 he records the revelation. Chapters 46 and 47 seem to be a continuation of the same general theme and may be part of the same revelation; chapter 46 concerns the gods of Babylon, and chapter 47 concerns Babylon's fall, which came at the hands of Cyrus. Thus these three chapters are treated together here. A more detailed outline follows:

1. Cyrus will subdue nations before him (45:1-4).
   a. The Lord will go before him (45:2).
   b. Cyrus will know that the Lord is the God of Israel (45:3).
   c. The Lord will bless Cyrus for Israel's sake although Cyrus has not known him (45:4).
2. There is no God beside the Lord (45:5-19).
   a. The Lord armed Cyrus that the nations might know of God from the east to the west (45:5-6).
   b. The Lord is the creator and governor of all things (45:7-12).
   c. He will raise up Cyrus and direct him, and all nations

   will be confounded and acknowledge that the God of Israel is with Cyrus (45:13-16).
   d. But Israel will be saved with an everlasting salvation (45:17).
   e. The Lord has spoken the truth openly (45:18-19).
3. All who escape from the nations are invited to come to the Lord (45:20-25).
   a. The graven images cannot save them (45:20).
   b. Every knee will bow and every tongue confess the Lord (45:21-23).
   c. In the Lord will all the seed of Israel be justified (45: 24-25).
4. The Babylonian gods could not deliver Babylon (46:1-2).
5. The Lord gave Israel birth and growth, and will deliver Israel (46:3-13).
   a. There is no one like the Lord; there is no other God (46:5-9).
   b. He knows the end from the beginning (46:10).
   c. He will call Cyrus from the east for his purposes (46:11).
   d. Salvation for Israel will be in Zion (46:12-13).
6. Babylon will be brought down and will no longer be the lady of kingdoms (47:1-15).
   a. Judah was given to Babylon, who showed no mercy (47:6).
   b. Babylon will become childless and a widow (47:7-9).
   c. Babylon trusted in its own wickedness and knowledge, and was lifted up in pride (47:10).
   d. Evil and desolation will come to Babylon, whose gods will not deliver its inhabitants (47:11-15).

Notes and Commentary

The best source of help in understanding these chapters is the New Testament. President Joseph Fielding Smith commented on two passages in chapter 45 and referred to the Book of Mormon to provide an insight into one of these. The Jewish historian Josephus also made an enlightening statement about Cyrus.

Isaiah 45:1-4. As previously noted, this prophecy foretelling the mission of Cyrus has led many to reject Isaiah as its author. However, the Jewish historian Josephus wrote that the prophecy was Isaiah's and that it was given 140 years before the destruction of the temple. This would have been nearly 200 years before Cyrus issued the decree for the Jews to return. The account in Josephus is as follows:

> In the first year of the reign of Cyrus, which was the seventieth from the day that our people were removed out of their own land into Babylon, God commiserated the captivity and calamity of these poor people, according as he had foretold to them by Jeremiah the prophet, before the destruction of the city, that after they had served Nebuchadnezzar and his posterity, and after they had undergone that servitude seventy years, he would restore them again to the land of their fathers, and they should build their temple, and enjoy their ancient prosperity; and these things God did afford them; for he stirred up the mind of Cyrus, and made him write this throughout all Asia:—"Thus saith Cyrus the King:—Since God Almighty hath appointed me to be king of the habitable earth, I believe that he is that God which the nation of the Israelites worship; for indeed he foretold my name by the prophets, and that I should build him a house at Jerusalem, in the country of Judea."
>
> This was known to Cyrus by his reading the book which Isaiah left behind him of his prophecies; for this prophet said that God had spoken thus to him in a secret vision:—"My will is, that Cyrus, whom I have appointed to be king over many and great nations, send back my people to their own land, and build my temple." This was foretold by Isaiah one hundred and forty years before the temple was demolished. Accordingly, when Cyrus read this, and admired the divine power, an earnest desire and ambition seized upon him to fulfil what was so written; so he called for the most eminent Jews that were in Babylon, and said to them, that he gave them leave to go back to their own country, and to rebuild their city Jerusalem, and the temple of God, for that he would be their assistant, and that he would write to the rulers and governors that were in the neighbourhood of their country of Judea, that they should contribute to them gold and silver for the building of the temple, and, besides that, beasts for their sacrifices. (Flavius Josephus, *Josephus: Complete Works*, trans. William Whiston [Grand Rapids, Mich.: Kregel Publications, 1972], Antiquities of the Jews, 11.1.1-2.)

President Joseph Fielding Smith cited this passage as evidence of the Lord's foreordaining not only prophets but other leaders as well (*AQ*, 5:181).

Isaiah 45:5, 21. The declaration that "there is no God beside me" was paraphrased by one of the Jewish scribes in response to the Savior's declaration that man should love God with all his heart, soul, mind, and strength. Jesus' response to the scribe was that he was "not far from the kingdom of God" (Mark 12:28-34). What the scribe apparently did not recognize was that Jesus was that God. Verse 21 adds that he is "a just God and a *Saviour*" (italics added). Jesus Christ was the Administrator of the world by "divine investiture of authority," as explained by the First Presidency in an official statement in 1916 (see *Messages of the First Presidency*, 6 vols. [Salt Lake City: Bookcraft, Inc., 1965-75], 5: 31-34).

Isaiah 45:7. The statement that God creates evil may be misunderstood and seems to contradict Moroni 7:12: "that which is evil cometh of the devil." The declaration in Isaiah may have reference to the Lord's bringing destruction upon a people "ripe in iniquity." This idea is supported by the RSV, which says, "I make weal and create woe." Another text, Amos 3:6, asks, "Shall there be evil in a city, and the Lord hath not done it?" But the JST reads "and the Lord hath not *known* it?" The Lord is not the author of evil, but is fully aware of all evil and of the consequences which follow. As Mormon says, "It is by the wicked that the wicked are punished" (Mormon 4:5).

Isaiah 45:8. This verse, declaring another evidence of the omniscience of God, probably has reference to the coming forth of the Book of Mormon. The instruction to "drop down, ye heavens, from above, and let the skies pour down righteousness" is fulfilled in the visitations of angels (such as the angel Moroni) and the giving of other types of revelation. To "let the earth open, and let them bring forth salvation" is to bring forth a record such as the Book of Mormon, which contains the fulness of the gospel. In words similar to these, Enoch was given a promise concerning that which would lead to the building of the New Jerusalem in the latter days (see Moses 7:62). In commenting on the passage in Moses, Joseph Smith said: "And now, I ask, how righteousness and truth are going to sweep the earth as with a flood? I will answer. Men and angels are to be co-workers in bringing to pass this great work, and Zion is to be prepared, even a new Jerusalem, for the elect that are to be gathered from the four quarters of the earth, and to be established an holy city, for the tabernacle of the Lord shall be with them." (*TPJS*, p. 84.) The Psalmist also spoke of the time when "Truth shall spring out of the earth; and righteousness shall look down from heaven" (Psalm 85:11).

Isaiah 45:9. This verse is similar to Isaiah 29:16, and Paul quoted one or the other in his epistle to the Romans (9:20).

Surely your turning of things upside down shall be esteemed as the potter's clay: for shall the work say of him that made it, He made me not? or shall the thing framed say of him that framed it, He had no understanding? (Isaiah 29:16.)

Woe unto him that striveth with his Maker! Let the potsherd strive with the potsherds of the earth. Shall the clay say to him that fashioneth it, What makest thou? or thy work, He hath no hands? (Isaiah 45:9.)

Nay but, O man, who art thou that repliest against God? Shall the thing formed say to him that formed it, Why hast thou made me thus? (Romans 9:20.)

Isaiah 45:14. In writing to the Saints at Corinth, Paul made a statement similar to the one at the end of this verse, but the occurrence he described was not given as a fulfillment of the prophecy in Isaiah.

Thus saith the Lord, the labour of Egypt, and merchandise of Ethiopia and of the Sabeans, men of stature, shall come over unto thee, and they shall be thine: they shall come after thee; in chains they shall come over, and they shall fall down unto thee, they shall make supplication unto thee, saying, Surely God is in thee; and there is none else, there is no God. (Isaiah 45:14.)

And thus are the secrets of his heart made manifest; and so falling down on his face he will worship God, and report that God is in you of a truth. (1 Corinthians 14:25.)

Isaiah 45:23. "That unto me every knee shall bow, every tongue shall swear" is another statement showing clearly that Jesus Christ is the Administrator of the Old Testament. Paul quoted this passage with reference to Christ in writing to the Romans and the Philippians:

I have sworn by myself, the word is gone out of my mouth in righteousness, and shall not return, That unto me every knee shall bow, every tongue shall swear. (Isaiah 45:23.)	For it is written, As I live, saith the Lord, every knee shall bow to me, and every tongue shall confess to God. (Romans 14:11.)	That at the name of Jesus every knee should bow, of things in earth, and things in heaven, and things in earth, and things under the earth; And that every tongue should confess that Jesus Christ is Lord, to the glory of God the Father. (Philippians 2:10-11.)

The prophet Abinadi gave an indication of the time when this prophecy will be fulfilled (see Mosiah 16:1-4), and his text was used by President Joseph Fielding Smith to show that those who "bow" and "confess" are not celestial beings who will receive exaltation, but primarily telestial beings who will have to acknowledge the Savior and admit that his judgments are just (see *DS*, 2:30-31). The Doctrine and Covenants also uses similar language in reference to the telestial beings (see D&C 76:110; compare 88:104).

Isaiah 47:7-9. The book of Revelation uses similar phraseology to describe the fall of Babylon in the latter days (see Revelation 18:7-8).

Isaiah 47:15. Again the Lord uses similar language to describe Babylon's fall in the latter days (Revelation 18:3).

Judah and the Furnace of Affliction

18

Isaiah 48

Chapter 48 is the first chapter of Isaiah quoted in the book of Mormon to "more fully persuade them [Nephi's brethren and the house of Israel] to believe in the Lord their Redeemer." For this purpose Nephi "did read unto them that which was written by the prophet Isaiah; for I did liken all scriptures unto us, that it might be for our profit and learning.

"Wherefore I spake unto them, saying: Hear ye the words of the prophet, ye who are a remnant of the house of Israel, a branch who have been broken off; hear ye the words of the prophet, which were written unto all the house of Israel, and liken them unto yourselves, that ye may have hope as well as your brethren from whom ye have been broken off; for after this manner has the prophet written." (1 Nephi 19:23-24.) Isaiah 40-47 provides an overview, identifies the "servant," and foretells of Cyrus and the fall of Babylon. While these were important, they were not as relevant to Nephi's people or to the latter-day readers of his record as chapters 48 and 49. Chapter 48 foretells the destiny of Judah and declares the omniscience of God; an outline of the chapter will show these two prominent themes.

1. The baptized members of Judah have apostatized (48:1-2).
   a. They swear by the name of the Lord, but not in truth or righteousness (48:1).
   b. They claim to be of the holy city, but do not rely on the Lord (48:2).

2. The Lord foretold Judah's destiny even from the beginning (48:3-8).
    a. They were shown the things which would happen before they happened (48:3).
    b. They were shown these things because they were obstinate and stubborn (48:4).
    c. They were shown them so they could not give credit to their idols (48:5).
    d. They have seen prophecy fulfilled and have been told of the future, and yet would not hear; this the Lord also knew (48:6-8).
3. The Lord will defer his anger and not cut Judah off (48:9-11).
    a. They will be sent through the furnace of affliction (48:10).
    b. The Lord will not allow his name to be polluted (48:11).
4. Jacob and Israel are invited to hearken unto God, who is the first and the last (48:12-22).
    a. He has created the earth and the heavens, and they obey him (48:13).
    b. He will fulfill his word on the Gentiles (48:14).
    c. Israel will declare God's word, and he will make Israel prosperous (48:15).
    d. The Lord has spoken of this from the beginning (48:16-17).
    e. If Israel had hearkened to the commandments, they would not have been destroyed (48:18-19).
    f. The Lord has delivered his people before (48:20-21).
    g. There will be no peace for the wicked (48:22).

Notes and Commentary

Every verse of this chapter is quoted differently in the Book of Mormon. Some of these differences are significant. Neither Nephi nor Mormon commented on this chapter, so the only help for understanding it comes from studying the differences in the Book of Mormon retentions. The modern prophets have said little about this chapter.

Isaiah 48:1.

Hear *ye* this, O house of Jacob, which are called by the name of Israel, and are come forth out of the waters of Judah, which swear by the name of the Lord, and make mention of the God of Israel, *but* not in truth, nor in righteousness. (Isaiah 48:1.)	*Hearken and* hear this, O house of Jacob, who are called by the name of Israel, and are come forth out of the waters of Judah, *or out of the waters of baptism*, who swear by the name of the Lord, and make mention of the God of Israel, *yet they swear* not in truth nor in righteousness. (1 Nephi 20:1.)

The phrase "out of the waters of Judah" refers to those of Judah who are baptized into the Church. The Prophet Joseph Smith added the phrase "or out of the waters of baptism" to the text in the third edition of the Book of Mormon (1840). This clarifies the meaning of the term "waters of Judah."

Isaiah 48:2.

For they call themselves of of the holy city, and stay themselves upon the God of Israel; The Lord of hosts is his name. (Isaiah 48:2.)	*Nevertheless*, they call themselves of the holy city, *but they do not* stay themselves upon the God of Israel, *who is the Lord of Hosts; yea*, the Lord of Hosts is his name. (1 Nephi 20:2.)

The Book of Mormon retains the words "but they do not," which help us see the apostate conditions of Judah. It also retains the phrase "who is the Lord of Hosts" to further identify or describe the God of Israel, but this does not add meaning to the text.

Isaiah 48:3. The Book of Mormon retains the word "show" in the KJV expression "I did them suddenly." That the Lord "did *show* them suddenly" places the responsibility for their actions upon the people.

Isaiah 48:6. The Book of Mormon "Thou hast *seen and* heard" is a plainer rendering.

Isaiah 48:3-8. This whole concept of why the Lord shows the future to individuals or a people is important. The principle of foreknowledge is difficult to understand, but is affirmed by several prophets who have been shown the end of the world from the beginning (see 1 Nephi 14:24-26). The Lord shows the future so that false gods will not be worshipped or credited with his operations. This understanding is an important contribution by Isaiah.

Isaiah 48:9. The Book of Mormon wording "will I refrain *from* thee" instead of "*for* thee" shows the Lord will withdraw from Judah rather than intercede for her.

Isaiah 48:10. The Book of Mormon does not include the KJV phrase "but not with silver." The Anchor Bible (20:94) translates the phrase "I have tested you like silver." This phrase may have been added to the original text as an explanation.

Isaiah 48:11. The Book of Mormon reads "*I will not suffer* my name *to* be polluted" in place of "how should my name be polluted?" This is much more logical reading.

Isaiah 48:12. Again, it is shown that Jesus Christ is the one who is speaking, and he calls his servant Israel to hearken. The Lord spoke to John on the Isle of Patmos and called himself by the same name revealed to Isaiah (see Revelation 1:8, 17: 22:13).

Isaiah 48:14.

All ye, assemble yourselves, and hear; *which* among them hath declared these things? The Lord hath loved him: he will do his pleasure on Babylon, and his arm shall *be on* the Chaldeans. (Isaiah 48:14.)

All ye, assemble yourselves, and hear; *who* among them hath declared these things *unto them*? The Lord hath loved him; *yea, and he will fulfill his word which he hath declared by them; and* he will do his pleasure on Babylon, and his arm shall *come upon* the Chaldeans. (1 Nephi 20:14.)

The Book of Mormon retention "unto them" identifies Israel, whom the Lord loved. This shows that the referent of "him" is not Cyrus, as many scholars say. "Babylon" and "the Chaldeans" appear to represent the Gentiles rather than those countries specifically.

Isaiah 48:15. The Book of Mormon reading "I have called him *to declare*" is consistent with the identification of Israel in verse 14, for Israel is to declare God's word.

Isaiah 48:16-17. The Book of Mormon retention "have sent him" in verse 17 shows that all of these verses are speaking of Israel as the servant who is called (see verse 12).

Come ye near unto me, *hear ye this*; I have not spoken in secret from the beginning; from the time that it was, *there am I*: and *now* the Lord God, and his Spirit, hath sent me.

Thus saith the Lord, thy Redeemer, the Holy One of Israel; I *am* the Lord thy God which teacheth thee to profit, which leadeth thee by the way *that* thou shouldest go. (Isaiah 48:16-17.)

Come ye near unto me; I have not spoken in secret; from the beginning, from the time that it was *declared have I spoken*; and the Lord God, and his Spirit, hath sent me.

And thus saith the Lord, thy Redeemer, the Holy One of Israel; I *have sent him*, the Lord thy God who teacheth thee to profit, who leadeth thee by the way thou shouldest go, *hath done it*. (1 Nephi 20:16-17.)

Isaiah 48:20-22. Verse 22 is almost identical with Isaiah 57:21. The Book of Mormon retains some transitional wording which provides a context for the idea presented here:

There is no peace, saith the Lord, unto the wicked. (Isaiah 48:22.)

And notwithstanding he hath done all this, and greater also, there is no peace, saith the Lord, unto the wicked. (1 Nephi 20:22.)

The wicked people who will not respond to Israel's declaration (in verse 20) to come out from Babylon—which is the world, as identified by President Joseph Fielding Smith (see *DS*, 3:30)—are the ones who will have no peace.

The House of Israel Nursed by the Gentiles

19

Isaiah 49

Before Nephi recorded the words of Isaiah on the plates which concluded his book called 1 Nephi, he spoke these words to all the house of Israel who should obtain his writings:

> For behold, I have workings in the spirit, which doth weary me even that all my joints are weak, for those who are at Jerusalem; for had not the Lord been merciful, to show unto me concerning them, even as he had prophets of old, I should have perished also.
>
> And he surely did show unto the prophets of old all things concerning them; and also he did show unto many concerning us; wherefore, it must needs be that we know concerning them for they are written upon the plates of brass. (1 Nephi 19:20-21.)

Nephi then recorded what is now Isaiah chapter 48 as evidence that the Lord had shown the prophets of old concerning the people of Jerusalem, and he recorded what is now Isaiah chapter 49 as evidence that the Lord had also shown the Nephites to some of the prophets of old.

Chapter 49 is one of the most important chapters in the whole book of Isaiah, because it also clearly foretells the mission of the Latter-day Saints and the destiny of the land of America in connection with the house of Israel. Nephi interpreted the chapter as foretelling that the land of America would receive some of scattered Israel, while his brother Jacob applied it both to the Jews in Jerusalem and to the

Gentiles. Chapter 49 is of such importance that it ought to be studied diligently by every member of the Church. The outline below will hopefully assist in such a study.

1. Israel is the servant of the Lord in whom he will be glorified (49:1-4).
   a. The children of Israel have been scattered upon the isles of the sea (49:1).
   b. They were foreordained to their work (49:1).
   c. Their message will be cutting because it is the word of God (49:2).
   d. The Lord has kept them hidden (49:2).
   e. He will polish them and preserve his servant (49:3).
   f. Although Israel's former efforts have been in vain, they will now do the Lord's work (49:4).
2. Israel's mission is to gather Jacob in the strength of the Lord (49:5-12).
   a. They are to raise up the tribes of Jacob (49:6).
   b. They are to restore the preserved of Israel (49:6).
   c. They are also to be a light unto the Gentiles (49:6).
   d. Kings will see, and princes will worship (49:7).
   e. The Lord will give Israel his servant to establish them as a covenant people in the isles of the sea; then they will "inherit the desolate heritages" (49:8).
   f. The "prisoners" will be led by the Lord, and the way will be opened for them (49:9-11).
   g. The house of Israel will gather from all lands (49:12).
3. The Lord will show that he has not forgotten his promises to Zion (the Americas) (49:13-17).
   a. Heaven and earth will rejoice when the Lord comforts his people (49:13).
   b. The Lord's promises are never forgotten (49:15).
   c. He has engraven them upon the palms of his hands (49:16).
   d. Joseph's children shall prosper over the Gentiles (49:17).
4. Many will gather to Zion, who will be adorned as a bride (49:18-23).

   a. People will come from far away and build up Zion's waste and desolate places (49:19).
   b. They will come seeking freedom or fewer restrictions (49:20).
   c. The Lord will lift up his standard to the Gentiles (49:22).
   d. The gentile kings and queens will nurse Israel's children (49:22-23).
   e. The Gentiles will bow down to Israel (49:23).
5. Israel will be delivered from the hands of the Gentiles (49:24-26).
   a. The Lord will contend with those who fight against Israel (49:25).
   b. The wicked will fight among themselves (49:26).
   c. All flesh will know that the Lord is the Redeemer (49:26).

Notes and Commentary

This entire chapter is quoted by Nephi, and part of it is quoted by Jacob. The commentary by both of these prophets is of great worth to our current study, and there are many significant retentions in the Book of Mormon which help us understand Isaiah's words more clearly and fully. The New Testament, the Doctrine and Covenants, and modern Church leaders also add significantly to our understanding.

Isaiah 49:1. About half of this verse has been lost from the KJV.

	And again: Hearken, O ye house of Israel, all ye that are broken off and are driven out, because of the wickedness of the pastors of my people; yea, all ye that are broken off, that are scattered abroad, who are of my people, O house of Israel.
Listen, O isles, unto me; and hearken, ye people, from far; The Lord hath called me from	Listen, O isles, unto me, and hearken ye people from far; the Lord hath called me from the

the womb; from the bowels of my mother hath he made mention of my name. (Isaiah 49:1.)	womb; from the bowels of my mother hath he made mention of my name. (1 Nephi 21:1.)

The Book of Mormon retention designates those who are "broken off" or "scattered abroad" as the segment of the house of Israel which is invited to hearken. This retention clarifies what the Lord means with the KJV "Listen, O isles." Nephi told his brothers that these verses referred to things which were spiritual and temporal and that they were given to the prophet by the Spirit to reveal what would "come upon the children of men according to the flesh." He further said that the house of Israel would be scattered upon all the face of the earth and among all nations, that many had already been led away and were scattered upon the isles of the sea, and that many more would be (see 1 Nephi 22:1-5). Jacob also reminded his brethren that they (the Nephites) had been scattered and were "upon an isle of the sea" (see 2 Nephi 10:20-22).

The "me" in this verse is identified in verse 3 as the servant Israel. This will be discussed more fully in the notes on verses 2 and 3. "The Lord hath called me from the womb: from the bowels of my mother hath he made mention of my name" is an obvious reference to foreordination. The wording is similar to that which tells of the foreordination of Jeremiah (see Jeremiah 1:4-5).

Isaiah 49:2. The statement that the mouth of the servant will be made "like a sharp sword" is a reference to the message he will bear, which is the word of God (see D&C 6:2; 11:2; 12:2; 14:2; 15:2; 16:2; 33:1). The sword analogy reflects the cutting nature of the truth of the word of God. As Nephi wrote, "the guilty taketh the truth to be hard, for it cutteth them to the very center" (1 Nephi 16:2). The book of Revelation also uses the sword analogy (see Revelation 1:16).

The Lord's hiding Israel in "the shadow of his hand" is clarified in the Doctrine and Covenants, where the Lord declares that the priesthood holders of this last dispensation are "lawful heirs, according to the flesh, and have been hid from the world with Christ in God" (D&C 86:8-9). This description of priesthood bearers as "lawful heirs according to the flesh" is a reference to the covenant which the Lord made with Abraham that all nations of the earth would be blessed through the literal seed of his body, who would bear the ministry and the priesthood (see Abraham 2:9-11). The Doctrine and Covenants also identifies latter-day Israel as the "seed of Abraham" (D&C 103:17). The world did not know where scattered Israel was, but the Lord knew and had concealed them in his protective hand.

The "polished shaft" hidden in the Lord's quiver may be a direct reference to Joseph Smith. As the "choice seer" of the latter day, he was to be the Lord's servant in a special sense (see 2 Nephi 3:6; 3 Nephi 21:10). The Prophet Joseph's description of himself is interesting in this light:

> I am like a huge, rough stone rolling down from a high mountain; and the only polishing I get is when some corner gets rubbed off by coming in contact with something else, striking with accelerated force against religious bigotry, priestcraft, lawyer-craft, doctor-craft, lying editors, suborned judges and jurors, and the authority of perjured executives, backed by mobs, blasphemers, licentious and corrupt men and women—all hell knocking off a corner here and a corner there. Thus I will become a smooth and polished shaft in the quiver of the Almighty, who will give me dominion over all and every one of them, when their refuge of lies shall fail, and their hiding place shall be destroyed, while these smooth-polished stones with which I come in contact become marred. (*TPJS*, p. 304.)

The arrow shaft is polished that it might fly truer and faster, and the shaft that is polished is generally reserved for one's most important shot. The last dispensation, when all things are gathered in one, is the Lord's most important "shot," so he saved his "polished shaft" for this latter-day work. Joseph was called to give this generation the word of God (see D&C 5:10), which recalls also the sharp sword analogy mentioned in verse 2.

Isaiah 49:3. The servant here identified as Israel was previously discussed (see especially the explanatory notes for Isaiah 41:8-9 and 42:17-25). The servant spoken of here is actually Ephraim, who holds the birthright of the twelve tribes (see D&C 133:30-34; Jeremiah 31:9), but specifically it is the Prophet Joseph Smith, who heads the dispensation of the fulness of times (see D&C 90:3-4).

Isaiah 49:4. This verse has perplexed scholars through the years. It seems to refer to the Ephraimites who have been devout members of the various Christian churches. But their membership, ordinances, and efforts in those churches have been to no avail as far as obtaining salvation is concerned because the churches have no authority. They must now turn their efforts to the work of their God under the restoration of his authority, and they will be judged or held accountable for this responsibility.

Isaiah 49:5-6. Through the strength of the Lord, Ephraim is to accomplish three things: (1) He will raise up the tribes of Jacob. These twelve tribes constitute the lost tribes, the Jews, and the Lamanites. Although they remained intact after their dispersion, they were not producing fruit unto the Lord at the time of the Restoration (see Jacob 5:38-39). (2) He will restore the preserved of Israel. These are those who have the blood of Israel but have been scattered among all the nations of the earth, as prophesied by Amos (9:8-9), and have lost their identity (see Jacob 5:52-54). (3) He will be a light to the Gentiles. At the same time that Ephraim will gather those of the blood of Israel from among the nations of the world, he will give the Gentiles an opportunity to be adopted into Israel. Thus the blessing of Abraham to all nations will be under way, and salvation will be extended "unto the end of the earth." The Doctrine and Covenants also calls the priesthood holders of this dispensation to be "a light unto the Gentiles" and "a savior unto my people Israel" (D&C 86:11).

Paul and Barnabas quoted the last part of verse 6 to show that the Gentiles were to receive the gospel after the Jews had rejected it (see Acts 13:47). This did not completely fulfill Isaiah's prophecy, but was an application made by Paul and Barnabas.

Isaiah 49:7.

Thus saith the Lord, the Redeemer of Israel, *and* his Holy One, to him whom man despiseth, to him whom the nation abhorreth, to a servant of rulers, Kings shall see and arise, princes also shall worship, because of the Lord that is faithful, *and the Holy One of*	Thus saith the Lord, the Redeemer of Israel, his Holy One, to him whom man despiseth, to him whom the nation abhorreth, to servant of rulers: Kings shall see and arise, princes also shall worship, because of the Lord that is faithful. (2 Nephi 21:7.)

Israel, and he shall choose thee.
(Isaiah 49:7.)

The Book of Mormon deletes several words, as noted above, but these do not change the meaning of the verse.

Isaiah 49:8.

Thus saith the Lord, In an acceptable time have I heard thee, and in a day of salvation have I helped thee: and I will preserve thee, and give thee for a covenant of the people, to establish the earth, to cause to inherit the desolate heritages;
(Isaiah 49:8.)

Thus saith the Lord: In an acceptable time have I heard thee, *O isles of the sea*, and in a day of salvation have I helped thee; and I will preserve thee, and give thee *my servant* for a covenant of the people, to establish the earth, to cause to inherit the desolate heritages;
(1 Nephi 21:8.)

The message here, as shown by the important retentions in the Book of Mormon, is that scattered Israel will be established as a covenant people in the isles of the sea through the Lord's servant. Paul quotes part of this verse to the Corinthians to encourage them to accept the gospel in the day or time of their salvation (see 2 Corinthians 6:2). This again is an application and not a fulfillment of the prophecy in Isaiah.

Isaiah 49:9-12. These verses are interpreted in 1 Nephi 22:10-12. Nephi said these verses teach that the Lord will "make bare his arm," or show his power, in the eyes of all nations in bringing his covenants and his gospel to the house of Israel. The children of Israel will be brought out of the captivity of the Gentiles and gathered to their promised lands, where they will be identified as Israelites. They will be brought out of obscurity and darkness, will be taught the truth, and will come to know the Savior. This redeeming power will not be known to men, but will be the miraculous power of God. The Book of Mormon retention "and then, O house of Israel" at the beginning of verse 12 shows that the gathering will begin after the Lord has fulfilled verses 10 and 11.

In describing a "great multitude" who would be gathered out of "all nations" to serve the Lord, John used the same words as those found in verse 10, but the time period of John's description seems to be the end of the world rather than the beginning of the gathering (see Revelation 7:16).

Isaiah 49:13. The Book of Mormon retains two whole clauses which have been lost from the KJV:

Sing, O heavens; and be joyful, O earth; and break forth into singing, O mountains: for the Lord hath comforted his people, and will have mercy upon his afflicted. (Isaiah 49:13.)	Sing, O heavens; and be joyful, ful, O earth; *for the feet of those who are in the east shall be established;* and break forth into singing, O mountains; *for they shall be smitten no more*; for the Lord hath comforted his people, and will have mercy upon his afflicted. (1 Nephi 21:13.)

"Those who are in the east" seems to refer to Jerusalem, while the "mountains" appears to be a reference to Zion or America. Thus the Lord is declaring that the two capitals of Israel shall be established and smitten no more.

Isaiah 49:14-15.

But Zion said, The Lord hath forsaken me, and my Lord hath forgotten me.	But, *behold*, Zion *hath* said: The Lord hath forsaken me, and my Lord hath forgotten me—*but he will show that he hath not.*
Can a woman forget her sucking child, that she should not have compassion on the son of her womb? yea, they may forget, yet will I not forget thee. (Isaiah 49:14-15.)	*For* can a woman forget her sucking child, that she should not have compassion on the son of her womb? Yea, they may forget, yet will I not forget thee, *O house of Israel.* (1 Nephi 21:14-15.)

The Book of Mormon retention "but he will show that he hath not" at the end of verse 14 forms a logical transition to verse 15, bridging the gap that exists in the KJV.

In verse 14, Zion apparently bemoans a seeming lack of evidence that the Lord has comforted his people, or will have mercy on the afflicted (see verse 13), but the Lord will remember his promises. A woman's love for her offspring is considered to be one of the strongest bonds that exist, but the Lord's love and promises are even stronger and are never forgotten. Zion (the Americas) was the land given to the children of the house of Joseph (see 3 Nephi 15:12-13; Genesis 49:22-26). The Lord has promised that the New Jerusalem, the epitome of beauty, will be established upon this land (see 3

Nephi 20:22). The Prophet Joseph Smith said concerning the location of Zion:

> You know there has been great discussion in relation to Zion—where it is, and where the gathering of the dispensation is, and which I am now going to tell you. The prophets have spoken and written upon it; but I will make a proclamation that will cover a broader ground. *The whole of America is Zion itself from north to south, and is described by the Prophets, who declare that it is the Zion where the mountain of the Lord should be, and that it should be in the center of the land.* When Elders shall take up and examine the old prophecies in the Bible, they will see it. (*TPJS*, p. 362.)

Isaiah's representing the land of Zion as speaking in verse 14 is consistent with another scripture (see Moses 7:48-49). The Book of Mormon retains the identifying phrase "O house of Israel" at the end of verse 15.

Isaiah 49:16. The engraving upon the palms has two possible symbolic meanings. As the Jews used phylacteries to remind them continually of the commandments of God, they wrote the commandments and wore them where they were continually before their eyes (see Deuteronomy 6:6-9). The Lord declared that he was keeping the promises made to Zion continually before his eyes, and that he would fulfill them at the time and in the manner promised. Another deeper meaning would be that the covenant made by Christ (to atone for the sins of the world and to bring to pass the resurrection) would be sealed or completed by his being nailed to the cross. These nail prints in the palms of his hands would then be a sign to the world, and especially to the Jews, that he had kept his promise (see Isaiah 22:23, 25; Zechariah 12:10; 13:6; D&C 45:48-53).

Isaiah 49:17. The Book of Mormon retention "shall make haste *against* thy destroyers" shows that Joseph's children, unto whom the land of Zion was given, will gain control over those who previously oppressed them. As the Gentiles came to America and scattered the Lamanite children of Joseph, so Joseph's children will prosper against the Gentiles.

Isaiah 49:18-21. The Lord invites Zion to look into the future and behold the multitudes that will come and adorn its land as a bride. The analogy of a bride is used because a bride is traditionally very meticulous in her dress and grooming on her wedding day. The land which has lain waste and desolate will be built up until man will reason that it is too small for the multitude which will come to it. These multitudes will come from afar seeking freedom because their former lands were too restrictive, "too strait." This will happen after the time when the "first" of Joseph's children (note the Book of Mormon retention in verse 20)—the Nephites—shall have forfeited their blessings in this choice land above all other lands. The migrations to come are going to be so numerous that it will astonish the land of Zion, who was previously complaining that the Lord had forgotten her.

Isaiah 49:22-23. These verses have been interpreted for us by both Nephi and Jacob. Nephi spoke of their fulfillment by the Lamanites in the land of America, but he also included all of the house of Israel, and Jacob spoke of their fulfillment through both the Jews and the Lamanites (see 1 Nephi 22:6-9; 2 Nephi 6:8-12; 10:1-22). The fulfillment was to commence with the Lord's "standard" being raised up to the Gentiles (see verse 22). This standard or "ensign," as it is elsewhere called by Isaiah, is identified in the Doctrine and Covenants as the "everlasting covenant" (see D&C 45:9). Elder Marion G. Romney identified the standard spoken of by Isaiah as the Church, which teaching is consistent with Doctrine and Covenants 115:3-5 (see CR, Apr. 1961, p. 119). The Lord has also identified the standard as his words which would be spoken to Nephi's seed (see 2 Nephi 29:2). Thus the Church, the Book of Mormon, and the everlasting covenant may all be seen as the fulfillment of this prophecy in Isaiah.

Nephi said there would be a temporal and a spiritual fulfillment of the children's being carried in the Gentiles' arms and upon their shoulders. He spoke of the house of Israel's being scattered and confounded, which would be followed by the Lord's raising up a mighty nation among the Gentiles upon the land of America who would scatter the Lamanites (see 1 Nephi 22:6-7). This, of course, was fulfilled in the settling of America and the moving of the Lamanites onto reservations, where they were given government aid. Elder Spencer W. Kimball has described how the Lamanites have been carried in the arms of the Gentiles at various times (see CR, Oct. 1965, p. 72; see also CR, Oct. 1956, pp. 52-58).

Nephi described the spiritual fulfillment of this prophecy through "a marvelous work among the Gentiles" (the restoration of the gospel), which would be of great worth to Nephi's seed and that of his brethren. He further declared the great worth of this marvelous work to the Gentiles and to all the house of Israel which would fulfill the promise given to Abraham (see 1 Nephi 22:8-9). Elder Kimball also noted the spiritual fulfillment of these prophecies in his addresses cited in the previous paragraph.

Jacob spoke of the Jews' being carried into captivity after Lehi and his sons left Jerusalem, and of their returning and having the Lord manifest to them in the flesh. He spoke of their crucifying the Holy One of Israel and then being scattered and smitten until the time when they would be gathered again. Jacob then referred to the blessings which would come to the Gentiles through not fighting against Zion and the covenant people of the Lord. He also warned that those who would fight against Zion and the covenant people would "lick up the dust of their feet" (see 2 Nephi 6:8-13).

Jacob enlarged upon the idea that the Lamanites would become "a righteous branch unto the house of Israel" (2 Nephi 9:53). He spoke again of the coming crucifixion of Christ, of the gathering of the Jews from the four parts of the earth to the land of their inheritance, and of the kings of the Gentiles becoming nursing fathers to them. He then said that the land of America would be the land of inheritance for his seed, and that the Gentiles would be blessed upon it. Although there were to be no kings upon this land, the Gentiles would afflict the seed of Israel and become like a father to them. Following this, the land would become a choice land and the great promises of the Lord to the isles of the sea would be fulfilled (see 2 Nephi 10).

As there are three separate chapters which describe the fulfillment of Isaiah's prophecies, the following parallel or harmony will help us see how these events were to come about among the Jews, the Nephites, and others of the house of Israel and all nations.

. . . I will lift up mine hand to the Gentiles . . .

Jews	*Nephites*	*Others*
2 Nephi 6:8-11	2 Nephi 10:1-2	

. . . and set up my standard to the people . . .

Jews	*Nephites*	*Others*
	1 Nephi 22:8	1 Nephi 22:9-10

. . . and they shall bring thy sons in their arms, and thy daughters shall be carried upon their shoulders.

Jews	*Nephites*	*Others*
	2 Nephi 10:10-18	

And kings shall be thy nursing fathers, and their queens thy nursing mothers . . .

Jews	*Nephites*	*Others*
2 Nephi 10:3-9		

. . . they shall bow down to thee with their face toward the earth, and lick up the dust of thy feet. . . .

Jews	*Nephites*	*Others*
2 Nephi 6:12-13	2 Nephi 10:19-20	2 Nephi 10:21-22

Isaiah 49:24-25.

Shall the prey be taken from the mighty, or the lawful captive delivered?

But thus saith the Lord, even the captives of the mighty shall be taken away, and the prey of the terrible shall be delivered: for I will contend with him that contendeth with thee, *and I will save thy children.* (Isaiah 49:24-25.)

For shall the prey be taken from the mighty, or the lawful captive delivered?

But thus saith the Lord: Even the captives of the mighty shall be taken away, and the prey of the terrible shall be delivered; for *the Mighty God shall deliver his covenant people. For thus saith the Lord:* I will contend with them that contendeth with thee— (2 Nephi 6:16-17.)

The "prey" spoken of is the house of Israel, which has been captive to the "mighty" (the Gentiles). While it may seem unlikely that Israel could overcome the mighty gentile nations who have been ruling the world for several hundred years, the Lord, who is "mightier than all the earth" (1 Nephi 4:1), will be on Israel's side.

In quoting this verse in 2 Nephi 6:17, Jacob apparently inserted the following into the text: "the mighty God shall deliver his covenant people. For thus saith the Lord." Yet he failed to quote the last line, "and I will save thy children." (Compare 1 Nephi 21:24-25.)

Isaiah 49:26. In 1 Nephi 22:13-14, Nephi gave this verse two interpretations: the great and abominable church would war among themselves and become drunken with their own blood, and the nations who would fight against the house of Israel or against Zion would "fall into the pit which they digged to ensnare the people of the Lord."

1 Nephi 22:15-17. These verses, or part of them, may also have been a part of Isaiah's writings at one time. Although we recognize the similarity between verse 15 and Malachi 4:1, Nephi's words could not have come from this book. Malachi had not written his work at the time Lehi left Jerusalem, so it could not have been included on the plates of brass. It might very well be that Malachi, living several hundred years after Isaiah, was quoting from the original Isaiah text.

Israel Has Not Been Cast Off Forever

20

Isaiah 50-52:12

Isaiah 50-52:12 is a message of hope to the whole house of Israel, showing how the covenant of Abraham will be extended to them in the last days through two great gathering places, Zion and Jerusalem.

Isaiah 50:4-9 is designated by Bible scholars as another "servant song" to Christ. The servant in Isaiah 42:1-4 was identified as Christ. The servant in chapter 49 was definitely identified as latter-day Israel. The servant here is also latter-day Israel, but the passage has a dual meaning as it also describes the mission of the Savior among the Jews (and possibly the other tribes of Israel) in the meridian of time. There are also those who feel, with some justification, that the servant spoken of in these verses is Isaiah himself. The dual meaning of the servant as Israel and Christ fits into the context of the overall message, as outlined below.

1. The Lord has not cast off Israel forever (50:1-3).
    a. The mother's bill of divorcement does not apply now (50:1).
    b. The Lord has no creditors, so Israel was not sold (50:1).
    c. Those who are cast off sell themselves (50:1).
    d. Their mother (ancient Israel) was cast off for the same reason (50:1).
    e. The Jews did not respond when Christ came to them, and they were driven out (50:2).

   f. When Christ called again there was none to answer (50:2).
   g. The Lord has power to redeem Israel anyway (50:2-3).
2. The Lord God has given his servant power to redeem (50:4-11).
   a. The servant can speak and confound the wise (50:4).
   b. He listened and followed revelation in spite of persecution (50:5-6).
   c. He will smite the contenders with the message of the gospel (50:7-8).
   d. He will smite those who condemn him (50:9).
   e. Those who walk in the light of their own reasoning will lie down in sorrow (50:10-11).
3. The righteous are invited to look back to the covenant made with Abraham and Sarah (51:1-8).
   a. The Lord will comfort Zion physically and socially (51:3).
   b. A law (the Book of Mormon) will proceed from the Lord for a light unto Israel in the isles of the sea (51:4-5).
   c. The heavens and the earth and its inhabitants will vanish, but the Lord's salvation is forever (51:6-8).
   d. Those who have the Lord's law written in their hearts need not fear the reproach of men (51:7-8).
4. Zion will put on her strength as in ancient days (51:9-16).
   a. The redeemed will return with singing and everlasting joy (51:11).
   b. The Lord will be the one who comforts them (51:12-15).
   c. The Lord has directed them and hidden them in his hand to be his people (51:16).
5. Jerusalem will be comforted by two sons (51:17-23).
   a. She has drunk the cup of the Lord's fury, but has no sons to guide her (51:17-18).
   b. Two sons will come to her to strengthen her (51:19-20).
   c. The cup of fury will be put into the hands of those who afflict Jerusalem (51:21-23).
6. The Lord's people will know his name in that day (52:1-6).

a. Zion will loose herself from the bands of her neck (52:1-2).
b. Jerusalem will rise from the dust and become a holy city (52:1-2).
c. They sold themselves for nought and will be redeemed without money (52:3).
d. They were ruled over, and the Lord's name was blasphemed (52:4-5).

7. All the ends of the earth will see the salvation of the Lord (52:7-12).
   a. The watchman will publish peace and bring Zion again (52:7-8).
   b. The waste places of Jerusalem will sing together (52:9).
   c. Those who bear the vessels of the Lord will become clean (52:11).
   d. They will not go in haste or by flight, but the Lord will go before and behind (52:12).

Notes and Commentary

All of these chapters are quoted in the Book of Mormon with the exception of 52:4-5. The other verses in chapter 52 are frequently quoted. There are many significant retentions in the Book of Mormon which help us understand these passages. The Doctrine and Covenants also contains many enlightening references to these chapters, particularly chapter 52. The New Testament quotes several verses, also primarily from the 52nd chapter. Modern Church authorities have made a few statements which help us gain a proper understanding of these chapters. All in all, there is little reason not to understand this part of Isaiah's writings—particularly chapter 52, which is dealt with more frequently in other scriptures than most chapters in the book of Isaiah. This should signify its importance.

Isaiah 50:1-3. Isaiah 50-52:12 is a continuation of the theme of chapter 49, and is considered separately here only for convenience of study. Chapter 49 concluded with a declaration that the Lord would fight for his people Israel against those who contended with them or with Zion and that the great and abominable church would be warring within itself. Continuing in the same vein, the Lord here states his reasons for fighting in Israel's behalf: (1) the bill of divorcement which he gave to their "mother" (former-day Israel—see Jeremiah 3:1, 8) is not in effect for latter-day Israel; and (2) the Lord has not sold them to his creditors, for he has none.

The Lord uses the metaphor of the ancient law of divorce given by Moses, wherein a man who found uncleanness in his wife could put her away, but was required to give her a bill of divorcement; he could never remarry her thereafter, even if her second husband died (see Deuteronomy 24:1-4). While the Lord had divorced ancient Israel because of their iniquities, latter-day Israel was not included in that bill of divorcement. Some scholars consider that under ancient law, a man could sell his children into servitude, either directly or in marriage, to pay his creditors (see Exodus 21:7), but the Lord is in debt to no one, so this does not apply either. Therefore, there is no reason why the Lord would not deliver Israel from the hands of their oppressors, and certainly he had power to do so.

There will be those in modern Israel who are *not* delivered, however, because they will suffer from their own iniquities, just as did many in former-day Israel because of their transgressions. The Lord's teachings in this matter are clarified in the Doctrine and Covenants. The context is the day of the Lord's fighting for Israel—and the day spoken of by Moses and Malachi when those who hearken not to the voice of the Lord will be cut off, and the proud and the wicked will be burned, leaving them "neither root [ancestors] nor branch [posterity]." Thus they are no longer a part of Israel; their patriarchal lines are severed.

> And upon them that hearken not to the voice of the Lord shall be fulfilled that which was written by the prophet Moses, that they should be cut off from among the people.
>
> And also that which was written by the prophet Malachi: For, behold, the day cometh that shall burn as an oven, and all the proud, yea, and all that do wickedly, shall be stubble; and the day that cometh shall burn them up, saith the Lord of hosts, that it shall leave them neither root nor branch. (D&C 133:63-64; see also Deuteronomy 18:15, 18-19; Acts 3:23; 1 Nephi 22:20-21; 3 Nephi 20:23; 21:11; Malachi 4:1.)

Doctrine and Covenants 133:66-69 contains the Lord's answer to those of Israel who are "cut off," with slight variations from the words in Isaiah. The 2 Nephi reading is also included for comparison:

Thus saith the Lord, Where is the bill of your mother's divorcement, whom I have put away? or which of my creditors is it to whom I have sold you? Behold, for your iniquities have ye sold yourselves, and for your transgressions is your mother put away.	Yea, for thus saith the Lord: Have I put thee away, or have I cast thee off forever? For thus saith the Lord: Where is the bill of your mother's divorcement? To whom have I put thee away, or to which of my creditors have I sold you? Yea, to whom have I sold you? Behold, for your iniquities have ye sold yourselves, and for your transgressions is your mother put away.	
Wherefore, when I came, *was there* no man? when I called, *was there* none to answer? Is my hand shortened at all, that it cannot redeem? or have I no power to deliver? behold, at my rebuke I dry up the sea, I make the rivers a wilderness: their fish stinketh, because there is no water, and dieth for thirst.	Wherefore, when I came, *there was* no man; when I called, *yea, there was* none to answer. *O house of Israel,* is my hand shortened at all that it cannot redeem, or have I no power to deliver? Behold, at my rebuke I dry up the sea, I make *their* rivers a wilderness *and* their fish to stink because the waters are dried up, and they die because of thirst.	*In that day* when I came *unto mine own*, no man *among you received me, and you were driven out.* When I called *again* there was none of you to answer; yet my arm was not shortened at all that I could not redeem, neither my power to deliver. Behold, at my rebuke I dry up the sea. I make the rivers a wilderness; their fish stink, and die for thirst.
I clothe the heavens with black-	I clothe the heavens with black-	I clothe the heavens with black-

ness, and I make sackcloth their covering. (Isaiah 50:1-3.)	ness, and I make sackcloth their covering. (2 Nephi 7:1-3.)	ness, and make sackcloth their covering. (D&C 133:66-69.)

When Christ came to his own in the meridian of time, the Jews collectively rejected the gospel. When he calls again, it will be his second appearance to them. Although the Jews will still not be ready for revelation, the Lord will have power to redeem them. This idea is amplified in chapter 51.

As Nephi commented on Isaiah 49 in 1 Nephi 22, he quoted or paraphrased three verses from "the prophet," obviously Isaiah. We do not have these verses in the present Bible text, but they fit very well into the context of Isaiah 49 and 50. We can illustrate this by placing the passage between the last verse of chapter 49 and the first verse of chapter 50:

> And I will feed them that oppress thee with their own flesh; and they shall be drunken with their own blood, as with sweet wine: and all flesh shall know that I the Lord am thy Saviour and thy Redeemer, the mighty One of Jacob. (Isaiah 49:26.)
>
> For behold, saith the prophet, the time cometh speedily that Satan shall have no more power over the hearts of the children of men; for the day soon cometh that all the proud and they who do wickedly shall be as stubble; and the day cometh that they must be burned.
>
> For the time soon cometh that the fulness of the wrath of God shall be poured out upon all the children of men; for he will not suffer that the wicked shall destroy the righteous.
>
> Wherefore, he will preserve the righteous by his power, even if it so be that the fulness of his wrath must come, and the righteous be preserved, even unto the destruction of their enemies by fire. Wherefore, the righteous need not fear; for thus saith the prophet, they shall be saved, even if it so be as by fire. (1 Nephi 22:15-17.)
>
> *Yea, for thus saith the Lord: Have I put thee away, or have I cast thee off forever? For* thus saith the Lord: Where is the bill of your mother's divorcement? *To* whom *have I* put *thee* away, or *to* which of my creditors *have I* sold you? *Yea, to whom have I sold you?* Behold, for your iniquities have ye sold yourselves, and for your transgressions is your mother put away. (2 Nephi 7:1.)

The italicized words above are retentions which the Book of Mormon has preserved. In 2 Nephi 6, Jacob quoted Isaiah 49, interspersing several of his own comments. (He also inserted Isaiah 11:11 between Isaiah 49:23 and 49:24.) This was similar to the pattern of Nephi's commentaries on Isaiah, although the intrusions dealt with different subjects.

Isaiah 50:4-9. As already stated, this so-called servant song probably had a dual meaning. This claim is supported by Doctrine and Covenants 133:66-70, which quotes Isaiah 50:2-3 and the last sentence of verse 11, suggesting that a change of thought has been inserted between verses 3 and 11. Verses 4 through 10 may have been inserted to show how the Lord was going to redeem the house of Israel through his "servant" (restored Israel, as explained in chapter 49). The Book of Mormon reading of verse 4 (2 Nephi 7:4) clearly shows that the servant is addressing the house of Israel.

Isaiah 50:4.

The Lord God hath given me the tongue of the learned, that I should know how to speak a word in season to him that is weary: he wakeneth morning by morning, he wakeneth mine ear to hear as the learned. (Isaiah 50:4.)

The Lord God hath given me the tongue of the learned, that I should know how to speak a word in season unto thee, O house of Israel. When ye are weary he waketh morning by morning. He waketh mine ear to hear as the learned. (2 Nephi 7:4.)

This verse has been interpreted as a reference to the twelve-year-old Christ as he sat in the temple in the midst of the doctors, who were "astonished at his understanding and answers" (Luke 2:46-47). Others, citing 2 Chronicles 36:15-16, have said that the verse refers to prophets' being called to preach to Jerusalem, but the Chronicles reference pertain to a later time than that of Isaiah—although the patterns of the prophets are similar (see Isaiah 30:8-11). Verse 4 also fits the calling and mission of Joseph Smith and the elders of restored Israel, who were to cause the wisdom of the wise men to perish (see Isaiah 29:14). It would be consistent with chapter 49 to identify the servant "me" as restored Israel.

Isaiah 50:5-7. In the JST, verse 5 reads, "The Lord God hath *appointed* mine ears" rather than "opened mine ear."

The subject still seems to be the servant Israel. The persecution of the Latter-day Saints, particularly in the days of Joseph Smith, is very similar to the events in these verses. The passage may also describe the persecution of the Savior as he was condemned. According to tradition, Isaiah also faced persecutors, eventually being sawn asunder with a wooden saw.

Isaiah 50:8-9.

He is near *that* justifieth me; who will contend with me? let us stand together: who is mine adversary? let him come near to me.	*And the Lord* is near, *and he* justifieth me. Who will contend with me? Let us stand together. Who is mine adversary? Let him come near me, *and I will smite him with the strength of my mouth.*
Behold, the Lord God will help me; who is he that shall condemn me? lo, they all shall wax old as a garment; the moth shall eat them up. (Isaiah 50:8-9.)	*For* the Lord God will help me. *And all they who* shall condemn me, behold, all they shall wax old as a garment, and the moth shall eat them up. (2 Nephi 7:8-9.)

The Book of Mormon identifies the pronoun "he" as the Lord and retains the clause "and I will smite him with the strength of my mouth." Verse 9 also reads more clearly in declaring the fate of those who condemn.

Isaiah 50:10-11. The Book of Mormon reading does not contain the last line of verse 10:

Who is among you that feareth the Lord, that obeyeth the voice of his servant, that walketh in darkness, and hath no light? let him trust in the name of the Lord, and stay upon his God. (Isaiah 50:10.)	Who is among you that feareth the Lord, that obeyeth the voice of his servant, that walketh in darkness and hath no light? (2 Nephi 7:10.)

Without it, verse 11 becomes a warning in the context of Isaiah 50:2-3 as clarified by section 133 of the Doctrine and Covenants. Those who will not follow revelation or heed the voice of the Lord's servant, but walk in their own light of reason, will lie down in sorrow, having been cut off from Israel.

Behold, all ye that kindle a fire, that compass yourselves about with sparks: walk in the light of your fire, and in the sparks that ye have kindled. This shall ye have of mine hand; ye shall lie down in sorrow. (Isaiah 50:11.)	And this shall ye have of my hand—ye shall lie down in sorrow. (D&C 133:70.)

The Lord gives a further description of their fate in the verses which follow:

> Behold, and lo, there are none to deliver you; for ye obeyed not my voice when I called to you out of the heavens; ye believed not my servants, and when they were sent unto you ye received them not.
>
> Wherefore, they sealed up the testimony and bound up the law, and ye were delivered over unto darkness.
>
> These shall go away into outer darkness, where there is weeping, and wailing, and gnashing of teeth.
>
> Behold the Lord your God hath spoken it. Amen. (D&C 133:71-74.)

Isaiah 51:1-2. A careful analysis of the covenant made with Abraham and Sarah shows that it will be fulfilled in the last days. The Doctrine and Covenants reveals that Abraham's covenant is now being fulfilled (see D&C 103:17; 132:30-31). Isaiah's invitation for the righteous to look to Abraham and Sarah pertains to this same time period.

Isaiah 51:3. President Charles W. Nibley once quoted this verse and said it referred to Utah and the missionary program, which was gathering Saints to Zion (see CR, Apr. 1930, p. 29). This idea is consistent with the Prophet Joseph Smith's designation of North and South America as the Zion spoken of by the Old Testament prophets (see *TPJS*, p. 362). But Utah would be only a part of this Zion, and these same physical and social blessings are to come to all the gathering places of the Saints in the land of Zion. The blessings pronounced upon Zion's waste places, wilderness, and deserts are reminiscent of the physical blessings which the Lord has promised those who keep the Sabbath in the land of Zion. These things will be given "to please the eye and to gladden the heart," and will all come "according to the law and the prophets" (D&C 59:16-19, 22).

Isaiah 51:4-5. The "law" which will come from the Lord is undoubtedly the Book of Mormon. This law is associated with judgment in both verses 4 and 5, and it will come forth from the "isles." The Book of Mormon is to judge the nations as well as individuals (see 2 Nephi 25:22; D&C 20:13-15).

Isaiah 51:6-8. In his second general epistle, the apostle Peter expressed teachings similar to these verses:

Lift up your eyes to the heavens, and look upon the earth beneath; for the heavens shall vanish away like smoke, and the earth shall wax old like a garment; and they that dwell therein shall die in like manner. But my salvation shall be forever, and my righteousness shall not be abolished.	But the day of the Lord will come as a thief in the night; in the which the heavens shall pass away with a great noise, and the elements shall melt with fervent heat, the earth also and the works that are therein shall be burned up.
Hearken unto me, ye that know righteousness, the people in whose heart *I have written* my law, fear ye not the reproach of men, neither be ye afraid of their revilings.	Seeing then that all these things shall be dissolved, what manner of persons ought ye to be in all holy conversation and godliness,
For the moth shall eat them up like a garment, and the worm shall eat them like wool. But my righteousness shall be forever, and my salvation from generation to generation. (2 Nephi 8:6-8.)	Looking for and hasting unto the coming of the day of God, wherein the heavens being on fire shall be dissolved, and the elements shall melt with fervent heat?
	Nevertheless we, according to his promise, look for new heavens and a new earth, wherein dwelleth righteousness. (2 Peter 3:10-13.)

The Book of Mormon retention shown by the italicized words calls to mind the promise given in Jeremiah that a new covenant will be established with Judah and Israel in the future, a further indication that this chapter refers to the last days (see Jeremiah 31:31-33). President Joseph Fielding Smith taught that verses 6 and 7 speak of the earth's being a living body which must die and become resurrected like man (see *DS*, 1:72-73).

Isaiah 51:9-10. The Book of Mormon retains the word "he" for the KJV "it" in both of these verses. In verse 10 Isaiah cites acts of strength which the Lord has accomplished in times past.

Isaiah 51:11. The "redeemed of the Lord" who were to "return, and come with singing unto Zion" with "everlasting joy" are identified in the Doctrine and Covenants as the Latter-day Saints (see D&C 45:71; 66:11; 101:18). The return has begun, but it will not be completed until the center place of Zion is built up "that the prophets might be fulfilled" (D&C 101:19).

Isaiah 51:16. This verse is similar to Isaiah 49:2; see the earlier note on that verse. That Zion will be recognized as the Lord's people is also part of the promise of the "new covenant" spoken of in Jeremiah 31:31-33.

Isaiah 51:18. Because Judah's sons are without the priesthood, there is no proper leadership. This is the same thought contained in Isaiah 50:2, as interpreted in Doctrine and Covenants 133:67; both refer to Judah (see the note on Isaiah 50:1-3).

Isaiah 51:19-20. The Book of Mormon identifies the two "things" in verse 19 (italicized in the KJV) as "sons." Because the people of Judah have no sons with the priesthood among them, two other sons (who have the priesthood) are to be sent to them.

These two *things* are come unto thee; who shall be sorry for thee? desolation, and destruction, and the famine, and the sword: by whom shall I comfort thee?

Thy sons have fainted, they lie at the head of all the streets, as a wild bull in a net: they are full of the fury of the Lord, the rebuke of thy God. (Isaiah 51:19-20.)

These two *sons* are come unto thee, who shall be sorry for thee—*thy* desolation and destruction, and the famine and the sword—*and* by whom shall I comfort thee?

Thy sons have fainted, *save these two;* they lie at the head of all the streets; as a wild bull in a net, they are full of the fury of the Lord, the rebuke of thy God. (2 Nephi 8:19-20.)

Because these "sons" are to bear the priesthood, they have to come from among the Latter-day Saints. They will be the "two witnesses" spoken of in Revelation 11 who will testify in Jerusalem, will be killed and left lying in the streets, and then will be resurrected to meet the Messiah as he appears to the Jews. These two prophets are also spoken of in Zechariah 4:3, 11-14. Elder Bruce R. McConkie has stated, "No doubt they will be members of the Council of the Twelve or of the First Presidency of the Church" (*DNTC*, 3:509).

Isaiah 51:21-23. Elder Orson Hyde applied verses 22 and 23 to the persecutors of the Church in the early days of the Restoration (see *JD*, 10:73-74). While the application was certainly valid, these verses refer to those who come against Judah in the last days.

Isaiah 52:1-2. These two verses demonstrate that what the Lord said in Isaiah 51 was addressed to the two gathering places of Zion and Jerusalem. Jacob included them as the conclusion of his quotation from Isaiah (see 2 Nephi 8:24-25). They are also quoted in two other places in the Book of Mormon. When the Savior visited the Nephites, he specified that these verses would be fulfilled when the Jews were gathered to Jerusalem in the last days. He also added one word to the text which was not quoted by Jacob: "Awake, awake *again*, and put on thy strength, O Zion" (3 Nephi 20:36-37). This was probably because Zion, or America, was "awakening" at the time of the Savior's visit and "putting on her strength," but the Savior knew that within 400 years the Nephites would lose that strength and fall again into a spiritual sleep. The use of the word "again" indicates a dual interpretation of the Isaiah text in this instance, and supports the idea that there are other dual interpretations throughout Isaiah. Moroni, in his final admonition, paraphrased these verses as prophecy which would be fulfilled (see Moroni 10:31).

In March 1838, the Prophet Joseph Smith gave the following interpretation of these verses in answer to a question about what Isaiah meant by "Put on thy strength, O Zion":

> He had reference to those whom God should call in the last days, who should hold the power of priesthood to bring again Zion, and the redemption of Israel; and to put on her strength is to put on the authority of the priesthood, which she, Zion, has a right to by lineage; also to return to that power which she had lost. (D&C 113:8.)

He also gave the meaning of "Zion loosing herself from the bands of her neck":

> We are to understand that the scattered remnants are exhorted to return to the Lord from whence they have fallen; which if they do, the promise of the Lord is that he will speak to them, or give them revelation. See the 6th, 7th, and 8th verses. The bands of her neck are the curses of God upon her, or the remnants of Israel in their scattered condition among the Gentiles. (D&C 113:10.)

Doctrine and Covenants 82:14 also declares that "Zion must arise and put on her beautiful garments."

Isaiah 52:3-6. These verses are not fully quoted in the Book of Mormon. Only verses 3 and 6 are quoted by the Savior (see 3 Nephi 20:38-39). The fact that verses 4 and 5 refer to Israel's bondage in Egypt and their unjust oppression by the Assyrians, and did not apply specifically to the Nephites, is probably a reason for their exclusion. The Anchor Bible (20:121) translates the last phrase of verse 4 as follows: ". . . and then Assyria oppressed them violently." This follows the Septuagint reading and is more consistent with history, as Assyria was an instrument in the Lord's hand to humble Israel. On the other hand, the KJV reading could mean that Assyria did not acknowledge the "cause" of their actions because they failed to respond to the Lord or recognize his hand in the conquest of Israel (see Isaiah 10:12-13). Because the Lord's name was blasphemed during these historical occurrences, he will cause his people to know his name—and to know that he does give revelation. This is confirmed in Doctrine and Covenants 113:10 and is a fitting introduction to verses 7 through 12, which show how in the last days the Lord will establish the knowledge that he exists. Paul applied verse 5 to the Roman Saints who were blaspheming the name of God (see Romans 2:24). It was an appropriate application which is true of every time period and should be a lesson to Church members today.

Isaiah 52:7. This verse is probably best known because of Handel's *Messiah*. Its interpretation is given to us in the Book of Mormon, and the time of its fulfillment is provided in the Doctrine and Covenants. The wicked priests of King Noah asked the prophet Abinadi what Isaiah 52:7-10 meant (see

Mosiah 12:20-24). In a delayed response, Abinadi identified Christ as the "founder of peace" and all those who declare the message of the gospel as the publishers of peace (see Mosiah 15:13-18). Paul bore the same testimony to the Romans concerning those who preach the gospel (see Romans 10:14-15). In the Doctrine and Covenants, the Lord quoted the words of verse 7 in sending out modern-day priesthood holders to do missionary work (D&C 19:29; 31:3; 79:1). The Savior also cited this verse as the response of those who come to know his name and his revelations, as described in verse 6—indicating that it is the message of the gospel which will bring his people to that knowledge (see 3 Nephi 20:39-40).

Isaiah 52:8-10. These verses are quoted four times in the Book of Mormon, and always as a unit, although the Savior once interpolated a comment between verses 8 and 9 when he quoted them (see 3 Nephi 20:33). Although verse 8 speaks about Zion while verse 9 speaks about Jerusalem, the Savior quoted all three verses twice to the Nephites and said they would be fulfilled through both the Nephites and the Jews. This again shows the dual nature of Isaiah's prophecies. The Savior first quoted this passage following his declaration that the land of America was to be given to Lehi's descendants after the Gentiles reject the fulness of the gospel and are "trodden under foot" by the house of Israel; he said this would fulfill the words of the prophet Isaiah (see 3 Nephi 16:10-20). He later quoted the passage while instructing the Nephites concerning the restoration of the Jews. He changed the wording from "thy watchmen" to "their watchmen," as he was referring to Jerusalem's watchmen in this case rather than those of Zion (see 3 Nephi 20:29-35). Abinadi also recognized the universal application of this passage in teaching that "the salvation of the Lord shall be declared to every nation, kindred, tongue, and people" and quoting these three verses as evidence (see Mosiah 15:28-31). Joseph Smith designated Jackson County, Missouri, as the Zion spoken of in verse 8 (see *TPJS*, pp. 79-80). The "watchmen" are those who preach the gospel, as indicated in verse 7. The song to be sung in Zion will be a new song, sung when all will know Christ (i.e., during the Millennium). The words of the song, which will include parts of verse 8, are recorded in Doctrine and Covenants 84:99-102.

The Lord will "make bare his holy arm in the eyes of all the nations" at his second coming (see D&C 133:2-3). Doctrine and Covenants 133:4 admonishes the members of the Church to sanctify themselves in preparation for that day.

Simeon, the devout temple worker at the time of the Savior's birth, declared, "mine eyes have seen thy salvation" (Luke 2:30), which is the designation given to the Savior by Isaiah. But that event obviously did not fulfill Isaiah's prophecy that "all the ends of the earth shall see the salvation of our God."

Isaiah 52:11. There are two admonitions in this verse: the Lord's people are instructed to depart from evil, and those who "bear the vessels of the Lord" (the watchmen or preachers of the gospel) are instructed to be clean. The place from which they are to depart is "Babylon" (D&C 133:5)—that is, "from the midst of wickedness, which is spiritual Babylon" (D&C 133:14; see also 38:42). The process of becoming clean is shown in Doctrine and Covenants 133:6: the Saints are to call solemn assemblies, teach each other, and call upon the name of the Lord. This verse in Isaiah is often quoted by modern Church leaders as an admonition to priesthood holders and Church members to live high moral standards. Paul paraphrased it in writing to the Corinthians with the same objective (see 2 Corinthians 6:17). The book of Revelation speaks of the fall of Babylon in the same time period as does Isaiah (see chapter 9 of this book), and also invites the Lord's people to come out of Babylon (see Revelation 18:4).

Isaiah 52:12. This verse is quoted almost verbatim in the Book of Mormon. The Doctrine and Covenants gives a similar but more extended wording:

For ye shall not go out with haste, nor go by flight: for the Lord will go before you; and the God of Israel will be your rearward. (Isaiah 52:12.)	For ye shall not go out with haste nor go by flight; for the Lord will go before you, and the God of Israel shall be your rearward. (3 Nephi 20:42.)	But verily, thus saith the Lord, let not your flight be in haste, but let *all things be prepared before you*; and he that goeth, let him not look back lest sudden destruction shall come upon him. (D&C 133:15.)

The "flight" from Babylon should be organized and well prepared, and it will be final—there is to be no looking back. The Lord promises to go before his people and to follow after them.

Isaiah Testifies of Christ's Earthly Ministry

21

Isaiah 52:13-54:17

Chapter 53 is probably the best-known chapter in the entire book of Isaiah because of its prophecies of the life of Christ. Scholars look upon this chapter as a fourth servant song to Christ, but most consider that the song begins with Isaiah 52:13. We have also begun there, not because others do, but because the last three verses of chapter 52 fit better into the context of the next chapter. However, the "servant" spoken of in Isaiah 52:13 is actually two different servants, as shown by the Savior's interpretation given to the Nephites. Chapter 53 is considered by Christians to be a prophecy of Christ, although the standard Jewish interpretation is that it describes the suffering of Israel or Judah as a people. This prophecy is written mostly in the past tense as if it had already happened. Abinadi, in commenting on Isaiah 53, recognized that it spoke of future things as if they had already come to pass (see Mosiah 16:6). An outline of Isaiah 52:13 through 54:17 gives us an overall perspective:

1. The Lord's servant will be exalted and extolled (52:13-15).
   a. He will be marred but not hurt (52:14).
   b. Kings will be astonished by his work (52:15).
2. The Jews will reject the mission of the Savior (53:1-3).
   a. They will not believe the testimony of the prophets (53:1).
   b. They will not believe the miracles which attest to his divinity (53:1).

   c. He will be raised up by the Father as a mortal (53:2).
   d. The Jews will despise and reject him (53:3).

3. The Savior will suffer these things to save the world (53:4-9).
   a. The world will esteem him to be smitten of God (53:4).
   b. All will have gone astray and will need his atonement (53:6).
   c. He will be afflicted and oppressed, but will not retaliate (53:7).
   d. His life will be cut short upon the earth (53:8).
   e. He will be buried with the wicked and the rich (53:9).

4. His sacrifice will be a freewill offering (53:10-11).
   a. He will see his seed, or those who will accept his atonement (53:10).
   b. He will satisfy the demands of justice (53:11).

5. He will be exalted and extolled because he will fulfill his mission (53:12).
   a. He will voluntarily give his life.
   b. He will suffer to gain an understanding of people.
   c. He will pay the price for the atonement.

6. More of the children of Israel will be gathered than are already gathered (54:1-17).
   a. Their borders will be enlarged and their stakes strengthened (54:2).
   b. They shall inhabit the desolate gentile cities (54:3).
   c. The covenant (marriage) between Christ and Israel will be reestablished (54:4-6).
   d. The gathering is as sure as the covenant made with Noah that there would be no more flood (54:7-9).
   e. The earth will be restored as it was before the curse (54:10).
   f. Great material blessings will be poured out upon Israel (54:11-12).
   g. Their children will be taught of the Lord and will have peace (54:13).
   h. Those who gather against Israel will not prosper (54:14-17).

Notes and Commentary

The Savior quoted and interpreted Isaiah 52:13-15 for the Nephites when he visited them. The prophet Abinadi quoted Isaiah 53 to the wicked priests of King Noah and added extensive comments on the meaning of the chapter. The Savior also quoted Isaiah 54 to the Nephites after describing events which would fulfill that chapter.

The New Testament quotes verses from Isaiah 53 extensively, and also contains a few quotations from Isaiah 52:13-15 and Isaiah 54. In the Doctrine and Covenants there are six passages related to this section of the Isaiah text, four of which concern Isaiah 54. Most of the quotations from this part of Isaiah by modern Church authorities are not interpretive in nature, although there are a few enlightening ones.

Isaiah 52:13-15. Verse 13 is almost universally accepted by Christians as a description of the Savior's being exalted on high following his persecution and crucifixion. The following two verses seem to describe his mortal life, and could well be left at that were it not for latter-day revelation which shows that these verses also apply to Joseph Smith, the prophet of the Restoration in the last days. After the Savior quoted these verses to the Nephites, he gave a sign to them to show when these things were to take place. Since he had already been persecuted, crucified and resurrected, his quoting these verses shows that they had not yet been completely fulfilled. He said the prophecy would begin to be fulfilled when the works of the Nephites (the Book of Mormon) would come forth among the Gentiles (see 3 Nephi 21:2-9). He also said that when the Lamanites began to know of the Book of Mormon, the fulfilling of the prophecy would already have commenced. That the prophecy speaks of another servant besides Christ is clear from the Savior's explanation in 3 Nephi 21:10-11, which fairly well limits its fulfillment to the time of Joseph Smith. He then explained how these verses would be fulfilled.

Christ also interpreted verse 15 for the Nephites; a comparison of the Isaiah text and his explanation will show that interpretation. We have also added a Doctrine and Covenants passage which speaks of the same conditions.

So shall he sprinkle many nations; the kings shall shut their mouths at him: for that which had not been told them shall they see; and that which they had not heard shall they consider. (Isaiah 52:15; 3 Nephi 20:45.)

And when that day shall come, it shall come to pass that kings shall shut their mouths; for that which had not been told them shall they see; and that which they had not heard shall they consider.

For in that day, for my sake shall the Father work a work, which shall be a great and a marvelous work among them; and there shall be among them those who will not believe it, although a man shall declare it unto them. (3 Nephi 21:8-9.)

What I have said unto you must needs be, that all men may be left without excuse;

That wise men and rulers may hear and know that which they have never considered;

That I may proceed to bring to pass my act, my strange act, and perform my work, my strange work, that men may discern between the righteous and the wicked, saith your God. (D&C 101:93-95.)

Here Christ seems to be telling the Nephites that a sign of the Restoration would be a day when kings would no longer hold absolute power but would be figureheads, with parliaments controlling the governments (see 3 Nephi 21:1-7). That thing which they had not yet heard or been told about was the marvelous work and a wonder which was to come forth under the direction of the Father. Paul paraphrased this verse to show why he went as an apostle among those who had not yet heard the gospel (see Romans 15:20-21). This was an application, not a fulfillment, of Isaiah's prophecy.

The JST changes the word "sprinkle" in verse 15 to "gather." This fits the context of Isaiah 54, which will be discussed later.

Following his explanation of the kings' shutting their mouths, the Savior spoke of the servant's being in his hand, which clearly shows it is someone other than himself. The

Doctrine and Covenants seems to identify that servant as Joseph Smith.

As many were astonished at thee; his visage was so marred more than any man, and his form more than the sons of men: (Isaiah 52:14; cf. 3 Nephi 20:44.)	But behold, the life of my servant shall be in my hand; therefore they shall not hurt him, although he shall be marred because of them. Yet I will heal him, for I will show unto them that my wisdom is greater than the cunning of the devil. (3 Nephi 21:10.)	I will not suffer that they shall destroy my work; yea, I will show unto them that my wisdom is greater than the cunning of the devil. (D&C 10:43.)

The marring of the servant's "visage" referred to in Isaiah 52:14 and 3 Nephi 20:44 has sometimes been thought to refer to the tarring and feathering of Joseph at Hiram, Ohio, in 1832. However, Doctrine and Covenants 10:43 refers to the marring of his *work*. The work of Joseph Smith was marred because of the loss of the 116 pages of manuscript, but the Lord's wisdom was greater than man's, and he had another record prepared to replace that which was lost (see D&C 10:38-46; for a detailed account of the loss of these manuscript pages, see *HC*, 1:20-23).

Isaiah 53:1. Isaiah had previously referred to Christ by the title Immanuel, which means "God is with us" (see Isaiah 7:14; 8:8, 10). The prophet Abinadi, after quoting the entire chapter of Isaiah 53, declared to the priests of King Noah that "God himself shall come down among the children of men, and shall redeem his people" (Mosiah 15:1). All the prophets since the time of Adam had testified of Christ, yet the people would not believe that he was the Messiah spoken of by these prophets (see Romans 10:16). They would not believe, in spite of the miracles he performed among them, which revealed his power to be "the arm of the Lord" (see John 12:37-38). This phrase is also used to designate the power of the Lord's second coming (see 1 Nephi 22:10-11; D&C 45:47).

Isaiah 53:2. This verse describes the early childhood or upbringing of Jesus. Scholars agree that this does not describe his physical appearance, but rather teaches that people would misjudge him because they were expecting their Messiah to come in a more glorious or supernatural way. His growing up would be watched over by the Father, just as a gardener cares for a tender plant. Luke records that "the child grew, and waxed strong in spirit, filled with wisdom: and the grace of God was upon him" (Luke 2:40). Jesus' declaration to his mother when he was only twelve years of age is ample evidence that he had been nurtured and prepared by his Father in Heaven during his years in Nazareth (see Luke 2:41-49; see also *The Promised Messiah*, pp. 477-78).

Jesus identified himself as the "root . . . of David" in Revelation 22:16. The "dry ground" out of which he was to come was representative of the spiritual barrenness of apostate Judaism at that time. He was not nurtured by the Jews, but by his Father in Heaven.

President Joseph Fielding Smith interpreted the Lord's having "no form nor comeliness" as his not being distinctive or different from others so that the Jews would not recognize him as the Son of God, for his appearance would be as a mortal man (see *DS*, 1:23). This is supported by John 6:42, which records the people's response to Christ's declaration that he had come down from heaven: "Is not this Jesus, the son of Joseph, whose father and mother we know?"

A deeper theological concept was taught by Abinadi as a commentary on this verse. Although Christ was a God before he was born, he was the son of God because he came to earth and dwelt in the flesh. Yet he was here to do the will of the Father, and in representing him through "divine investiture of authority" he could properly be referred to as the Father. So he ministered as the Son of God but represented the Father, and thus was called both the Father and the Son. Further, being born of a mortal mother, he was of mortal flesh and had power to lay down his life, or to die. Yet being conceived by the Father, he had the power to break the bands of death and take up his life again as an immortal being. Thus he had the power of the Father and the Son, and was one God with the attributes of both Father and Son. (See Mosiah 15:2-4; for a fuller treatise see *Messages of the First Presidency*, 6 vols. [Salt Lake City: Bookcraft, Inc., 1965-75], 5:23-34.)

Isaiah 53:3-4. These verses describe the Savior's three-year ministry, or at least the beginning of it. As Elder S. Dilworth Young interpreted verse 3, Jesus was "despised" because he was a Nazarene (see CR, Apr. 1974, p. 87; see also John 1:46; Matthew 2:23).

Matthew quoted the first part of verse 4 and said that it was fulfilled when many were brought to Jesus and were healed or had evil spirits cast out of them (Matthew 8:16-17; compare Mosiah 3:5-6; Alma 7:11). Peter was apparently paraphrasing the first part of verse 4 to show that it was fulfilled when Christ was lifted up on the cross, which was the culmination of his physical suffering (see 1 Peter 2:24). Yet when he was on the cross, people thought his suffering was the judgment of God coming upon him, a common belief about suffering in that age (see Mosiah 3:9).

Isaiah 53:5-6. According to Abinadi, the prophets had foretold that Christ's coming would bring about the resurrection, and that he would be oppressed and afflicted (see Mosiah 13:35). Abinadi also equated verses 5 and 6 with the breaking of the bands of death and with Christ's taking upon himself the iniquities and transgressions of all people. In other words, Abinadi taught that these verses foretold the Savior's resurrection and atonement (see Mosiah 15:8-9). Paul also gave this interpretation (see Romans 4:24-25), as did Peter (see 1 Peter 2:24-25; compare Mosiah 3:7; Alma 7:12-13). These New Testament writings are here compared with the Isaiah text:

But he was wounded for our transgressions, he was bruised for our iniquities: the chastisement of our peace was upon him; and with his stripes we are healed.	Who his own self bare our sins in his own body on the tree, that we, being dead to sins, should live unto righteousness: by whose stripes ye were healed.	Who was delivered for our offences, and was raised again for our justification. (Romans 4:25.)

All we like sheep have gone astray; we have turned every one to his own way; and the Lord hath laid on him the iniquity of us all. (Isaiah 53:5-6.)

For ye were as sheep going astray; but are now returned unto the Shepherd and Bishop of your souls. (1 Peter 2:24-25.)

All who have lived on this earth have sinned except Christ, who took upon himself all of our sins (see Romans 3:23; 1 John 1:8-2:2; Hebrews 4:15).

Isaiah 53:7. This verse depicts the trials of Jesus before the high priest, the Sanhedrin, Pilate, and Herod. Abinadi equated this verse with Jesus' submission even to an ultimate crucifixion according to the will of the Father (see Mosiah 15:6-7). That he was oppressed and afflicted is shown in the accounts of his trials (see Matthew 26:67-68; 27:29-30; Mark 14:65; 15:19-20; Luke 22:63-65). His not opening his mouth was completely fulfilled when he stood silent before Herod (see Luke 23:8-11). However, he did answer some questions put to him by Pilate (see Matthew 27:11-14) and the high priest (see Mark 14:56-62). Peter paraphrased this verse in telling of Christ's suffering (see 1 Peter 2:23). The eunuch Philip found was reading Isaiah 53:7-8, and when Philip testified of Jesus, he was baptized (Acts 8:26-38).

Isaiah 53:8. This verse is a prophecy that Christ's life would be taken before its normal time. Abinadi also asked, "Who shall declare his generation?" (Mosiah 15:10), but he did not provide a direct answer. However, in quoting Isaiah 52:7, he indirectly answered that the prophets and all who would teach the gospel would "declare his generation" (see Mosiah 15:13-18).

Isaiah 53:9. His grave's being with the wicked is a prophecy of Christ's being crucified between two thieves (see Luke 23:32-33; Matthew 27:38; Mark 15:27; John 19:18). His grave's being with the rich is a prophecy of his being buried in the tomb of the rich man Joseph of Arimathea (see Matthew 27:57-60; Mark 15:42-46; Luke 23:50-53; John 19:38-42).

Isaiah said the Savior would be so buried or killed because he had done no violence. The Book of Mormon retains the word "evil" instead of "violence" (see Mosiah 14:9). Peter quoted this part of the verse as follows: ". . . who did no sin, neither was guile found in his mouth" (1 Peter 2:22). This seems to be a prophecy of Pilate's finding no fault in him (see Matthew 27:22-24; Mark 15:14-15; Luke 23:1-4, 13-24; John 18:38). The statement that there was no deceit in his mouth may have reference to Jesus' statement before Pilate that he came to "bear witness unto the truth. Every one that is of the truth heareth my voice." To this testimony Pilate responded, "What is truth?" He then went out again to the Jews and declared that he found no fault in the man (see John 18:37-38).

Isaiah 53:10-11. "It pleased the Lord to bruise him" is a declaration that Christ's sacrifice was a freewill offering, on the part of both the Father and the Son. In John 3:16-17, Jesus declared that the Father had sent his Son to be sacrificed because of his love for the world. In Doctrine and Covenants 34:3, Jesus declared that he voluntarily gave his life because of his own love for the world.

The phrase "make his soul an offering for sin" was paraphrased by the Savior when he said to his ancient apostles that the Son of Man had come to minister and to "give his life a ransom for many" (Matthew 20:28).

Who are the "seed" Christ was to see? Abinadi said that those who hearken to the words of the prophets and believe in Christ are his seed (see Mosiah 15:10-13). His seed consists of those who are "spiritually begotten" as his sons and daughters (see Mosiah 5:7; see also *The Promised Messiah*, pp. 359-62).

Isaiah 53:10-11 also provides a possible insight into the Savior's atonement. The passage may be suggesting that, when Christ was in the Garden of Gethsemane, he in some way placed himself in the stead of the inhabitants of the world and suffered the agony required to pay the demands of justice for their sins (see also Alma 7:13; 2 Nephi 9:20-23). This extreme agony caused him to bleed at every pore (see Luke 22:44; Mosiah 3:7; D&C 19:18).

Isaiah 53:12. Because Christ fulfilled his mission, he was to ascend into heaven and reign in glory with the Father. There he would disperse mercy to those who would accept him, repent, and live the gospel. He would be able to do this for three reasons: (1) he gave up his life and overcame death; (2) he was "numbered with the transgressors" (he knows what it is like to suffer pain and affliction); and (3) he atoned for the sins of the transgressors.

According to Mark 15:28, Christ's being "numbered with the transgressors" was fulfilled when he was lifted up on the cross between two thieves. This interpretation is borne out by the Lord's statement in the Garden of Gethsemane, just prior to his arrest, that he had yet to fulfill this prophecy (see Luke 22:37). However, Alma 7:11 shows that Christ's sufferings included even more than his trials and crucifixion.

Isaiah 54:1. That this chapter is a continuation of the revelation beginning in Isaiah 52:13 is shown by the JST reading of 52:15: "So shall he *gather* many nations." The Savior told the Nephites that the prophecies in chapter 54 would come to pass after the Father's work commenced among all nations (see 3 Nephi 22:1). Isaiah 54 is therefore an explanation of the gathering which will be completed in the last days as the covenant of Israel is fulfilled.

The "children of the desolate" represent the large number of people from the tribes of Israel who will gather to Zion following the building of the New Jerusalem (see 3 Nephi 21:22-29). There will be many more of them than the remnant who will already have gathered and built the New Jerusalem, or those whom Isaiah calls the "children of the married wife." The symbolic marriage of Christ to Israel is here represented, with the members of the Church being considered the children of that covenant relationship.

Isaiah 54:2. The large influx of people who will gather to Zion will give her strength and cause her borders to be enlarged. This idea is supported by the Lord's invitation for the people to gather out from the gentile nations to Zion, and for the Jews to gather to Jerusalem, as outlined in Doctrine and Covenants 133:7-13 (wherein verse 9 paraphrases Isaiah 54:2). Moroni also paraphrased verse 2 in his final admonition to Jerusalem and Zion as he closed the Book of Mormon record (see Moroni 10:31). The concept of a tent with its cords and stakes comes from the tent or tabernacle of Moses, and all Israel is being invited to seek shelter under it. The stakes are thus the strongholds surrounding Zion, or Jackson

County. They are also a "refuge from the storm" and from the wrath of God which will be poured out upon the world (see D&C 115:6; Isaiah 4:5-6).

Isaiah 54:3. The extending of Zion will see the children of Israel inhabit the gentile cities which will have become desolate, probably because those of the "great and abominable church" will war among themselves (see 1 Nephi 22:13).

Isaiah 54:5-6. The Lord, as the symbolic husband of Israel, is again identified as Christ by Isaiah. In the book of Revelation, John used the same symbolism as he saw the heavenly New Jerusalem, the city of Enoch, return to Zion "as a bride adorned for her husband" (Revelation 21:2).

Isaiah 54:7-10. These verses further describe the latter-day gathering. Verse 9 is a significant verse, as it speaks of the sureness of the Lord's covenant and also confirms the historicity of the biblical flood. The quotation of this verse in 3 Nephi 22 adds another witness to three other Book of Mormon references (Alma 10:22; Ether 6:7; 13:2) which also verify that the biblical flood occurred. Verse 10 speaks of the restoration of the earth to the condition in which it existed before it was cursed, as explained by President Joseph Fielding Smith (see *DS*, 2:316-17). The Book of Mormon retains the word "people" instead of "peace" in the same verse.

Isaiah 54:11-12. These precious stones symbolize the material blessings which the Lord will pour out upon the city of Zion. The book of Revelation uses similar symbolism (see Revelation 21:19-21).

Isaiah 54:13. The promise of Israel's children being taught by the Lord and having great peace is also given in the Doctrine and Covenants 45:58. This is a promise pertaining to the millennial era, so it confirms the time period of which Isaiah speaks.

Isaiah 54:15. The Book of Mormon retains the words "against thee," in the first clause, clarifying that the gathering spoken of in this case is not the gathering of Israel, but the gathering of the wicked against the Lord's people. The Lord gives the assurance here that his people will prosper.

Behold, they shall surely gather together, but not by me: whosoever shall gather together against thee shall fall for thy sake. (Isaiah 54:15.)

Behold, they shall surely gather together *against thee*, not by me; whosoever shall gather together against thee shall fall for thy sake. (3 Nephi 22:15.)

Isaiah 54:17. This same promise—that no weapon will prosper against the Lord's people who gather to Zion, and that those who speak against them will be condemned—was given to the Latter-day Saints when the first letters against the Church were published in 1831:

No weapon that is formed against thee shall prosper; and every tongue that shall rise against thee in judgment thou shalt condemn. This is the heritage of the servants of the Lord, and their righteousness is of me, saith the Lord. (Isaiah 54:17; cf. 3 Nephi 22:17.)

Verily, thus saith the Lord unto you—there is no weapon that is formed against you shall prosper;

And if any man lift his voice against you he shall be confounded in mine own due time. (D&C 71:9-10.)

The Doctrine and Covenants phrase "in mine own due time" could well be the millennial era of which Isaiah speaks. The Prophet Joseph Smith paraphrased the opening words of this verse—"That no weapon formed against them shall prosper"—in his inspired prayer at the dedication of the Kirtland Temple (see D&C 109:25).

A New Nation of Israel

22

Isaiah 55-57

Most modern scholars now claim that the Book of Isaiah was written by three different authors, and they call chapters 56 through 66 Trito or Third Isaiah. They do this because they believe that the message, language, and writing style are different in these later chapters than in chapters 40 through 55. We reject this theory and assert that chapters 55 through 57 provide evidence of a single author. (See also Appendix A for further evidence against the multiple-authorship theory.) There is a cohesive message contained within these three chapters which could not be seen clearly if we had to separate chapter 55 from the other two.

Chapter 55 identifies some eternal principles which may be isolated and independent, but the chapter as a whole is the foundation upon which chapters 56 and 57 are built. This unity is shown in the outline below.

1. A new nation will be established with an everlasting covenant (55:1-5).
   a. Thirst and hunger of the soul will be satisfied without payment (55:1-2).
   b. The throne of David will lead the people (55:3-4).
   c. Those of other nations will gather to create this new nation (55:5).
2. The opportunity to enter that nation is offered by covenant and should be taken when it is offered (55:6-13).

 a. The wicked must forsake his ways and return to the Lord (55:7).
 b. The nation will follow the Lord's ways and not man's (55:8-11).
 c. Joy, peace, and prosperity will be established in the Lord's name (55:12-13).
3. This nation will be established near the time of the Lord's coming (56:1-57:12).
 a. Those who keep the commandments will be blessed (56:1-2).
 b. The Gentiles who accept the covenant will be adopted into Israel (56:3-8).
 c. The gentile nations will follow their own ways (56: 9-12).
 d. The righteous and honorable will find peace in death (57:1-2).
 e. The Gentiles will adulterate themselves with the kings of the earth (57:3-12).
4. Those who trust in the Lord will possess the land and inherit his holy mountain (57:13-21).
 a. Those who are contrite and humble will dwell with him (57:15).
 b. Those who are led there will have peace and will be healed (57:16-19).
 c. There will be no peace for the wicked (57:20-21).

Notes and Commentary

Isaiah 55:1-2 is quoted twice in the Book of Mormon, but only once in a context which is useful to our study. There are a few New Testament references which help us indirectly to understand some of the Isaiah passages, and there is one reference in the Doctrine and Covenants. Several General Authorities have quoted Isaiah 55:6-9 or parts of it; they have used it primarily as a description of a characteristic of God, but not in the context of Isaiah's message.

Isaiah 55:1-2. A comparison of the two quotations of this passage in the Book of Mormon shows retentions from the

Isaiah text used by Jacob. Nephi apparently only paraphrased the passage.

Ho, every one that thirsteth, come ye to the waters, and he that hath no money; come ye, buy, and eat; yea, come, buy wine and milk without money and without price.	*Come, my brethren*, every one that thirsteth, come ye to the waters; and he that hath no money, come buy and eat; yea, come buy wine and milk without money and without price.	Behold, doth he cry unto any, saying: Depart from me? Behold, I say unto you, Nay; but he saith: Come unto me all ye ends of the earth, buy milk and honey, without money and without price. (2 Nephi 26:25.)
Wherefore do ye spend money for that which is not bread? and your labour for that which satisfieth not? hearken diligently unto me, and eat ye that which is good, and let your soul delight itself in fatness. (Isaiah 55:1-2.)	Wherefore, *do not* spend money for that which is *of no worth*, nor your labor for that which cannot satisfy. Hearken diligently unto me, *and remember the words which I have spoken; and come unto the Holy One of Israel, and feast upon that which perisheth not, neither can be corrupted*, and let your soul delight in fatness. (2 Nephi 9:50-51.)	

Nephi's paraphrase refers to the last days, when the Book of Mormon is to come forth among the Gentiles. This time period is also the context of chapter 55 in Isaiah. Jacob quoted the passage in a discourse on the Atonement, as an invitation to partake of Christ's redemption. A similar invitation to come to the Lord is used in variant forms in three different places in the book of Revelation: one is to the church of the Laodiceans in the days of John (see Revelation 3:18); the other two occur in the context of the latter days, although at a later period than Isaiah and Nephi referred to (see Revelation

21:6; 22:17). The Savior himself issued similar invitations (John 4:13-14; 6:47-51). When we have all the records, we will undoubtedly see that such invitations have been extended from the beginning of the world.

Isaiah 55:3-5. Paul related "the sure mercies of David" (verse 3) to Christ's resurrection (see Acts 13:34; see also *The Promised Messiah*, pp. 271-75). The new nation spoken of in verse 5, which will be glorified by the Holy One of Israel, is obviously restored Israel, which will eventually be ruled over by Jesus Christ, the King of Kings, a descendant of David. This will fulfill the promise given to David that his seed would be established forever (see 2 Samuel 7:16; Psalm 89:28-37; Revelation 17:14; 19:16; D&C 58:22).

Isaiah 55:6-7. The Lord gave the same commandment to "call upon me while I am near" to the faithful priesthood holders of the Church as he instructed them to fulfill their stewardships in this dispensation (see D&C 88:62-63). Isaiah's invitation is to the wicked inhabitants of the nations, the gentile nations, to call upon the Lord so that they may receive his mercy and receive a remission of their sins. The modern priesthood holders were called to go to those wicked nations and cry repentance. Thus the two references fit into the same time period and context.

Several of the Brethren have quoted these two verses to illustrate the principles of revelation and repentance.

Isaiah 55:8-9. These verses, showing that the Lord will establish the latter-day nation of restored Israel according to his ways and not the ways of man, are often used to show the character of God and his greatness. Jacob taught the same principle in the Book of Mormon—that God will give revelation to bring about his purposes.

For my thoughts are not your thoughts, neither are your ways my ways, saith the Lord. (Isaiah 55:8.)

Behold, great and marvelous are the works of the Lord. How unsearchable are the depths of the mysteries of him; and it is impossible that man should find out all his ways. And no man knoweth of his ways save it be revealed unto him; wherefore, brethren, despise not the revelations of God. (Jacob 4:8.)

Elder Boyd K. Packer's invitation to the ministers of the Christian churches to consider how the Lord would correct the problems of disharmony in the churches (by restoration through revelation rather than ecumenical council) is an example of how the Brethren use these verses (see CR, Apr. 1967, pp. 129-30).

Isaiah 55:10-13. These verses, an extension of the principle taught in verses 8 and 9, give another interesting analogy to illustrate the word of God. Such analogies are used throughout the scriptures. Just as the rains and the snows come and produce growth, so will the word of God by revelation to man bring joy, peace, and prosperity to restored Israel.

Isaiah 56:3-8. These verses seem to clearly describe the times of the Gentiles when those who are not of Israel will be given the opportunity to come and be numbered with Israel (see 3 Nephi 30:1-2; D&C 45:28). The strangers are those not of Israel who represent the gentile nations where the gospel is restored. The eunuchs, literally those who could not produce offspring, may refer to those who have no posterity in the Church and no other relatives who will join; yet they will become the sons or daughters of Jesus Christ (see Mosiah 5:7; Galatians 4:1-7).

Isaiah 56:7. The reference to the Lord's house has given historical trouble to commentators. This verse was quoted by the Savior when he cleansed the temple the second time (see Matthew 21:13; Mark 11:17; Luke 19:46). That event was obviously not the fulfillment of Isaiah's prophecy, but Christ quoted the passage while expressing his wrath over the temple's being made "a den of thieves." The prophecy points to the time when all people or nations would come up to worship and their sacrifices would be acceptable. This is undoubtedly the same time period to which Isaiah referred in chapter 2 when he spoke of "the mountain of the Lord's house" and said that "all nations shall flow unto it" (Isaiah 2:2-3).

Isaiah 56:9-12. There is no general agreement among scholars about the identity of the "beasts," the "watchmen," and the "greedy dogs" in these verses. Many interpret the beasts as the surrounding nations, and the watchmen and dogs as the leaders of Israel who are not protecting their flock but are asleep. However, the context of the preceding and the following verses points to the gentile nations whose hearts and minds are turned to material things, and who depend on their own intellects rather than the higher thoughts and ways of the Lord. The majority of the Gentiles will reject the gospel (see D&C 45:29) and continue in their ignorant and wicked ways.

Isaiah 57:1-2. These verses are an extension of the last four verses of chapter 56. There are many good people living among the Gentiles. While collectively the nations have rejected the gospel, these honorable men who have not had a full opportunity to accept it in this life will have a full opportunity in the spirit world. Thus they will find peace in death. The Anchor Bible (20:154), in commenting on Isaiah 57:1, says: "The lines are obscure, but the sense seems to be that the death of the righteous brings them into security." This obscurity vanishes before a knowledge that the work of the Lord goes on in the spirit world.

Isaiah 57:3-12. These lengthy and descriptive verses suggest immorality in temple prostitution, which involved even the kings. The message was condensed by the angel who announced the fall of Babylon; he declared that "all nations" and the kings of the earth had committed fornication with Babylon (see Revelation 18:3). In other words, the nations honor the Lord with their mouths, but their hearts are far from him, and they turn to the worship of a king or government for security.

Isaiah 57:13-21. The revelation ends with a message of hope to those who will follow the Lord and inherit his holy mountain, the place of restored Israel. There they will have his presence and enjoy peace and the healing of the soul. The wicked, on the contrary, will have no peace. President Harold B. Lee quoted verses 19 through 21 as an example of Isaiah's attempts to "fortify his people against the wickedness of the world" (CR, Oct. 1973, p. 4).

The Sins of the House of Jacob

23

Isaiah 58-60

Whether chapters 58 and 59 are prophecies against the people of Isaiah's time or those of the latter days is not certain. If Isaiah is describing the latter days, he could be referring to 1820, when the whole world was still in apostasy, or he could be describing the cleansing of restored Israel. Since 59:16 seems to be describing the complete apostasy of Israel, the restoration spoken of in the end of chapter 59 is undoubtedly a reference to the last days. Consequently, the sins of the house of Jacob would represent the corruption of Israel prior to the latter-day restoration. All this may well apply to Isaiah's time also, as a dual prophecy. Chapter 60 definitely speaks of the latter-day Zion or New Jerusalem. However, some of its verses may also be of a dual nature.

Regardless of the time period, the eternal nature of the gospel makes it appropriate to "liken" chapters 58 and 59 to ourselves "for our profit and learning" (see 1 Nephi 19:23-24). The law of the fast as taught in the Church today is basically that which Isaiah taught in chapter 58. Likewise, the sins of Jacob enumerated by Isaiah have application to this day, as an outline of his message will show.

1. The prophet will proclaim the sins of Jacob (58:1-2).
2. Israel will fast and claim that the Lord doesn't notice (58:3-5).
    a. They will find pleasure in the day they fast (58:3).
    b. They will fast for strife and debate (58:4).
    c. They will afflict their souls before men (58:5).

3. There are four purposes of the Lord's fast (58:6-7).
   a. It looses the bands of wickedness (58:6).
   b. It undoes heavy burdens (58:6).
   c. It lets the oppressed go free (58:6).
   d. It eliminates the poor by dealing bread to the hungry (58:7).
4. Isaiah proclaims the blessings of the fast (58:8-12).
   a. Your "light" will break forth—the Spirit will attend you (58:8).
   b. You will have health (58:8).
   c. Righteousness will go before you and be an influence for good (58:8).
   d. The glory of the Lord will follow you and confirm your actions (58:8).
   e. Your prayers will be answered (58:9).
   f. The Lord will guide you continually (58:10-11).
   g. Your posterity will be blessed, and they will bless you (58:12).
5. The purpose and blessings of the Sabbath are given (58:13-14).
   a. You are not to do your pleasures, but the Lord's (58:13).
   b. You will "ride upon the high places of the earth" (58:14).
   c. You will be fed with the "heritage of Jacob" (58:14).
6. Revelation has ceased among Israel because of their sins (59:1-15).
   a. The Lord has not changed, but Israel has (59:1-8).
   b. The people grope in darkness, and the Lord is displeased (59:9-15).
7. The Lord will intervene because there is "no man" (a complete apostasy) (59:16-21).
   a. The Lord will arm himself and recompense Israel (59:17-18).
   b. He will lift up a standard to Israel (59:19).
   c. He will come to Zion (59:20).
   d. He will establish the everlasting covenant with Israel (59:21).

8. Zion will arise and be glorious (60:1-22).
   a. Darkness will cover the rest of the earth (60:2).
   b. The Gentiles and kings will come to Zion's light (60:3).
   c. They will bring their wealth and adorn Zion (60:4-11).
   d. The nations who do not serve Zion will perish (60:12).
   e. Zion will be beautified and will have peace (60:13-18).
   f. The Lord will be their light instead of the sun and the moon (60:19-20).
   g. Zion will become a mighty nation in the Lord's time (60:21-22).

Notes and Commentary

Chapter 58 was quoted almost entirely by Bishop John H. Vandenberg and Bishop Victor L. Brown in two different general conferences with added interpretations and applications. There are also other quotations by General Authorities from this chapter, but they usually just make reference to the law or blessing of fasting and do not interpret the text.

There are some New Testament references. and one from the Doctrine and Covenants, which help us understand chapter 59. The Prophet Joseph Smith and Elder Orson Pratt gave us a fuller understanding of Isaiah 60.

Isaiah 58:4. Bishop John H. Vandenberg said the reward of their improper fasting was "strife, debate, and wickedness" (see CR, Apr. 1963, p. 28). They may also have been fasting for the wrong reasons, seeking strength for arguments or sinful endeavors.

Isaiah 58:6-7. Bishop Vandenberg also equated these verses with the two great commandments to love God and our neighbor:

> I suppose when he speaks of "loosing the bands of wickedness" of "undoing the heavy burdens," and the "breaking of every yoke" that he is referring to the wickedness of people who think only of themselves in selfishness, vanity, pride, and having hearts so set upon the things of this world that the two great commandments of loving God and loving neighbor are entirely forgotten. The principles of loving thy neighbor and of loving God are encompassed in the true purpose of the fast.

> Certainly, it takes no imagination to understand what is meant when he says, ". . . that thou bring the poor that are cast out to thy house? when thou seest the naked, that thou cover him; and that thou hide not thyself from thine own flesh?"
>
> He meant that in addition to taking care of the poor, that we should watch over our own kin and be responsible for our father, mother, brother, and sister when they are in need.
>
> It is here that I would like to state that the Lord has caused a day of fasting and prayer to be set up in this day so that collectively the Church might join together to fulfill the purposes of fasting.
>
> In the general letter from the Council of the Twelve to the Church under date of May 17, 1845, which Orson Pratt read to the Saints, these words appear:
>
> "Let this be an ensample to all saints, and there will never be any lack for bread: When the poor are starving, let those who have, fast one day and give what they otherwise would have eaten to the bishops for the poor, and every one will abound for a long time; and this is one great and important principle of fasts, approved of the Lord. And so long as the saints will all live to this principle, with glad hearts and cheerful countenances they will always have an abundance." (*DHC* 7:413.)
>
> The bishop should frequently encourage the members of his ward to observe the fast day and voluntarily contribute a generous offering. The Lord knows in his wisdom that individually we are generally not prone to seek out the poor, the hungry, and those in need, and individually attend to their needs on a continuing basis. By fasting collectively there is no end to the good that can be done; that no one need suffer; that such assistance as might be given is rendered through the bishop in love and mercy and that full dollar value is rendered without any administrative cost. (CR, Apr. 1963, p. 28.)

Bishop Victor L. Brown interpreted verse 6 to mean "to overcome the temptations of Satan as the Savior did." He also said that verse 7 means "to assist the poor and the needy." (*Ensign*, Nov. 1977, p. 83.)

A breakdown of verse 6 shows three purposes of the fast: (1) "to loose the bands of wickedness," or to help us overcome personal sins which have engulfed us; (2) "to undo the heavy burdens," or to help us gain strength for difficult assignments or problems; and (3) "to let the oppressed go free," or to petition the Lord to intervene in behalf of our loved ones, such as Alma did when fasting for the salvation of his son (see Mosiah 27:13-24).

Isaiah 58:8. Bishop Brown said this verse describes the achievement of "success in life" (*Ensign*, Nov. 1977, p. 83).

Isaiah 58:9-11. In quoting parts of these verses, Bishop Vandenberg inserted several interpretive comments. The text is here quoted with his comments as he inserted them:

> . . . If thou take away from . . . thee the yoke, (or wickedness) the putting forth of the finger, (or accusing others) and speaking vanity;
>
> And if thou draw out thy soul to the hungry, and satisfy the afflicted soul; then shall thy light rise in obscurity, and thy darkness be as the noon day:
>
> And the Lord shall guide thee continually, (or the Holy Ghost will direct your daily life) and satisfy thy soul in drought, (This is your personal security in times of need and difficulty.) and make fat thy bones: (I believe this has to do with health. In the bone there is marrow and marrow manufactures the blood that is vital to the strength and well-being of the body.) and thou shalt be like a watered garden, and like a spring of water, whose waters fail not (or inspiration and wisdom will flow from you continually). (CR, Apr. 1963, p. 29.)

Bishop Brown interpreted these three verses to mean "To humble and prepare ourselves to communicate with the Lord" (*Ensign*, Nov. 1977, p. 83).

Isaiah 58:12. Bishop Vandenberg said the following about this verse:

> To me this is a promise to those working with the members of the Church who are in need physically and spiritually, "they that shall be of thee," or that you may be able to help them—to do what? "Build the old waste places," and as you help them to build "thou shalt raise up the foundations of (their) many generations (to follow); and then thou shalt be called, The repairer of the breach." In other words, you have helped them overcome their weaknesses, to restore their souls, to bridge the gap through reactivating, rehabilitation, and "restoring" the path for them to walk in.
>
> To those responsible for the leadership of the Saints in every unit of the Church, I say, teach the people the principle

of fasting, in love, in gentleness, in firmness, and in humility. Fasting will give them spiritual strength and help them to develop self-control. (CR, Apr. 1963, p. 29.)

Isaiah 59:1-2. Elder Mark E. Petersen quoted these verses as a sign of the lack of new revelation and new scripture, both of which are marks of man's having drifted from the path of truth and right (see CR, Oct. 1964, p. 122).

Isaiah 59:7. Paul quoted part of this verse to the Romans (see Romans 3:15-16) along with several other scriptures to show that all were under sin, both Jew and Gentile.

Isaiah 59:17. Paul referred to the "armour of God" in writing to the Ephesians (see Ephesians 6:13-17) and to the Thessalonians (see 1 Thessalonians 5:8). The Lord also used a description of this "armor" in a revelation to Joseph Smith (see D&C 27:15-18). However, this verse in Isaiah refers to the Lord's putting armor on himself to pour out vengeance, while the New Testament and the Doctrine and Covenants speak of the Saints' arming themselves to "withstand the evil day."

Isaiah 59:20-21. Paul said that these verses would be fulfilled after the fulness of the Gentiles had come in (see Romans 11:26-27). The passage in Romans contains a different ending than the one in Isaiah.

	For I would not, brethren, that ye should be ignorant of this mystery, lest ye should be wise in your own conceits; that blindness in part is happened to Israel, until the fulness of the Gentiles be come in.
And the Redeemer shall come to Zion, and unto them that turn from transgression in Jacob, saith the Lord.	And so all Israel shall be saved: as it is written, There shall come out of Sion the Deliverer, and shall turn away ungodliness from Jacob:
As for me, this is my covenant with them, saith the Lord; My spirit that is upon thee, and my words which I have put in thy mouth, shall not depart out of thy mouth, nor out of the	For this is my covenant unto them, when I shall take away their sins. (Romans 11:25-27.)

mouth of thy seed, nor out of
the mouth of thy seed's seed,
saith the Lord, from henceforth
and for ever. (Isaiah 59:20-21.)

When Joseph Smith went to the Hill Cumorah on 22 September 1823, following the visit of the angel Moroni, Moroni appeared to him again and told him, among other things, that persecution would rage against the Church, "but it will increase the more opposed, and spread farther and farther, increasing in knowledge till they shall be sanctified and receive an inheritance where the glory of God shall rest upon them; and when this takes place, and all things are prepared, the ten tribes of Israel will be revealed in the north country, whither they have been for a long season; and when this is fulfilled will be brought to pass that saying of the prophet . . . [quotes Isaiah 59:20]." (Oliver Cowdery, *MA*, Oct. 1835, p. 199.) This would be consistent with Paul's declaration that these verses would be fulfilled after the fulness of the Gentiles had come in.

Elder Orson Pratt reasoned that the coming of this Redeemer, or "Deliverer" as rendered in Romans, was not fulfilled by Jesus Christ in the meridian of time.

> Who will be that Deliverer? Certainly Jesus, when he came eighteen centuries ago, did not turn away ungodliness from Jacob, for they then were filling up their cup with iniquity. They have remained in unbelief from that day to this; hence, there did not come a Deliverer out of Zion eighteen centuries ago. But the Zion of the last days, that Zion that is so frequently and so fully spoken of by the ancient prophets, especially by Isaiah, is the Church and kingdom of God; and out of that Church or kingdom or Zion is to come a Deliverer, who will turn away ungodliness from Jacob after the times of the Gentiles are fulfilled. (*JD*, 14:64.)

Isaiah 60:1-2. Elder Orson Pratt interpreted verse 1 as a reference to the latter-day Zion:

> The passage which I have quoted from Isaiah has reference to the latter-day Zion. . . . The Zion that is here spoken of is called to "arise and shine, for the glory of the Lord is risen upon thee." There is no one thing more fully revealed in the Scriptures of eternal truth, than the rise of the Zion of our

> God in the latter days, clothed upon with the glory of God from the heavens—a Zion that will attract the attention of all the nations and kindreds of the whole earth. It will not be something that takes place in a corner on some distant island of the sea, or away among some obscure people; but it will be something that will call forth the attention of all people and nations upon the face of the whole earth. (*JD*, 16:78.)

This Zion to which the Redeemer would come (see 59:20) was to be established in the glory of the Lord at a period of time when darkness would cover the people of the earth. The words of verse 2 are quoted by the Lord in Doctrine and Covenants 112:23 as a description of the conditions on the earth in 1837. The Prophet Joseph Smith said the following about verse 2:

> Consider for a moment, brethren, the fulfillment of the words of the prophet; for we behold that darkness covers the earth, and gross darkness the minds of the inhabitants thereof—that crimes of every description are increasing among men—vices of great enormity are practiced—the rising generation growing up in the fullness of pride and arrogance—the aged losing every sense of conviction, and seemingly banishing every thought of a day of retribution—intemperance, immorality, extravagance, pride, blindness of heart, idolatry, the loss of natural affection; the love of this world, and indifference toward the things of eternity increasing among those who profess a belief in the religion of heaven, and infidelity spreading itself in consequence of the same—men giving themselves up to commit acts of the foulest kind, and deeds of the blackest dye, blaspheming, defrauding, blasting the reputation of neighbors, stealing, robbing, murdering; advocating error and opposing the truth, forsaking the covenant of heaven, and denying the faith of Jesus—and in the midst of all this, the day of the Lord fast approaching when none except those who have won the wedding garment will be permitted to eat and drink in the presence of the Bridegroom, the Prince of Peace! (*TPJS*, p. 47.)

The crimes and vices spoken of by the Prophet have continued to increase. Only "those who have won the wedding garment," he said, "will be permitted." This shows that he saw Isaiah's prophecy being completely fulfilled in a future day, and also that the inhabitants of Zion would have to be cleansed and prepared for Christ's coming. This period is described in Doctrine and Covenants 45 as the time of the establishment of the New Jerusalem, which will occur at a time when all the world except Zion will be at war (see D&C 45:62-75). The Prophet Joseph also described this period:

> We ought to have the building up of Zion as our greatest object. When wars come, we shall have to flee to Zion. The cry is to make haste. The last revelation says, Ye shall not have time to have gone over the earth, until these things come. It will come as did the cholera, war, fires, and earthquakes; one pestilence after another, until the Ancient of Days comes, then judgment will be given to the Saints.
>
> . . . Look to the Presidency and receive instruction. Every man who is afraid, covetous, will be taken in a snare. The time is soon coming, when no man will have any peace but in Zion and her stakes.
>
> I saw men hunting the lives of their own sons, and brother murdering brother, women killing their own daughters, and daughters seeking the lives of their mothers. I saw armies arrayed against armies. I saw blood, desolation, fires. The Son of Man has said that the mother shall be against the daughter, and the daughter against the mother. These things are at our doors. They will follow the Saints of God from city to city. Satan will rage, and the spirit of the devil is now enraged. I know not how soon these things will take place; but with a view of them, shall I cry peace? No; I will lift up my voice and testify of them. How long you will have good crops, and the famine be kept off, I do not know; when the fig tree leaves, know then that the summer is nigh at hand.
>
> We may look for angels and receive their ministrations, but we are to try the spirits and prove them, for it is often the case that men make a mistake in regard to these things. God has so ordained that when He has communicated, no vision is to be taken but what you see by the seeing of the eye, or what you hear by the hearing of the ear. When you see a vision, pray for the interpretation; if you get not this, shut it up; there must be certainty in this matter. An open vision will manifest that which is more important. Lying spirits are going forth in the earth. There will be great manifestations of spirits, both false and true. (*TPJS*, pp. 160-61.)

Elder Orson Pratt said that the darkness would be caused "Because the salt of the earth is gathered out; the children of light are gathered together to Zion, and those who are left behind are in darkness, that is, a great many of them. No doubt there will be honest ones, and vast numbers who will come to Zion, notwithstanding the darkness that covers the earth." (*JD*, 14:355.)

Isaiah 60:3. Elder Orson Pratt commented concerning this verse: "Inquires one—'Is Zion going to become popular, so that Gentiles and kings and great men will come to her light?' Yes, certainly; and not only Gentiles, kings and great men, but many of all the nations of the earth have got to come to Zion. . . ." (*JD*, 18:153.)

The wise men who came from the east because they had seen the new star at Christ's birth are thought by some scholars to have fulfilled this prophecy (see Matthew 2:1-2). However, an examination of the entire prophecy shows that Isaiah is speaking of a later time period and a different geographic area, although, due to the nature of dual prophecy, it could also have had reference to the Savior's birth.

Isaiah 60:4-5. Zion is invited to see the gathering to her, which is not limited to people but also includes the wealth of the nations. A marginal note in the KJV gives "wealth of the Gentiles" as an alternate reading for "forces of the Gentiles." The Anchor Bible (20:173) translates the last half of the verse as follows: "For the riches of the sea will be turned to you; the wealth of the nations will come to you."

Isaiah 60:6-7. Verse 6 is often cross-referenced with the visit of the wise men to the Christ child (see Matthew 2:11). Again, this could be a dual prophecy, but the context of Isaiah is the latter days, when the wealth of the gentile nations will be brought to Zion. These verses thus seem to describe the transporting of wealth from these nations to Zion, where it will be used to adorn the temple ("the house of my glory").

Isaiah 60:8-10. These verses also describe the gathering of the people to latter-day Zion. Elder John Longden interpreted verse 8 as a description of an airplane (see CR, Apr. 1964, p. 116). Verse 9 specifies the area under discussion as the "isles," which would be the land of America (see 2 Nephi 10:20). That ships will bring the Lord's sons and their wealth from Tarshish suggests a great distance. The building of the walls of Zion by the "sons of strangers" has reference to the contribution the Gentiles and their kings will make to the building up of Zion.

Isaiah 60:11-12. John also described the gates of New Jerusalem as being open continually (see Revelation 21:25). Elder Orson Pratt interpreted this passage in Isaiah as a description of the latter days, when all nations will have to serve Zion or be "utterly wasted." Even the United States, said Elder Pratt, will have to comply with the ordinances of Zion, repent of her sins, and be prepared for the great and glorious day of the Lord's coming in order to be saved from destruction (see *JD*, 14:355). President Spencer W. Kimball said in a general conference, "We continue to warn the people and plead with them, for we are watchmen upon the towers, and in our hands we have a trumpet which we must blow loudly and sound the alarm." He then quoted verse 12. (See CR, Oct. 1975, p. 8.)

Isaiah 60:13-18. These verses further describe the beautification of "the city of the Lord, The Zion of the Holy One of Israel" (verse 14). Elder Orson Pratt said this will be a time of great abundance of precious metals, when "God will give the keys of the treasures of the earth and he will open them up to the people." After quoting verse 17, he continued, "Gold and silver will be so plentiful that they will be used for the pavement of streets" (*JD*, 18:154).

Isaiah 60:19-20. John also said that, although the New Jerusalem will have no sun, there will be no night. Thus the gates will be open continually, as mentioned in Isaiah 60:11 (see Revelation 21:23, 25). Elder Orson Pratt said:

> Zion will not need the sun when the Lord is there, and all the city is lighted up by the glory of his presence. When the whole heavens above are illuminated by the presence of his glory we shall not need those bright luminaries of heaven to give light, so far as the city of Zion is concerned. But there will be a great people round about, dwelling in other cities that will still have need of the light of the sun and the moon; but the great capital city where the Lord will establish one of his thrones—for his throne is not to be in Jerusalem alone, it will also be in Zion. . . . When therefore, he shall establish his throne in Zion and shall light up the habitations thereof

> with the glory of his presence, they will not need this light which comes from the bright luminaries that shine forth in yonder heavens, but they will be clothed upon with the glory of their God. When the people meet together in assemblies like this, in their Tabernacles, the Lord will meet with them, his glory will be upon them; a cloud will overshadow them by day and if they happen to have an evening meeting they will not need gas light or lights of an artificial nature, for the Lord will be there and his glory will be upon all their assemblies. (*JD*, 14:355-56.)

Isaiah 60:22. The Doctrine and Covenants interprets this verse for us.

	And for this cause, that men might be made partakers of the glories which were to be revealed, the Lord sent forth the fulness of his gospel, his everlasting covenant, reasoning in plainness and simplicity— To prepare the weak for those things which are coming on the earth, and for the Lord's errand in the day when the
A little one shall become a thousand, and a small one a strong nation: I the Lord will hasten it in his time. (Isaiah 60:22.)	weak shall confound the wise, and the little one become a strong nation, and two shall put their tens of thousands to flight. (D&C 133:57-58.)

Thus the remnant of Israel which will be gathered in the last days will become the mighty nation of Israel. Elder Orson Pratt quoted this verse to support the teaching that Zion will become a great people, destined to fill the mountains in the last days (see *JD*, 18:153). The JST changes the last line to read, "I the Lord will hasten it in *my* time."

Isaiah's Appendix 24

Isaiah 61-64

Chapters 61 through 64 are grouped together because parts of chapters 62 through 64 concern the Second Coming and are quoted in Doctrine and Covenants 133. The Savior quoted Isaiah 61:1-2 in the synagogue in Nazareth and told his hearers that these verses had been "fulfilled in your ears" (Luke 4:16-21). However, the rest of verse 2 and verse 3 also prophesy of the Savior's mission and extend to the day of the vengeance of God, or the Second Coming. Therefore, chapter 61 also fits the overall pattern of the other three chapters, even though most of it discusses the ministry of Jesus in the flesh. An outline of these four chapters will show their relationship to each other and their unity of thought:

1. The mission of Christ is described (61:1-3).
   a. It begins in the meridian of time (61:1-2).
   b. It is completed in the fulness of times (61:1-3).
2. Zion will be established in the latter days (61:4-11).
   a. The wastelands will be rebuilt with the Gentiles' help (61:4-5).
   b. The priesthood will be restored and acknowledged by the Gentiles (61:6).
   c. Israel will become socially acceptable through the everlasting covenant (61:7-9).
   d. Zion will adorn herself as the bride in preparation for the Bridegroom (61:10-11).

3. The lands of Jerusalem and Zion will be reunited by the Lord as they were before (62:1-12).
   a. Both lands will become holy cities, or New Jerusalem (62:1-2).
   b. They will crown their inhabitants with the glory of the temple endowment (62:3).
   c. The watchmen of the Lord will be over Jerusalem until it becomes a holy city (62:6-9).
   d. Zion will lift up a standard in a distant land to which many will come (62:10-12).
4. The Lord will come and destroy the wicked in justice (63:1-16).
   a. His garments will be red like those of one who treads the winepress (63:1-6).
   b. Those who are not destroyed will recognize his mercy (63:7-9).
   c. Those who are destroyed will be those who rebelled against him (63:10).
   d. The people will lament and turn to the Lord for help (63:11-16).
5. The servants of the Lord will plead for his second coming (63:17-64:12).
   a. The return of the tribes to their lands will be requested (63:17-19).
   b. The servants will plead for the mountains to flow down and for other great blessings to come (64:1-4).
   c. The servants will acknowledge their unrighteousness, but will submit to the Lord (64:5-8).
   d. They will plead for mercy in the restoration of Israel and the temple (64:9-12).

Notes and Commentary

An understanding of these chapters rests almost entirely upon Doctrine and Covenants 133. Parts of chapters 62, 63, and 64 are quoted there, but in a different sequence. It would be well for students of Isaiah to study section 133 along with these chapters. The Savior's quoting of Isaiah

61:1-2a in Nazareth is a great help, of course, but can be misunderstood if not read carefully. Elder Orson Pratt gave some important insights into the last three verses of chapter 62 which are uplifting as well as instructive. There are also a few other helps from the New Testament and other sections in the Doctrine and Covenants.

Isaiah 61:1-3. The Savior's attributing verses 1-2a to Isaiah is a witness for the single authorship of the book of Isaiah, and speaks against the so-called Third Isaiah theory. A comparison of the Isaiah and Luke texts is revealing:

Isaiah	Luke
	And there was delivered unto him the book of the prophet Esaias. And when he had opened the book, he found the place where it was written,
The Spirit of the Lord God is upon me; because the Lord hath anointed me to preach good tidings unto the meek; he hath sent me to bind up the broken-hearted, to proclaim liberty to the captives, and the opening of the prison to them that are bound;	The Spirit of the Lord is upon me, because he hath anointed me to preach the gospel to the poor; he hath sent me to heal the brokenhearted, to preach deliverance to the captives, and recovering of sight to the blind, to set at liberty them that are bruised,
To proclaim the acceptable year of the Lord, and the day of vengeance of our God; to comfort all that mourn;	To preach the acceptable year of the Lord. (Luke 4:17-19.)
To appoint unto them that mourn in Zion, to give unto them beauty for ashes, the oil of joy for mourning, the garment of praise for the spirit of heaviness; that they might be called trees of righteousness, the planting of the Lord, that he might be glorified. (Isaiah 61:1-3.)	

When Jesus sat down following his reading and "the eyes of all them that were in the synagogue were fastened on him," he announced, "This day is this scripture fulfilled in your ears" (Luke 4:20-21). Thus he proclaimed these verses to be a prophecy of his mission. It is significant that he read only part of the prophecy, thus showing that this text of Isaiah prophesies of his entire mission, which extends to his second coming. His mission, as characterized by these verses, may be categorized as follows:

1. To preach the gospel to the poor (to proclaim the plan of salvation).
2. To heal the brokenhearted (to provide forgiveness of sin).
3. To preach deliverance to the captives (to open the spirit world for the preaching of the gospel).
4. To recover sight to the blind (to perform miracles of healing and to overcome ignorance and superstition).
5. To open the prison to those who are bound (to provide vicarious ordinances for the dead).
6. To proclaim the acceptable year of the Lord (to identify the earthly ministry of the Messiah).
7. To declare the day of vengeance of our God (to foretell his second coming).
8. To comfort all who mourn (to give the Holy Ghost as a companion).
9. To appoint certain blessings to those who mourn in Zion (to deliver the keys necessary for establishing Zion).

Although only part of these nine aspects of the Savior's mission applied to the meridian of time, they all pertain to the latter days. The Prophet Joseph declared: "It [these last days] is the acceptable year of the Lord: liberate the captives that they may sing hosanna" (*TPJS*, p. 77). Peter's reference to Christ's preaching to the spirits in prison confirms this as a part of his ministry (see 1 Peter 3:18-19). Isaiah 61:1-3 and Luke 4:18-19 are often quoted by the General Authorities to show that both Isaiah and the Savior taught of work for the dead. Joseph Smith used the concept of freeing the prisoners in his epistle on baptism for the dead (see D&C 128:22).

When John's disciples came to Jesus to learn whether he was the Christ, he sent them back to John with a message of the miracles they had seen and a summary of Isaiah's prophecy, which would enable them to know that he was the Messiah and not an imposter (see Matthew 11:2-5; Luke 7:19-22).

Isaiah 61:4-6. The last half of verse 3 describes Zion, and these verses seem to elaborate on the building of Zion. They may also refer to Jerusalem's being rebuilt, but the passage deals primarily with Zion because it speaks of "strangers" (the Gentiles) being associated with them. Verse 6 is also an obvious reference to the priesthood's being restored in Zion.

Isaiah 61:7-9. While verses 6 through 8 describe the physical restoration of Zion and the priesthood which her men will exercise, these verses seem to describe the reversal of Israel's desolate social condition in the world to the extent that they will have everlasting joy and acceptance among the Gentiles. This new status will be brought about through the "everlasting covenant" which the Lord will make with Israel (the gospel).

Isaiah 61:10-11. These verses show the reaction of Zion to the prophetic promises and conditions which have been described in the preceding verses. Israel's preparation for her marriage to the Lamb in the last days, as described by John the Revelator (see Revelation 19:7-9; 21:2), is also described here by Isaiah.

Isaiah 62:1-2. The new name which is to come upon Zion and Jerusalem is a result of the righteousness of their people in the New Jerusalem (see Revelation 3:12). As Jerusalem means city of peace, the New Jerusalem is the new or perhaps renewed city of peace, or "holy city," as prophesied in Ether 13:5.

Isaiah 62:3. In Doctrine and Covenants 133:32 the "servants of the Lord, even the children of Ephraim"—that is, the Latter-day Saints—are designated as those who will crown the lost tribes with glory when they return from the north countries.

Isaiah 62:4. The JST translates the Hebrew "Hephzi-bah" as "Delightful," and "Beulah" as "Union." This is supported by marginal readings in the KJV. The Doctrine and Covenants describes this event of the land's being "married" in more modern terms:

> He shall command the great deep, and it shall be driven back into the north countries, and the islands shall become one land;

> And the land of Jerusalem and the land of Zion shall be turned back into their own place, and the earth shall be like as it was in the days before it was divided. (D&C 133:23-24.)

This catastrophic event of the last days will occur in conjunction with the return of the lost tribes out of the north countries (see D&C 133:26-30; 3 Nephi 21:23-26). Incidentally, this passage from the Doctrine and Covenants confirms that the division of the earth recorded in Genesis 10:25 was a literal division and not just a spiritual or ideological one, as some critics suppose.

Isaiah 62:5. The JST changes the word "sons" to "God," making this verse read "so shall thy God marry thee." The two lands will be brought together by the power of the voice of the Lord, just as a marriage is sealed by the voice of one who has the authority to join a man and wife.

Isaiah 62:6-9. Just as Doctrine and Covenants 133, which is called the Appendix to the Doctrine and Covenants, speaks of the two gathering places of the house of Israel, so does Isaiah. These verses speak of the Lord's continual watch over Jerusalem until the promise of her becoming a holy city is fulfilled.

Isaiah 62:10-12. Elder Orson Pratt often quoted these verses in reference to the establishing of Zion in the Rocky Mountains. "I have no idea but what Isaiah, in gazing down upon future generations, saw the time when a long train of carriages would be whirled across a continent, without any apparent animal force or power. He perhaps did not understand the modern terms for tunnel through a rock, and hence he calls them gates." (*JD*, 18:183.) On another occasion Elder Pratt said: "I have no doubt that the prophet saw the construction of this highway in vision, in fact he must have seen it or he could not have predicted it to such a nicety. He must also have seen these trains crossing this great continent, 'dodging' into what seemed to be holes in the mountains, and after watching a little while see them come out at the opposite side." (*JD*, 14:69.) He further suggested that the casting up of the highway and the gathering out of the stones, mentioned in verse 10, described the construction of the railroad highway through the mountains by the Saints when they blasted out the rocks and gathered out the stones (see *JD*, 14:69).

Elder Pratt interpreted the phrase "unto the end of the world" to show that Isaiah was standing in Jerusalem and seeing the standard lifted up by the Lord from a very distant land to all the inhabitants of the earth (see *JD*, 18:184). And he interpreted verse 12 to be referring to Zion in the mountains because of the words "Sought out, A city not forsaken":

> How different from old Jerusalem! Was that sought out? No; Jerusalem was built up a long time before Israel came out of Egypt, and was there ready for them to take possession of when they entered the Holy Land. Was Jerusalem ever forsaken? Yes, forsaken for many generations. But not so with Zion, that should get up into the mountains; they should seek out a location, so much so that the city should be called "Sought out;" and instead of being forsaken, as many people suppose the "Mormons" will be, the Lord God will protect them. (*JD*, 18:184.)

On another occasion, Elder Pratt spoke of "the people who dwell in the mountains" as those who were called a "holy people" by the prophet Isaiah, in spite of the world's looking upon them (at the time of Elder Pratt) as a corrupt people (see *JD*, 16:86).

Isaiah 63:1-2. The "day of vengeance of our God" (61:2) is now elaborated upon by Isaiah. This day, of course, is the Lord's second coming. Doctrine and Covenants 133:46-49 provides an interesting comparison:

Who is this that cometh *from Edom*, with dyed garments *from Bozrah*? this that is glorious in his apparel, travelling in the greatness of his strength? I that speak in righteousness, mighty to save.	*And it shall be said:* Who is this that cometh *down from God in heaven* with dyed garments; *yea, from the regions which are not known*, clothed in his glorious apparel, traveling in the greatness of his strength? *And he shall say:* I *am he* who spake in righteousness, mighty to save.
Wherefore art thou red in thine apparel, and thy garments like him that treadeth in the winevat? (Isaiah 63:1-2.)	*And the Lord shall be* red in his apparel, and his garments like him that treadeth in the wine-vat.

> And so great shall be the glory of his presence that the sun shall hide his face in shame, and the moon shall withhold its light, and the stars shall be hurled from their places. (D&C 133:46-49.)

Whether the garments of the Savior will literally be red, or whether this is a figurative expression of his having trodden down the wicked, is not clear. Certainly the symbolism is taught here, regardless of the actual color of the garment. Doctrine and Covenants 133:49 is a paraphrase or combination of Isaiah 13:10 and 13 and Isaiah 24:23, which also speak of the Lord's second coming. The book of Revelation also describes this event in similar language (see Revelation 19:13, 15; 14:20).

Isaiah 63:3-9. These verses are also quoted in the Doctrine and Covenants, but with slight variations:

I have trodden the winepress alone; and of the people there was none with me: *for* I *will* tread them in mine anger, and trample them in my fury; and their blood *shall be* sprinkled upon my garments, and *I will* stain all my rainment.	*And his voice shall be heard:* I have trodden the wine-press alone, *and have brought judgment upon all people*; and none were with me;
For the day of vengeance is in mine heart, and the year of my redeemed is come.	
And I looked, and there was none to help; and I wondered that there was none to uphold: therefore mine own arm brought salvation unto me; and my fury, it upheld me.	And I *have* trampled them in my fury, *and* I *did* tread upon them in mine anger, and their blood *have I* sprinkled upon my garments, and stained all my rainment; for *this was* the day of vengeance which *was* in my heart.
And I will tread down the people in mine anger, and make them drunk in my fury, and I will bring down their strength to the earth.	

I will mention the lovingkindnesses of the Lord, and the praises of the Lord, according to all that the Lord hath bestowed on us, and the great goodness toward the house of Israel, which he hath bestowed on them according to his mercies, and according to the multitude of his lovingkindnesses.	And *now* the year of my redeemed is come; and *they shall* mention the loving kindness of their Lord, and all that he has bestowed upon them according to his goodness, and according to his loving kindness, forever and ever.
For he said, Surely they are my people, children that will not lie: so he was their Saviour.	
In all their affliction he was afflicted, and the angel of his presence saved them: in his love and in his pity he redeemed them; and he bare them, and carried them all the days of old. (Isaiah 63:3-9.)	In all their afflictions he was afflicted. And the angel of his presence saved them; and in his love, and in his pity, he redeemed them, and bore them, and carried them all the days of old; (D&C 133:50-53.)

These verses announce the completion of the Lord's destruction of the wicked and his atonement for the sins of the repentant. The Doctrine and Covenants further describes the righteous Saints who lived before the time of Christ, received the great blessings of his atonement, and also were resurrected at the time of his resurrection. These will appear with Christ when he comes and calls forth others from the grave (see D&C 133:54-56).

Elder John Taylor contrasted the Lord's first coming, when he was led as a lamb to the slaughter as prophesied by Isaiah (53:7), with his second coming, a day of vengeance, when he will come as a man of war and tread down the wicked because of the wickedness of the earth and the justice of God (see *JD*, 10:115).

Section 76 of the Doctrine and Covenants uses the first part of Isaiah 63:3, "I have trodden the winepress alone," in describing the destruction of the telestial beings at Christ's coming, then adds this descriptive phrase: "even the winepress of the fierceness of the wrath of Almighty God" (D&C 76:107). Also, Doctrine and Covenants 88 says that the various trumps which will be sounded at the second coming of Christ will include the announcement that Christ's work is finished: "The Lamb of God hath overcome and trodden the wine-press alone, even the wine-press of the fierceness of the wrath of Almighty God" (D&C 88:106).

Isaiah 63:10-16. These verses, which are perplexing to the scholars, undoubtedly need some clarification or textual restorations. They seem to be a lamentation or a plea for the Lord to remember his people and perform some of the miracles which he had previously done for them.

Isaiah 63:17-19. The JST contains a significant change in verse 17:

O Lord, why hast thou *made* us to err from thy ways, and *hardened* our heart from thy fear? Return for thy servants' sake, the tribes of thine inheritance. (KJV, Isaiah 63:17.)	O Lord, why hast thou *suffered* us to err from thy ways, and *to harden* our heart from thy fear? Return for thy servants' sake, the tribes of thine inheritance. (JST, Isaiah 63:17.)

This is still a part of the lament of the people, but it also exemplifies the eternal principle of agency, given unto men in the Garden of Eden, whereby man may choose for himself (see Moses 3:17). President David O. McKay taught that agency is the greatest gift next to life itself (see CR, Oct. 1965, p. 8). Verses 10 through 19 probably preceded verses 1 through 9 in the original text. This conclusion is drawn from the fact that Isaiah 64:1-5 is quoted in Doctrine and Covenants 133 before Isaiah 63:1-9 (see D&C 133:40-45), and Isaiah 64:1-5 is a continuation of Isaiah 63:10-19. The last part of verse 17 may be a plea for the return of the ten tribes, which is also spoken of in Doctrine and Covenants 133:26.

Isaiah 64:1-5. These verses are all quoted in the Appendix to the Doctrine and Covenants (section 133), where they precede the quotation of Isaiah 63:1-9, as mentioned above. They are quoted in the context of the servants of God preaching the gospel to every nation (which will occur in fulfillment of a prophecy recorded in Revelation 14:6-7).

> And this gospel shall be preached unto every nation, and kindred, and tongue, and people.

Oh that thou wouldest rend the heavens, that thou wouldest come down, that the mountains might flow down at thy presence,

As when the melting fire burneth, the fire causeth the waters to boil, to make thy name known to thine adversaries, that the nations may tremble at thy presence!

When thou didst terrible things which we looked not for, thou camest down, the mountains flowed down at thy presence.

For since the beginning of the world men have not heard, nor perceived by the ear, neither hath the eye seen, O God, beside thee, what he hath prepared for him that waiteth for him.

Thou meetest him that rejoiceth and worketh righteousness, those that remember thee in thy ways: behold, thou art wroth; for we have sinned: in those is continuance, and we shall be saved. (Isaiah 64:1-5.)

And the servants of God shall go forth, saying with a loud voice: Fear God and give glory to him, for the hour of his judgment is come;

And worship him that made heaven, and earth, and the sea, and the fountains of waters—

Calling upon the name of the Lord day and night, saying: O that thou wouldst rend the heavens, that thou wouldst come down, that the mountains might flow down at thy presence.

And it shall be answered upon their heads; for the presence of the Lord shall be as the melting fire that burneth, and as the fire which causeth the waters to boil.

O Lord, thou shalt come down to make thy name known to thine adversaries, and all nations shall tremble at thy presence—

When thou doest terrible things, things they look not for;

Yea, when thou comest down, and the mountains flow down at thy presence, thou shalt meet him who rejoiceth and worketh righteousness, who remembereth thee in thy ways.

For since the beginning of the world have not men heard nor perceived by the ear, neither hath any eye seen, O God, besides thee, how great things thou hast prepared for him that waiteth for thee. (D&C 133: 37-45.)

In Doctrine and Covenants 133:22 the Lord said that, at the time of his appearance, his voice "shall break down the mountains." This information may also have preceded the verses we have quoted from the original text of Isaiah.

The last part of Isaiah 64:2 is quoted elsewhere in the Doctrine and Covenants in relationship to the Lord's second coming: "And it shall be a great day at the time of my coming, for all nations shall tremble" (D&C 34:8). Paul quoted verse 4 to the Corinthian Saints in an attempt to encourage them to have faith in God. The textual differences in his quotation enlighten our understanding of that verse: "But as it is written, Eye hath not seen, nor ear heard, neither have entered into the heart of man, the things which God hath prepared for them that love him" (1 Corinthians 2:9).

Isaiah 64:5-6. The Prophet changed these verses somewhat. He basically rearranged the phrases, further demonstrating that these chapters may not be as they were originally.

Thou meetest him that rejoiceth and worketh righteousness, those that remember thee in thy ways: behold, thou art wroth; for we have sinned: in those is continuance, and we shall be saved.	Thou meetest him that worketh righteousness, and rejoiceth him that remembereth thee in thy ways; in righteousness there is continuance, and such shall be saved.
But we are all as an unclean thing, and all our righteousnesses are as filthy rags; and we all do fade as a leaf; and our iniquities, like the wind, have taken us away. (KJV, Isaiah 64:5-6.)	But we have sinned; we are all as an unclean thing, and all our righteousnesses are as filthy rags; and we all do fade as a leaf; and our iniquities, like the wind, have taken us away. (JST, Isaiah 64:5-6.)

Isaiah 64:11. The Anchor Bible translates "our holy and our beautiful house" as "our holy and beautiful *temple*."

The Millennial Reign 25

Isaiah 65-66

Because chapter 64 ends with a question, chapter 65 is usually considered to be the answer. However, if chapter 64 is out of place chronologically, as suggested by the arrangement of verses in Doctrine and Covenants 133, chapter 65 should be considered the beginning of a new revelation—especially in light of the changes made by the Prophet Joseph in the JST. This revelation could be seen as a summary or conclusion to the book of Isaiah. Chapters 61 through 64 are comparable to section 133 of the Doctrine and Covenants, which was given as an Appendix to the Doctrine and Covenants, and chapters 65 and 66 seem to serve as a summary which follows Isaiah's "appendix." These chapters include a description of the Millennium. While the appendix, as in the Doctrine and Covenants, deals with the Second Coming, these chapters summarize the events from the Restoration to the Second Coming, which will usher in the Millennium.

1. Those who seek the Lord will find him, whether they are Israelites or Gentiles (65:1-16).
   a. The Lord sent his servant to the Gentiles because Israel had rejected his ways (65:2-5).
   b. The Lord brought his justice and judgments upon Israel (65:6-7).
   c. The Lord preserved a remnant of Israel and Judah to inherit his mountains and to be his servants (65:8-10).
   d. The remnant will also be cleansed through the justice and judgment of the Lord (65:11-16).

2. The Lord will renew the earth and bring about its paradisiacal glory (create new heavens and a new earth) for his righteous servants (65:17-25).
    a. There will be rejoicing in Jerusalem and no more sorrow (65:18-19).
    b. Every man will live to the age of 100, and then will be changed to a celestial or terrestrial being (65:20).
    c. Men will build and plant without interruption throughout their entire lives (65:21-22).
    d. The fruits of men's labors will continue with their seed (65:23).
    e. Great knowledge will be poured out by revelation (65:24).
    f. Enmity between man and beast will cease (65:25).

3. As heaven is the Lord's throne and the earth his footstool, man can build nothing that will adequately honor the Lord, for he created all things (66:1-17).
    a. God looks with favor upon the man who is poor and humble in spirit and who trembles at his word (66:2).
    b. Those who suffer ritualistic sacrifices but follow their own ways and hearken not to his voice are an abomination to him (66:3-4).
    c. Those who ridicule Israel because of Jehovah will be ashamed when he appears in retribution (66:5-6).
    d. The Lord will miraculously give birth to the kingdom of God in Zion (66:7-9).
    e. Jerusalem will rejoice over the deliverance in Zion because she will be comforted by Zion (66:10-14).
    f. The Lord will come with fire and destroy many wicked people (66:15-17).

4. The Lord will gather the house of Israel from all nations to witness his glory (66:18-24).
    a. A sign (the Book of Mormon) will be sent among them (66:19).
    b. The priesthood will be given to those who are gathered (66:21).
    c. Their seed and their names will endure forever (66:22).

d. Their worship will be constant (66:23).
e. They will see the carcasses of those who were destroyed (66:24).

NOTES AND COMMENTARY

The primary source of help for understanding chapter 65 is Doctrine and Covenants 101. Also, the changes in the JST give the chapter its proper beginning. The New Testament quotes two passages from chapter 65, supporting the Doctrine and Covenants and JST interpretations. Modern Church leaders have often referred to this chapter in identifying the conditions of the Millennium; they have also provided some interpretations.

Not as much help is available for chapter 66. The New Testament and the Doctrine and Covenants contain a few quotes or paraphrases, but they are not very specific. We have only one interpretation from a General Authority, but it is significant.

Isaiah 65:1-2. Paul quoted these verses in writing to the Romans, but with slight differences. The JST gives these two verses yet a different reading.

I am *sought* of them *that asked not for me*; I am found of them that sought me not: I said, Behold me, *behold* me, unto a nation that was not called by my name.	I am *found* of them *who seek after me, I give unto all them that ask of me*; I am *not* found of them that sought me not, *or that inquireth not* after me.	But Esaias is very bold, and saith, I was *found* of them that sought me not; I was *made manifest* unto them that asked not after me.
I have spread out my hands all the day unto a *rebellious* people, which walketh in *a way that was* not good, after their own thoughts; (KJV, Isaiah 65:1-2.)	I said *unto my servant*, Behold me, *look upon* me; *I will send you unto* a nation that is not called after my name, *for* I have spread out my hands all the day to a people who walketh not in *my ways, and their works are*	*But to Israel he saith*, All day long I have stretched forth my hands unto a *disobedient and gainsaying* people. (Romans 10:20-21.)

> *evil and* not good,
> and they walk after
> their own thoughts.
> (JST, Isaiah 65:1-2.)

Paul uses these verses to show the contrast between the Gentiles, who did not seek after God but responded to the call of the preachers of the gospel (verse 1), and Israel, who was "a disobedient and gainsaying people." The Prophet Joseph Smith provided a fuller text, showing that whoever seeks the Lord (Israelite or Gentile) will find him, and whoever does not seek him will not find him. The contrast presented by Paul is supported in verse 2 of the JST reading, which indicates that the Lord would send his servants to those not of Israel (the Gentiles) because Israel had not walked after his ways. The message, then, is that the gospel would be taken to the Gentiles because Israel had not responded to the call.

Isaiah 65:3-5. These verses describe the hypocrisy of the nation of Israel through the years, the reason for the Lord's anger with her, and his turning to the Gentiles. In verse 4, the JST uses the word "beasts" in place of the word "things" (italicized in the KJV). The Anchor Bible (20:194) translates the same word "unclean meat."

Isaiah 65:6-7. These verses are a declaration that Israel will have to pay for her transgressions because God will recompense evil. The scripture to which Isaiah refers is not readily recognized and may be one which has been lost. The Book of Mormon also teaches us this principle in Mormon 3:15. God is a God of justice, and so the demands of justice must be met.

Isaiah 65:8-10. Although Israel must be punished, the Lord promises to preserve a remnant from Jacob and also from Judah to be his elect, to inherit his mountains and be his servants.

Isaiah 65:11-16. The RSV translates the first part of verse 11 "But you who forsake the Lord, who forget my holy mountain." This helps to show the proper chronology: Isaiah is now addressing the remnant of Israel who have gathered to the Lord's holy mountain but have forsaken him and forgotten the covenants and blessings which are theirs. These too will face the destructive justice and judgment of the Lord as he cleanses his own house (see D&C 112:24-26). However, those who have kept their covenants will have great blessings in contrast to the destruction which will come upon the wicked element of Israel.

Isaiah 65:17. This is not a reference to the celestialized earth, but rather to the "paradisiacal" earth spoken of in the tenth article of faith. The earth will be restored to the condition in which it existed before Adam's transgression (see Joseph Fielding Smith, *ST*, pp. 36-37; *DS*, 3:94).

Elder Orson Pratt interpreted the last half of this verse as a reference to the people living during the Millennium:

> Now, that has reference to the creation that will be renewed, at the beginning of the millennium. People will not remember. Our children that will be born during the millennium will not remember all the wickedness and corruption that existed in the days of their fathers. It will not come into their minds, unless God puts it there; but when they become immortal, after the thousand years have ended, then I think they will comprehend the process by which this world was made. (*JD*, 21:327.)

The earth will be renewed by a pouring out of the glory of the Lord upon the earth which will cause the corrupted men and animals to be consumed, the elements of the earth to melt, and all things to become new (see D&C 101:23-25; 3 Nephi 26:3). Peter taught that these things would occur in fulfillment of a promise of the Lord (see 2 Peter 3:10-13).

Isaiah 65:18-19. The joy and rejoicing described here will take place in the New Jerusalem also, and will not be restricted to the Jerusalem of mortal earth. Indeed, this rejoicing will be found in all the cities of peace and righteousness where Israel, the Lord's people, dwell. So the passage has reference to more than the two great capitals, Zion and Jerusalem; this prophecy includes the many holy places of Zion and her stakes, where all the righteous Saints will have gathered in preparation for the Millennium. The joy these righteous people are to experience will come because whatever they ask for will be given them, and Satan will have no more power over them. There will be no weeping or sorrow, because there will be no death. (See D&C 101:27-29.)

Isaiah 65:20. This verse was clarified somewhat by the Prophet Joseph Smith:

There shall be no more thence an infant of days, nor an old man that hath not filled his days: for the child shall die an hundred years old; but the sinner being a hundred years old shall be accursed. (KJV, Isaiah 65:20.)

In those days there shall be no more thence an infant of days, nor an old man that hath not filled his days; for the child shall *not* die, *but shall live to be* an hundred years old; but the sinner, *living to be* an hundred years old, shall be accursed. (JST, Isaiah 65:20.)

During the Millennium, the life span of man will be extended to the "age of a tree," or approximately 100 years. There will be no infant mortality, but all people will live out their days and then be changed from mortality to immortality instantaneously, or "in the twinkling of an eye" (see D&C 101:30-31; 63:50-51). However, there will still be agency on the earth, and man must choose between an honorable terrestrial life and a glorified celestial one. There will be many, particularly during the beginning of the Millennium, who will not yet be members of the Church but will be honorable people by the earth's standards (see Joseph Fielding Smith, *DS*, 3:63-64; *AQ*, 2:20-21; 5:141-42).

Isaiah 65:21-22. The Lord paraphrased these verses in Doctrine and Covenants 101:99-101 when he instructed the Saints not to sell their properties in Jackson County, Missouri, and promised that they would be permitted to dwell upon these properties if they would "bring forth fruit and works meet for my kingdom." During the Millennium, there will be nothing to prevent or impair the inhabitants of the earth from establishing permanent homes and vineyards for their entire lives.

Isaiah 65:23. Elder LeGrand Richards interpreted this verse to show the eternal nature of families (see CR, Oct. 1973, pp. 75-76; CR, Oct. 1974, p. 73). Homes and vineyards will continue within families.

Isaiah 65:24. The Millennium will be a period of great revelation from the Lord. Knowledge of the creation, the heavens, the spirit world, and the true history of the earth will be revealed (see D&C 101:32-34).

Isaiah 65:25. This verse is condensed in Doctrine and Covenants 101:26, which merely states that the enmity of man and beasts and "of all flesh" will cease during the

Millennium. Isaiah also states that the lion (symbolizing carnivorous animals) will change its diet to that of cattle. There will be complete peace between man and animals, and also between the animals. President Joseph F. Smith taught that this enmity would cease if man would no longer seek to destroy the animals, and he cited the tame animals found in national parks as evidence (see *Gospel Doctrine* [Salt Lake City: Deseret Book Company, 1969], pp. 265-66). Of course, the outpouring of the glory of the Lord upon the earth will also further that ceasing of enmity, and the earth's being changed apparently will also have an effect.

Isaiah 66:1-2. Isaiah is here proclaiming the greatness of God to introduce a summary of the great things the Lord is going to do in the last days. Just before he was martyred, Stephen quoted these verses to show that, although Solomon had built the Lord a house, the Lord did not dwell in temples made with hands (see Acts 7:47-50). In a revelation given to Joseph Smith in January 1831, the Lord referred to the earth's being his footstool and noted that he would yet stand upon it (see D&C 38:17).

Isaiah 66:3-17. The interpretation of these verses given in the earlier outline was drawn from a careful analysis of various versions or translations of the text. Even though there is no unanimity of opinion among the translations or the commentators, the outline seems to be consistent with the chronology and theology of the events of the last days which are being summarized. The only help within other scriptures comes from Revelation 12:1-5, which sheds light on verse 7. Here John saw a woman in travail bringing forth a man child. Elder Bruce R. McConkie has identified this man child as the kingdom of God (see *DNTC*, 3:516). While the context of these verses in the book of Revelation is in the meridian of time, while Isaiah is speaking of the last days, the identification of the man child would still be the same.

Isaiah 66:18-21. Elder Orson Pratt said that these verses speak of the gathering of Israel from among all nations and languages. In so doing, they declare the glory of Jehovah among the Gentiles. Those gathered will be honored with the priesthood. Elder Pratt interpreted the sign which was to be sent among them to be the same sign given by the Savior to the Nephites when he ministered among them. This sign was the coming forth of the Book of Mormon, first among the Gentiles and then among the Lamanites (see *JD*, 18:16-17; 3 Nephi 21:1-6). Paul was apparently paraphrasing part of verse 20 in Romans 15:16 as justification for his preaching the gospel to the Gentiles.

Isaiah 66:22-23. Again Isaiah refers to "the new heavens and the new earth," but this time he points to their eternal nature as an illustration. The names of the children of Israel who have gathered and their seed will also be eternal. The scriptures speak of two different creations of a new heaven and a new earth. One is a renewal of the paradisiacal glory of the earth during the Millennium, spoken of in Isaiah 65:17 (see the note on that verse); the other is the bringing forth of the resurrected, celestialized earth. This verse may refer to either or both of these because of the eternal status mentioned. Scriptures which speak of the resurrected earth are Revelation 21:1 and Doctrine and Covenants 29:23.

Worship among the children of Israel during the Millennium will be as constant as the eternal nature of the earth, their seed, and their names.

Isaiah 66:24. Those who transgressed and were destroyed at the second coming of Christ are either those of a telestial nature or sons of perdition. The same terminology is used to describe those who are in hell (see Mark 9:44, 46, 48; Luke 16:24) and those who become sons of perdition (see D&C 76:44).

Appendix A
Authorship of Isaiah

Modern Bible scholars do not accept the idea that the entire book of Isaiah was written by one author, the prophet Isaiah. This questioning of the unity of the book began as early as the twelfth century and has progressed to the point of almost universal acceptance. The Anchor Bible is representative of that acceptance: "The distinction between First Isaiah and Second Isaiah is so widely accepted in modern scholarship that the argument against it need not be examined at length. The distinction between Second Isaiah and Third Isaiah is almost as widely accepted." (John L. McKenzie, "Second Isaiah," *The Anchor Bible* [New York: Doubleday and Company, Inc., 1968], 20:xv.)

The term "Second Isaiah" originally referred to Chapters 40 through 66 of Isaiah, which were considered to have been written by an author different from the one who wrote chapters 1 through 39. The term "Third Isaiah" is a later designation, applied to chapters 56 through 66 by scholars who claimed that these were the work of still another author. These three divisions have been further grouped into various sections, such as chapters 1 through 12, 13 through 23, 24 through 35, and 36 through 39. Some have also attempted to identify certain sections within chapters 40 through 66 as interpolations by other authors at various times. The arguments for these theories will not be discussed in depth here, but we will offer some basic reasons for our accepting the book of Isaiah as a unit written entirely by the prophet Isaiah. This is not to suggest that the text has come forth unmolested from the time of its writing. As noted within this study, there are many evidences that the text has suffered extensively through the years. If the original text were available, perhaps many of the objections now raised against the single authorship claim would be answered.

Actually, the authorship issue revolves around one's acceptance or rejection of divine revelation. The traditional acceptance of Isaiah as the single author is challenged by those who do not comprehend the foreknowledge of God, which includes his ability to name people yet unborn and describe events far in the future. The chief example is found in Isaiah 44:28 and 45:1, which record the name of Cyrus, the future king of Persia, and prophesy that he will be responsible for allowing the Jews to return from their captivity in Babylon. Cyrus lived approximately two hundred years after the time of Isaiah. The critics see this identification by name — and the event associated with that name, which is now historical fact — as definite evidence that Isaiah did not write this part of the text. They reason that a prophet may be able to predict events of the near future by analyzing social, economic, and political conditions, but that it is impossible for him to foretell specific names of individuals who will be involved in specific acts, particularly when these people are unborn at the time of the prediction. Their conclusion, therefore, is that this section of the book was written by someone who lived either during or after the days of Cyrus. (See James Muilenberg, "The Book of Isaiah, Introduction," chapters 40-66, *The Interpreters Bible* [New York: Abingdon Press, 1956], 5:382.)

To those who accept the Book of Mormon as revelation, such specific prophecies pose no problem. Book of Mormon prophets foretold the name of Jesus (see 2 Nephi 10:3; 25:19) and the name of Mary, the mother of Jesus (see Mosiah 3:8? Alma 7:10). The Book of Mormon records a prophecy of Joseph who was sold into Egypt in which he foretold the name of Moses, who would lead Israel out of Egypt, and also the name of Joseph, a seer of the latter days. Therefore, the Book of Mormon verifies that a prophet, when moved upon by the Spirit, is able to prophesy the names of people in the future, thus refuting the reasoning of scholars when they reject the stated authorship of certain biblical texts.

The acceptance of Isaiah as the one and only author of the book which bears his name is also challenged by those who consider the vocabulary, style, and thought of Isaiah 40 through 66 so different from that of the earlier chapters that they have to be the work of a different author. With the development of computers, vocabulary studies would seem to be able to settle this issue once and for all, but variant conclusions are being drawn from word studies. The more recent of the studies seem to be reversing the notion that these later chapters contain a significantly different vocabulary than the earlier ones, but the changed style and thought of the later chapters are still a major factor in the scholars' rejection of the single authorship of Isaiah.

It is quite obvious that Isaiah chapters 40 through 66 are in a different style from that of the first part of the book. However, this does not mean that the same author did not write both parts. The manner of revelation may dictate a different style of writing. To those who accept the Doctrine and Covenants as revelation, a significant difference is also noted there. The Lord revealed in his Preface to the Doctrine and Covenants that the revelations given thus far (sixty-five of which were included in the first printed compilation) were of him, but "were given unto my servants in their weakness, after the manner of their language, that they might come to understanding" (D&C 1:24; compare 2 Nephi 31:3).[1] On a later occasion, Joseph Smith and Sidney Rigdon were shown a vision of the various degrees of glory in the eternal world and "were commanded to write while we were yet in the Spirit" (D&C 76:113). This certainly exemplifies a difference in the manner of receiving revelation. Isaiah may well have had a similar experience which could account for the two styles of writing in his book. As evidence of this, 2 Chronicles 26:22 records that the rest of the acts of Uzziah were written by "Isaiah the prophet," whereas 2 Chronicles 32:32 records that the rest of the acts of Hezekiah were "written in the *vision* of Isaiah the prophet." If Isaiah's vision was written while he was "yet in the Spirit," this could well account for a different style of writing between the earlier and later chapters. (See chapter 3 for an analysis of the organization of the book of Isaiah.)

Many scholars divide the book into three parts because of the themes which run through the chapters within these divisions. The first thirty-nine chapters, which include the four chapters of history from the book of 2 Kings, deal with political issues of the nations in and around Isaiah's time (some delete chapters 34 and 35 from this section). The theme of chapters 40 through 55, in the analysis of these scholars, is a nonpolitical one, dealing with the gathering of Israel unto a new nation from their place of exile; this interpretation, along with the references to Cyrus, has led them to associate this portion of Isaiah with the captivity of Judah in Babylon. And the theme of chapters 56 through 66 is supposedly

1. This seems compatible with the thinking of the scholars, but actually it is not. The scholars' idea is that God is limited by the language and abilities of the man who is inspired, while the Doctrine and Covenants is saying that God will adjust the language to the level of man's ability to understand. The language does not therefore impose any limitation, but is revealed in such a way that man can comprehend the message. After receiving and writing section 76, Joseph Smith proclaimed that he "could explain a hundred fold more than I ever have of the glories of the kingdoms manifested to me in the vision, were I permitted, and were the people prepared to receive them" (*TPJS*, p. 305).

one of an established community seeking to strengthen itself into a Zion community. They recognize some overlapping between divisions, but emphasize the differences.

As for the themes found in the three parts of Isaiah identified by the scholars, it should be noted that subject matter often dictates different styles of writing. The three themes are realistic in light of the history of Israel. The early chapters of Isaiah do deal with the downfall of the nation or house of Israel. As Isaiah warned of this downfall, he also held out the message of hope — the promise of a restoration in the latter days. The middle chapters deal with the gathering of Israel to the lands of their inheritance. What the scholars have not recognized, however, is that there are *two* promised lands for the gathering — Zion and Jerusalem — and that Zion is the land of the Americas, which was given to the descendants of Joseph (see 3 Nephi 15:12-13; *TPJS*, p. 362). The loss of "many plain and precious things" from the record of the Jews seems to be the major cause of this oversight, but the Book of Mormon solves the dilemma (see 1 Nephi 13:20-41). The last eleven chapters do describe the building up of Zion after the children of Israel are gathered. Thus, the themes of the book of Isaiah are consistent with the revealed plan of the Lord for his people. Living in the day when these prophecies are being fulfilled enables Latter-day Saints to recognize and understand the message of Isaiah (see 2 Nephi 25:7), while those scholars who are not a part of this movement are unable to obtain this understanding.

Further evidence for the single authorship of Isaiah is found in statements within the Book of Mormon and the New Testament. But again, the validity of this evidence is based on acceptance of these scriptures as the revealed word of God.

The Book of Mormon plates preserved a text of Isaiah's writings at least five hundred years older than any other manuscript. This text assumes that the prophet Isaiah was the author of both First and Second Isaiah, as they are called. Thirteen complete chapters from First Isaiah are quoted in the Book of Mormon and identified as the work of Isaiah. Passages from two other chapters in this section of Isaiah are also quoted, although Isaiah is not named as the author in those cases. Seven chapters from so-called Second Isaiah are quoted in the Book of Mormon and definitely attributed to Isaiah himself; passages from one other chapter in Second Isaiah are also quoted, but here again the writer is not identified. Interestingly, no passages from so-called Third Isaiah are quoted in the Book of Mormon. However, Moroni, in writing about the covenant of Israel which would be restored in the latter days, admonished his readers to "search the prophecies of Isaiah" because he did not have the space to write them (see Mormon 8:23). That he gave this admonition without stipulating any restrictions suggests that there were several other prophecies in addition to those which had already been quoted in the record which spoke of the covenant of Israel in the latter days. Since the later chapters of Isaiah speak concerning latter-day Israel or Zion, Moroni may well have had reference to these chapters, particularly when we consider that Isaiah 49:1 through 55:2 had already been quoted within the Book of Mormon. Since the third section of Isaiah deals with the eventual establishment of a Zion community, it would be natural for the Book of Mormon prophets and the Savior to rely upon the earlier sections to establish their teachings. Israel was to be scattered and gathered again before Zion would be built up; to have stressed the Zion community in that day, although it was mentioned by Isaiah, would have been "putting the cart before the horse." The Doctrine and Covenants was apparently the book to bring about this Zion community, which has come forth in a day when the spiritual foundations of Zion are being laid, and does quote freely from the prophecies in the third section of Isaiah (see Appendix D). Although Isaiah is not named as the original author of these quoted prophecies, the Preface to the Doctrine and Covenants does state that one of the purposes of the latter-day restoration was "that it might be fulfilled, which was written by the prophets" (D&C 1:18). So it is understandable that many prophecies from so-called Third Isaiah are quoted in the Doctrine and Covenants.

The New Testament also witnesses that Isaiah was the single author of the work called by his name. The Savior himself, as well as his apostles, identified as Isaiah's own writings passages quoted from all three of the scholars' divisions of his work (see Appendix E). For example, Isaiah 6:9-10 is quoted in Matthew 13:14-15; Isaiah 42:1-3 is quoted in Matthew 12:17-20; and Isaiah 61:1-2 is quoted in Luke 4:17-19. Since the Book of Mormon does not quote from so-called Third Isaiah, it is significant that the New Testament does. The New Testament quotes eleven passages which are clearly from this section of Isaiah, and contains at least eighteen other passages which are paraphrases or possible quotations. Most of the eleven passages are introduced as scripture by the preface "It is written," and two of them are specifically identified as the words of Isaiah — one by the Savior himself in the synagogue in Nazareth (see Isaiah 61:1-2; Luke 4:17-19), and the other by Paul in his epistle to the Romans (see Isaiah 65:1-2; Romans 10:20-21).

In light of all these witnesses, we can see that the original work of Isaiah included all of our present-day text and possibly more, as has been indicated in this book. In the Book of Mormon,

Nephi testified that "many plain and precious things" were taken away from "the record of the Jews" (the Bible). He was also shown that other records were to come forth in the latter days to establish the truth of the first record, and to make known the plain and precious truths which had been lost (see 1 Nephi 13:20-41). These last records include the Book of Mormon and the Doctrine and Covenants, and they witness to the world that Isaiah is the author of the book called by his name.

Appendix B
Ancient and Modern Commentary on Isaiah

The chart in this appendix identifies where specific chapters and verses in the biblical Isaiah are recorded or alluded to in other scriptures or are commented on by General Authorities. For those passages it also shows degrees of difference between the biblical rendering on the one hand and the renderings in the Book of Mormon and the Joseph Smith Translation on the other hand and lists these comparisons by code (see below).

Code to Comparisons

S	Same as the biblical text
C	Change from the biblical text
SC	Slight wording change but no change in meaning
SBM	Same as Book of Mormon (in Joseph Smith Translation)
SCBM	Slight change from Book of Mormon (in Joseph Smith Translation)

Code to General Authorities' Name Abbreviations

BHR	B. H. Roberts
BRM	Bruce R. McConkie
BY	Brigham Young
DOM	David O. McKay
EGS	Eldred G. Smith
ETB	Ezra Taft Benson
GAS	George Albert Smith
GBH	Gordon B. Hinckley
GFR	George F. Richards
CWN	Charles W. Nibley
CWP	Charles W. Penrose
HBB	Hugh B. Brown
HBL	Harold B. Lee
HDT	Henry D. Taylor
HS	Hyrum Smith
HWH	Howard W. Hunter
JAC	James A. Cullimore
JFS	Joseph Fielding Smith
JFSmith	Joseph F. Smith
JHV	John H. Vandenberg

Code to General Authorities' Name Abbreviations

JL	John Longden	OC	Oliver Cowdery
JS	Joseph Smith	OH	Orson Hyde
JT	John Taylor	OP	Orson Pratt
LR	LeGrand Richards	PHD	Paul H. Dunn
MDH	Marion D. Hanks	RC	Rudger Clawson
MEP	Mark E. Petersen	SDY	S. Dilworth Young
MGR	Marion G. Romney	SWK	Spencer W. Kimball
MH	Martin Harris	TMB	Theodore M. Burton
MRH	Milton R. Hunter	TSM	Thomas S. Monson
NET	N. Eldon Tanner	VLB	Victor L. Brown

Isaiah	Book of Mormon		JST	New Testament	D&C	General Authorities
1:1-6						
1:7						OC, *MA*, Apr. 1835, pp. 109-110 (quotes Moroni)
1:8						
1:9				Rom. 9:29		
1:10-15						
1:16-17			SC	1 Pet. 3:11		JFS, *AQ* 1:51
1:18					50:10-12	JFS, *AQ* 2:179-80
1:19-20					64:34	
1:21-22						
1:23-24						OC, *MA*, Apr. 1835, p. 110 (quotes Moroni)
1:25-26						OC, *MA*, Apr. 1835, p. 110 (quotes Moroni) *TPJS*, p. 93
1:27-31						
2:1	2 Ne. 12:1	S				
2:2	2 Ne. 12:2	C	SBM		133:12-13	SDY, CR 4/74:88-89
2:3-4	2 Ne. 12:3-4	S			115:4-5	OC, *MA*, Apr. 1835 p. 110 LR, CR 10/62:109; CR 4/67:22; CR 10/70: 61-62; CR 4/71:143; TMB, CR 4/71:108; HBL, CR 4/73:5; *Ensign* 11/71:15; MEP, *Why the Religious Life*, pp. 200-201, 305-7; OP, *JD* 14:350; GBH, CR 10/74:144-45; JFS, *DS* 1:176; *ST*, p. 67; BRM, CR 10/67:43
2:5	2 Ne. 12:5	C	SBM			*TPJS*, pp. 248-52
2:6	2 Ne. 12:6	SC	SBM			
2:7	2 Ne. 12:7	S				
2:8	2 Ne. 12:8	SC				
2:9	2 Ne. 12:9	C	SBM			
2:10	2 Ne. 12:10	C	SCBM	Luke 23:30 2 Thes. 1:9 Rev. 6:15-16		
2:11	2 Ne. 12:11	SC	SCBM			
2:12-13	2 Ne. 12:12-13	C	SBM			

Isaiah	*Book of Mormon*		*JST*	*New Testament*	*D&C*	*General Authorities*
2:14	2 Ne. 12:14	C	SCBM			
2:15	2 Ne. 12:15	S	SCBM			
2:16	2 Ne. 12:16	C	SBM			
2:17-18	2 Ne. 12:17-18	S				
2:19	2 Ne. 12:19	C	SBM	See above (under 2:10)		
2:20	2 Ne. 12:20	SC	SBM			
2:21	2 Nc. 12:21	C	SCBM	See above (under 2:10)		
2:22	2 Ne. 12:22	S				
3:1	2 Ne. 13:1	SC	SBM			
3:2-3	2 Ne. 13:2-3	S				
3:4	2 Ne. 13:4	SC	SBM			
3:5	2 Ne. 13:5	S				
3:6	2 Ne. 13:6	C	SBM			
3:7	2 Ne. 13:7	SC	SBM			
3:8	2 Ne. 13:8	SC	SBM			
3:9	2 N3. 13:9	SC	SBM			MDH, CR 10/73:16
3:10	2 Ne. 13:10	SC	SBM			
3:11	2 Ne. 13:11	C	SBM			
3:12	2 Ne. 13:12	SC	SCBM			ETB, CR 10/70:21
3:13	2 Ne. 13:13	S				
3:14	2 Ne. 13:14	SC				
3:15	2 Ne. 13:15	SC	SBM			HBL, CR 10/71:58
3:16	2 Ne. 13:16	S				JFS, *AQ* 5:172-74
3:17	2 Ne. 13:17	S				
3:18	2 Ne. 13:18	SC	SBM			
3:19-22	2 Ne. 13:19-22	S				
3:23	2 Ne. 13:23	SC				
3:24	2 Ne. 13:24	SC	SBM			
3:25	2 Ne. 13:25	S				
3:26	2 Ne. 13:26	SC	SBM			
4:1	2 Ne. 14:1	S	3:27	Luke 1:25		
4:2	2 Ne. 14:2	SC	4:1 SCBM			
4:3	2 Ne. 14:3	SC	4:2		112:23-26	JFS, *DS* 1:169
4:4	2 Ne. 14:4	S	4:3			
4:5	2 Ne. 14:5	C	4:4 SBM		45:63-75	*TPJS*, p. 161
					84:2-5	OC, *MA*, Apr. 1835 (quotes Moroni); OP, *JD* 16:82

Isaiah	*Book of Mormon*		*JST*	*New Testament*	*D&C*	*General Authorities*
4:6	2 Ne. 14:6	SC	4:5		115:4-6	HBL, CR 4/73:5
5:1	2 Ne. 15:1	C	SBM		101:43-62	
5:2-3	2 Ne. 15:2-3					
5:4	2 Ne. 15:4	SC	SBM			
5:5	2 Ne. 15:5	SC	SBM			
5:6	2 Ne. 15:6					
5:7	2 Ne. 15:7	SC				
5:8	2 Ne. 15:8	C	SCBM			
5:9	2 Ne. 15:9	C	SBM			
5:10	2 Ne. 15:10	SC				
5:11	2 Ne. 15:11	SC	SCBM			
5:12	2 Ne. 15:12	S				
5:13-18	2 Ne. 15:13-18	S				
5:19	2 Ne. 15:19	SC				
5:20	2 Ne. 15:20					SWK, CR 10/62:56
5:21	2 Ne. 15:21	SC	SBM			NET, CR 10/68:49
5:22	2 Ne. 15:22	SC	SBM			
5:23	2 Ne. 15:23	SC				
5:24	2 Ne. 15:24	SC				
5:25	2 Ne. 15:25	S				
5:26	2 Ne. 15:26 2 Ne. 29:2	SC				
5:27	2 Ne. 15:27	SC				OP, *JD* 16:84; LR, *A Marvelous Work and a Wonder,* pp. 235-36; CR 10/75:77-78 JFS, *DS* 1:146
5:28	2 Ne. 15:28	SC	SCBM			
5:29	2 Ne. 15:29	SC	SBM			
5:30	2 Ne. 15:30	SC	SBM			
6:1	2 Ne. 16:1	S		Rev. 4:2		
6:2	2 Ne. 16:2	S		Rev. 4:8	38:1; 77:2-4	
6:3	2 Ne. 16:3	S		Rev. 4:8		
6:4	2 Ne. 16:4	S		Rev. 15:8		
6:5	2 Ne. 16:5	C				
6:6	2 Ne. 16:6	S				
6:7	2 Ne. 16:7	C	SBM			
6:8	2 Ne. 16:8	S				
6:9	2 Ne. 16:9	C	SBM	Matt. 13: 14-15; Mark 4:12; Luke		

Isaiah	*Book of Mormon*		*JST*	*New Testament*	*D&C*	*General Authorities*
				8:10; John 12:40-41		
6:10	2 Ne. 16:10	C	SBM	Acts 28:26-27; Rom. 11:8		
6:11	2 Ne. 16:11	C	SBM			
6:12	2 Ne. 16:12	C	SBM			
6:13	2 Ne. 16:13	C	SBM			
7:1	2 Ne. 17:1	SC				
7:2-5	2 Ne. 17:2-5	S				
7:6	2 Ne. 17:6	SC	SCBM			
7:7	2 Ne. 17:7	S				
7:8	2 Ne. 17:8	SC				
7:9-10	2 Ne. 17:9-10	S				
7:11	2 Ne. 17:11	SC				
7:12-13	2 Ne. 17:12-13	S				
7:14	2 Ne. 17:14 1 Ne. 11:13-21 Alma 7:10	SC	SBM	Matt. 1:23		HBB, CR 10/60:93 MEP, CR 10/65:60 HDT, CR 10/75:93
7:15	2 Ne. 17:15	SC	SBM			
7:16	2 Ne. 17:16	S				
7:17	2 Ne. 17:17	SC				
7:18	2 Ne. 17:18	SC				
7:19	2 Ne. 17:19	S				
7:20	2 Ne. 17:20	SC				
7:21	2 Ne. 17:21	SC				
7:22	2 Ne. 17:22	SC				
7:23	2 Ne. 17:23	SC	SCBM			
7:24	2 Ne. 17:24	S				
7:25	2 Ne. 17:25	SC				
8:1	2 Ne. 18:1	SC	SBM			
8:2-3	2 Ne. 18:2-3	S				
8:4	2 Ne. 18:4	SC	SBM			
8:5-11	2 Ne. 18:5-11	S				
8:12	2 Ne. 18:12	SC				
8:13	2 Ne. 18:13					
8:14	2 Ne. 18:14 Jacob 4:15	SC S		1 Pet. 2:8; Rom. 9:33; 1 Cor. 1:23		
8:15	2 Ne. 18:15	S				
8:16	2 Ne. 18:16	S			88:84	

Isaiah	*Book of Mormon*		*JST*	*New Testament*	*D&C*	*General Authorities*
					133:72	
8:17-18	2 Ne. 18:17-18	S		Heb. 2:13		
8:19	2 Ne. 18:19	SC	SBM			JFS, *AQ* 4:33
8:20	2 Ne. 18:20	SC				ETB, CR 10/63:16; *TPJS*, pp. 373-74
8:21	2 Ne. 18:21	S				
8:22	2 Ne. 18:22	SC				
9:1	2 Ne. 19:1	C	SCBM	Matt. 4:15-16		
9:2	2 Ne. 19:2	S				
9:3	2 Ne. 19:3	C	SCBM			
9:4	2 Ne. 19:4	C				
9:5	2 Ne. 19:5	S				
9:6	2 Ne. 19:6	C		Luke 2:10-11		
9:7	2 Ne. 19:7	SC	SCBM	Luke 1:32		
9:8	2 Ne. 19:8	C	SBM			
9:9-13	2 Ne. 19:9-13	S				
9:14	2 Ne. 19:14	SC				
9:15	2 Ne. 19:15	C				
9:16	2 Ne. 19:16	S				
9:17	2 Ne. 19:17	C	SBM			
9:18-21	2 Ne. 19:18-21	S				
10:1	2 Ne. 20:1	S				
10:2	2 Ne. 20:2	SC				
10:3-4	2 Ne. 20:3-4	S				
10:5	2 Ne. 20:5	C				
10:6	2 Ne. 20:6	SC				
10:7	2 Ne. 20:7	SC				
10:8-9	2 Ne. 20:8-9	S				
10:10	2 Ne. 20:10	SC	SBM			
10:11	2 Ne. 20:11	SC	SBM			
10:12	2 Ne. 20:12	SC	SBM			
10:13	2 Ne. 20:13	SC	SBM			
10:14	2 Ne. 20:14	S				
10:15	2 Ne. 20:15	SC				
10:16	2 Ne. 20:16	S				
10:17	2 Ne. 20:17	SC				
10:18-20	2 Ne. 20:18-20	S				
10:21	2 Ne. 20:21	SC	SBM			
10:22	2 Ne. 20:22	S		Rom. 9:27		

Isaiah	*Book of Mormon*		*JST*	*New Testament*	*D&C*	*General Authorities*
10:23	2 Ne. 20:23	SC				
10:24-34	2 Ne. 20:24-34	S				
11:1	2 Ne. 21:1	SC		Rev. 5:5 Rev. 22:16	113:1-4	JSH 1:40
11:2-3	2 Ne. 21:2-3	S				
11:4	2 Ne. 21:4	S		Rev. 2:16	19:15	JFS, *DS* 1:168
11:5	2 Ne. 21:5 2 Ne. 30:11	S S				
11:6	2 Ne. 21:6 2 Ne. 30:12	SC				*TPJS*, pp. 71, 93, 316
11:7	2 Ne. 21:7 2 Ne. 30:13	S S				JFS, *AQ* 1:xvii; 2:xiv; 2:22; 5:143-44
11:8	2 Ne. 21:8 2 Ne. 30:14	S S				
11:9	2 Ne. 21:9	S				OP, *JD* 16:47ff; 21:325; JFS, *DS* 3:65
11:10	2 Ne. 21:10	S		Rom. 15:12 Rev. 5:5	113:5-6 90:2-4	
11:11	2 Ne. 21:11 2 Ne. 25:17 2 Ne. 29:1 Jacob 6:2	S S S				*TPJS*, pp. 14-15; JFS, *AQ* 2:181; OP, *JD* 14:66; LR, CR 10/75:77
11:12	2 Ne. 21:12	S				
11:13	2 Ne. 21:13	SC				
11:14	2 Ne. 21:14	S				
11:15	2 Ne. 21:15	SC				OC, *MA*, Apr. 1835, p. 111; OP, *JD* 14:66
11:16	2 Ne. 21:16	S			133:26-32	JFS, *DS* 3:252
12:1	2 Ne. 22:1	S				
12:2	2 Ne. 22:2	C		Heb. 2:13		
12:3	2 Ne. 22:3	S		Rev. 21:6; John 7:38		
12:4	2 Ne. 22:4	S				
12:5-6	2 Ne. 22:5-6	S				
13:1	2 Ne. 23:1	S		Rev. 18:2-3	133-14	
13:2	2 Ne. 23:2	S	C	Rev. 18:4	133:4-13	
13:3	2 Ne. 23:3	C	SBM	Matt. 13:24-30	86:1-7	
13:4	2 Ne. 23:4	SC	SBM			
13:5	2 Ne. 23:5	SC	SBM			
13:6-7	2 Ne. 23:6-7	S				
13:8	2 Ne. 23:8	SC				

Isaiah	*Book of Mormon*		*JST*	*New Testament*	*D&C*	*General Authorities*
13:9	2 Ne. 23:9	S				
13:10	2 Ne. 23:10	C		Matt. 24:29	29:14 34:9 45:42 88:87 133:49	OC, *MA*, Apr. 1835, pp. 111-12
13:11	2 Ne. 23:11	SC				SWK, CR 4/74:6
13:12-13	2 Ne. 23:12-13	S			21:6; 35:24	
13:14	2 Ne. 23:14	SC				
13:15	2 Ne. 23:15	C	SCBM			
13:16	2 Ne. 23:16	S				
13:17	2 Ne. 23:17	SC				
13:18	2 Ne. 23:18	S				
13:19	2 Ne. 23:19 2 Ne. 25:15	S				
13:20-21	2 Ne. 23:20-21	S				
13:22	2 Ne. 23:22	C	SCBM			LR, CR 10/66:42
14:1	2 Ne. 24:1	C				
14:2	2 Ne. 24:2	C	SCBM			
14:3	2 Ne. 24:3	C	SBM			
14:4	2 Ne. 24:4	C	SBM			
14:5	2 Ne. 24:5	SC	SCBM			
14:6	2 Ne. 24:6	S				
14:7	2 Ne. 24:7 1 Ne. 22:26	S		Rev. 20:1-3	43:31; 88:110; 101:28	
14:8	2 Ne. 24:8	SC	SBM			
14:9	2 Ne. 24:9 Alma 34:34-35	S				*TPJS*, p. 297
14:10	2 Ne. 24:10	S				
14:11	2 Ne. 24:11	C				
14:12	2 Ne. 24:12	SC		Rev. 12:7-9	76:25-27	JS,[1] *TPJS*, pp. 297-98
14:13	2 Ne. 24:13	S				
14:14	2 Ne. 24:14 2 Ne. 2:17-18	S			88:35	 MGR, CR 4/71:23
14:15	2 Ne. 24:15	S				
14:16	2 Ne. 24:16	SC	SBM			
14:17	2 Ne. 24:17 Alma 30:60	SC	SBM			

1. See also Abr. 3:27-28; Moses 4:1-4.

Isaiah	*Book of Mormon*		*JST*	*New Testament*	*D&C*	*General Authorities*
14:18	2 Ne. 24:18	SC	SBM			
14:19	2 Ne. 24:19	SC	SBM			
14:20	2 Ne. 24:20	S				
14:21	2 Ne. 24:21	SC	SBM		88:21-35	
14:22-24	2 Ne. 24:22-24	S				
14:25	2 Ne. 24:25	C				
14:26	2 Ne. 24:26	SC				
14:27	2 Ne. 24:27	SC				
14:28-31	2 Ne. 24:28-31	S				
14:32	2 Ne. 24:32	SC	SCBM		97:21	
15:1-9						
16:1-4						
16:5				Luke 1:32		
16:6			SC			
16:7-14						
17:1-14						
18:1-7						HS, *HC* 6:322
19:1-25						BRM, *Ensign* 10/73: 82
20:1-6						
21:1-8						
21:9				Rev. 14:8		
21:10-17						
22:1-12						
22:13				1 Cor. 15:32		
22:14-19						
22:20						
22:21-22				Rev. 3:7		
22:23-25					45:48-53	
23:1-7						
23:8				Rev. 18:23		
23:9						
23:10			SC			
23:11-18						

Isaiah	*Book of Mormon*	*JST*	*New Testament*	*D&C*	*General Authorities*
24:1					
24:2					SWK, CR 4/71:9;
24:3					MGR, CR 4/68:113
24:4					JFS, *DS* 3:316
24:5			Heb. 13:20	1:15	JFS, *DS* 1:168
24:6					RC, CR 4/14:22-23; GFR, CR 4/30; *TPJS*, p. 15; LR, CR 10/77:30; JFS, *DS* 3:62
24:7					
24:8			Rev. 18:22		
24:9-14					
24:15	2 Ne. 10:20				
24:16-20				49:23 88:87	*TPJS*, 29, 71; OC, *MA*, Apr. 1835, pp. 111-12
24:21-22					
24:23			Rev. 21:23		OP, *JD* 20:12
25:1-5					
25:6				58:8-12	
25:7				121:26-33	
25:8			1 Cor. 15:54; Rev. 7:17; 21:4		
25:9-12					
26:1-2					
26:3					HWH, CR 10/66:15
26:4-16					
26:17			John 16:21		
26:18-19					
26:20-21				45:43-47	BHR, *Rasha the Jew;* CWP; CR 10/18:17; *TPJS*, p. 17
27:1			Rev. 20:2; 12:9		
27:2-13					
28:1-8					
28:9			1 Cor. 3:1-2 Heb. 5:11-14	19:21-22	
28:10	2 Ne. 28:30				

Isaiah	*Book of Mormon*		*JST*	*New Testament*	*D&C*	*General Authorities*
28:11				1 Cor. 14:21		
28:12-14						
28:15					5:19; 45:31; 97:23	
28:16				Rom. 9:33 1 Pet. 2:6		
28:17						
28:18-19						*TPJS*, p. 87
28:20						
28:21					95:4 101:95	OC, *MA*, Feb. 1835, p. 79; *TPJS*, p. 267
28:22				Rom. 9:28		
28:23-29						
29:1						
29:2		C				OP, *Works*, pp. 270-79 (covers entire chapter); LR, CR 4/67:21
29:3-4	2 Ne. 26:15-17	SC	SCBM	Luke 19:43-44		LR, CR 4/63:118; JFS, *DS* 3:211-13
29:5	2 Ne. 26:18	C	SC			MEP, CR 10/77:16
29:6	2 Ne. 27:2	SC	SCBM			LR, CR 4/76:123-24
29:7	2 Ne. 27:3a	C				
29:8	2 Ne. 27:3b	SC	SCBM			
29:9	2 Ne. 27:4	C	SBM			
29:10	2 Ne. 27:5	C	SBM	Rom. 11:8		
	2 Ne. 27:6-8		SBM			
	2 Ne. 27:9-10		SCBM			
	2 Ne. 27:11-14		SBM			
29:11	2 Ne. 27:15-18	C	SBM			
29:12	2 Ne. 27:19-20	C	SBM			
	2 Ne. 27:21-23		SBM			OC, *MA*, Feb. 1835, p. 80; JS-H 1:63-65; JFS, *DS* 3:213; *MEP*, CR 10/77:15-18;
29:13	2 Ne. 27:24-25	C	SCBM	Matt. 15:7-9 Mark 7:6-7		JS-H 1:17-19; OC, *MA*, Feb. 1835; JFS, *DS* 3:284; LR, CR 10/77:30-31; OFW, CR 4/14:41

Isaiah	*Book of Mormon*		*JST*	*New Testament*	*D&C*	*General Authorities*
29:14	2 Ne. 27:26	SC	SBM			OFW, CR 10/16:51-52; MEP, CR 10/77: 15-18; LR, CR 4/63: 116; CR 4/70:147; CR 4/73:100; SWK, CR 4/75:9
	2 Ne. 25:17-18 2 Ne. 29:1-2 3 Ne. 21:9			1 Cor. 1:19-20	4:1; 6:1; 11:1; 12:1; 14:1;18:44	
29:15	2 Ne. 27:27a	C	SBM			
29:16	2 Ne. 27:27b	C	SBM	Rom. 9:20		
29:17	2 Ne. 27:28	C	SCBM			OP, *Works*, pp. 276-77; JFS, *DS* 3:260-61; MEP, CR 10/65:61; CR 10/70:142
29:18-19	2 Ne. 27:29-30	SC	SBM			MEP, CR 10/65:61; LR, CR 4/76:124
29:20	2 Ne. 27:31	C	SBM			
29:21	2 Ne. 27:32	C	SBM			*TPJS*, p. 124
29:22	2 Ne. 27:33	S				
29:23	2 Ne. 27:34	S				
29:24	2 Ne. 27:35	S				ETB, CR 4/75:96
30:1-8	Jacob 4:10					JFS, *DS* 3:4
30:9-10						MDH, CR 4/72:127
30:11-17					(vs. 17)	TSM, CR 10/70:105
30:18						MDH, CR 4/72:126-27; CR 10/77:56
30:19-20						
30:21						MEP, CR 4/77:110; TSM, CR 4/75:23; MDH, CR 10/65:120
30:22-26				Rev. 21:23		
30:27-33						
31:1-9						
32:1-12					58:17-22	
32:13-14			C (32:14)			OP, *JD* 18:144-45, 149 (on 32:13-20)
32:15-16						
32:17						
32:18-20						EGS, CR 4/72:147
33:1-2			SC (33:2)			

Isaiah	*Book of Mormon*	*JST*	*New Testament*	*D&C*	*General Authorities*
33:3-14					
33:15					BRM, CR 10/73:55-56
33:16-17					
33:18		SC	1 Cor. 1:20		
33:19-20					*TPJS*, p. 33
33:21-24					
34:1-3					JFS, *ST*, pp. 150-51 (on 34:1-8)
34:4	3 Ne. 26:3		2 Pet. 3:10-13 Rev. 6:14		*TPJS*, p. 29
34:5-6				1:12-14 1:36	
34:7		SC			
34:8-9					
34:10			Rev. 14:11		
34:11-15					
34:16		C			OP, *JD* 18:145
34:17		C			
35:1-2				49:24-25 117:7	JFS, *DS* 3:346-47; MRH, CR 10/65:81; LR, CR 10/66:42; OP, *JD* 18:145
35:3-7			Heb. 12:12	81:5	HBB, CR 4/66:120; PHD, CR 10/68:52
35:8-10		C		101:18; 133:26-34 45:71; 66:11	DOM, CR 10/66:137; *TPJS*, pp. 17, 34
40:1-2					
40:3	1 Ne. 10:8		Matt. 3:3 Mark 1:3 Luke 1:76; 3:4 John 1:23	33:10 65:1 88:66	*TPJS*, pp. 319, 335 OP, *JD* 18:149, 183
40:4			Luke 3:5	133:22	OP, *JD* 18:149
40:5			Luke 3:6	101:23	JFS, *DS* 2:316-17
40:6-8			Pet. 1:24-25 Mark 13:31		
40:9-11			Rev. 22:12		OP, *JD* 18:150, 182-83
40:12-17			Rom. 11: 33-35		
40:18-27					
40:28-31				89:20	

Isaiah	*Book of Mormon*	*JST*	*New Testament*	*D&C*	*General Authorities*
41:1-3					
41:4			Rev. 1:8, 17; 22:13		
41:5-7					
41:8-9				93:46; 133:30-32	
41:10					JFS, *DS* 3:107
41:11-20					
41:21					BRM, CR 4/73:35
41:22-27					
41:28		SC			
41:29					
42:1-4			Matt. 12: 14-21		
42:5					
42:6-7			Luke 2:32 Acts 26: 17-18 1 Pet. 3:19	128:22	*TPJS*, p. 219; JFS, *DS* 2:155; TMB, CR 10/64:33
42:8-18					
42:19-25		C			
43:1-4					
43:5-7					*TPJS*, p. 183; JFS, *DS* 3:254; OP, *JD* 18:186
43:8-10				76:1	
43:11					
43:12					BRM, CR 10/69:82-83; CR 4/72:135; CR 4:73:36
43:13		SC			
43:14-28					
44:1-5					
44:6-20			Rev. 1:8, 17; 22:13		
44:21		SC			
44:22-28					
45:1-4					JFS, *AQ* 5:181
45:5			Mark 12:32		
45:6-8					*TPJS*, p. 84
45:9			Rom. 9:20		
45:10-13					
45:14			1 Cor. 14:25		
45:15-22					

Isaiah	*Book of Mormon*		*JST*	*New Testament*	*D&C*	*General Authorities*
45:23	Mos. 16:1-4			Rom. 14:11 Philip. 2: 10-11	76:110 88:104	JFS, *DS* 2:30-31
45:24-25						
46:1-13						
47:1-6						
47:7-9				Rev. 18:7-8		
47:10-14						
47:15				Rev. 18:3		
48:1-3	1 Ne. 20:1-3	C				
48:4-5	1 Ne. 20:4-5	SC				
48:6	1 Ne. 20:6	C				
48:7-8	1 Ne. 20:7-8	SC				
48:9-11	1 Ne. 20:9-11	C				
48:12	1 Ne. 20:12	SC		Rev. 1:8, 17; 22:13		
48:13	1 Ne. 20:13	SC				
48:14-17	1 Ne. 20: 14-17	C				
48:18-19	1 Ne. 20: 18-19	SC				JFS, *DS* 3:30
48:20	1 Ne. 20:20	SC				
48:21	1 Ne. 20:21	SC				
48:22	1 Ne. 20:22	C				
49:1	1 Ne. 21:1 1 Ne. 22:1-5 2 Ne. 10: 20-22	C				
49:2	1 Ne. 21:2	S		Rev. 1:16	5:10; 6:2; 86:8-9; 103:17	JS, Abr. 2:9-11; *TPJS*, p. 304
49:3	1 Ne. 21:3	S			133:30-34	
49:4-5	1 Ne. 21:4-5	SC				
49:6	1 Ne. 21:6	SC		Acts 13:47	86:11	
49:7	1 Ne. 21:7	C		1 Cor. 1:9		
49:8	1 Ne. 21:8	C		2 Cor. 6:2		
49:9	1 Ne. 21:9 1 Ne. 22: 10-12	SC				
49:10	1 Ne. 21:10	SC		Rev. 7:16		
49:11	1 Ne. 21:11	S				
49:12	1 Ne. 21:12	C				
49:13	1 Ne. 21:13	C				

Isaiah	*Book of Mormon*		*JST*	*New Testament*	*D&C*	*General Authorities*
49:14	1 Ne. 21:14	C				*TPJS*, p. 362
49:15	1 Ne. 21:15	C				
49:16	1 Ne. 21:16	S				
49:17	1 Ne. 21:17	C				
49:18	1 Ne. 21:18	SC				
49:19	1 Ne. 21:19	S				
49:20	1 Ne. 21:20	C				
49:21	1 Ne. 21:21	SC				
49:22	1 Ne. 21:22	S			45:9	MGR, CR 4/61:119;
	2 Ne. 6:6	S			115:3-5	OP, *JD* 16:85
	1 Ne. 22:6-9					
49:23	1 Ne. 21:23	SC	SCBM			SWK, CR 10/65:72;
	2 Ne. 6:7, 13	SC				CR 10/56:52-58
	2 Ne. 6:8-12					
	10:1-22					
49:24	1 Ne. 21:24	SC				
	2 Ne. 6:16	SC				
49:25	1 Ne. 21:25	S				
	2 Ne. 6:17	C				
49:26	1 Ne. 21:26	SC	Same as 2 Ne. 6: 18			
	1 Ne. 22:13-14					
	1 Ne. 22:15-17					
50:1	2 Ne. 7:1	C	SCBM			
50:2	2 Ne. 7:2	C	SCBM		133:66-68	
50:3	2 Ne. 7:3	S	SCBM		133:69	
50:4	2 Ne. 7:4	C	SCBM			
50:5	2 Ne. 7:5	S	C			
50:6	2 Ne. 7:6	SC	SC			
50:7	2 Ne. 7:7	S	SC			
50:8	2 Ne. 7:8	C	SCBM			
50:9	2 Ne. 7:9	C	SCBM			
50:10	2 Ne. 7:10	C	SCBM			
50:11	2 Ne. 7:11	SC	SCBM		133:70-74	
51:1	2 Ne. 8:1	SC	SCBM			
51:2	2 Ne. 8:2	SC				
51:3	2 Ne. 8:3	S				CWN, CR 4/30:29
51:4-5	2 Ne. 8:4-5	SC				
51:6	2 Ne. 8:6	S		2 Pet. 3: 10-13		JFS, *DS* 1:72-73
51:7	2 Ne. 8:7	C	SBM			

Isaiah	*Book of Mormon*		*JST*	*New Testament*	*D&C*	*General Authorities*
51:8	2 Ne. 8:8	S				
51:9-10	2 Ne. 8:9-10	C				
51:11-12	2 Ne. 8:11-12	SC	SCBM		101:18-19	
					45:71	
					66:11	
51:13-14	2 Ne. 8:13-14	S				
51:15	2 Ne. 8:15	C				
51:16	2 Ne. 8:16	SC	SCBM			
51:17	2 Ne. 8:17	SC				
51:18	2 Ne. 8:18	SC	SCBM			
51:19	2 Ne. 8:19	C	SCBM			BRM, *DNTC* 3:509;
51:20-23	2 Ne. 8:20-23	C	SBM	Rev. 11:1-12		OH, *JD* 10:73-74
52:1	2 Ne. 8:24	S			113:7-8	
	3 Ne. 20:36	C			82:14	
	Moro. 10:31					
52:2	2 Ne. 8:25	SC			113:9-10	
	3 Ne. 20:37	SC				
	Moro. 10:31					
52:3	3 Ne. 20:38	S				
52:4						
52:5				Rom. 2:24		
52:6	3 Ne. 20:39	SC	SCBM		113:10	
52:7	3 Ne. 20:40	C	SBM	Rom. 10:14-15	19:29	
	Mos. 12:21	S			31:3	
	Mos. 15:13-18				79:1	
	1 Ne. 13:37					
52:8	Mos. 12:22	S			84:98-99	*TPJS*, pp. 79-80
	Mos. 15:29	SC				
	3 Ne. 16:18	S				
	3 Ne. 20:32	SC				
52:9	Mos. 12:23	S				
	Mos. 15:19	S				
	3 Ne. 16:19	S				
	3 Ne. 20:34	C				
52:10	Mos. 12:24	S		Luke 2:30	133:2-4	
	Mos. 15:30	S				
	3 Ne. 16:20	SC				
	3 Ne. 20:35	C				
52:11	3 Ne. 20:41	SC		2 Cor. 6:17	38:42	
				Rev. 18:4	133:5-6	
52:12	3 Ne. 20:42	SC			133:15	
52:13	3 Ne. 20:43		S			
52:14	3 Ne. 20:44		S			

Isaiah	*Book of Mormon*	*JST*	*New Testament*	*D&C*	*General Authorities*
52:15	3 Ne. 21:10 3 Ne. 20:45 3 Ne. 21:8	C	Rom. 15:21	101:94	
53:1	Mos. 14:1 Mos. 15:1	S	John 12:38 Rom. 10:16		JFS, *DS* 1:23
53:2	Mos. 14:2 Mos. 15:2-4	SC	Rev. 22:16		
53:3	Mos. 14:3 Mos. 15:5	SC	Matt. 2:23 John 1:46		SDY, CR 4/74:87
53:4	Mos. 14:4	S	Matt. 8: 16-17 1 Pet. 2:24		
53:5	Mos. 14:5 Mos. 13:35 Mos. 15:8-9	S	Rom. 4:25 1 Pet. 2:24		
53:6	Mos. 14:6	SC	1 Pet. 2:25		
53:7	Mos. 14:7 Mos. 15:6-7	S	Luke 23:8- 11; 22:63- 65 Matt. 26: 67-68; 27: 11-14, 29-30 Mark 14: 56-62, 65; 15:19-20 1 Pet. 2:23 Acts 8:32		
53:8	Mos. 14:8 Mos. 15:10	SC	Acts 8:33		
53:9	Mos. 14:9	C	Matt. 27: 22-24, 38, 57-60 Mark 15: 14-15, 27, 42-46 Luke 23:1-4, 13-24, 32-33, 50-53 John 18: 37-38; 19:18, 20:38-42 1 Pet. 2:22		
53:10-11	Mos. 14:10-	S	John 3:	34:3	

Isaiah	*Book of Mormon*	*JST*	*New Testament*	*D&C*	*General Authorities*
	11		16-17		
	Mos. 15:10- 10-13		Matt. 20:28		
53:12	Mos. 14:12	SC	Mark 15:28		
	Mos. 15:8-9		Luke 22:37		
54:1	3 Ne. 22:1	S	Gal. 4:27		
	3 Ne. 21: 22-29				
54:2	3 Ne. 22:2	S		82:14; 133:9	
	Moro. 10:31				
54:3	3 Ne. 22:3	S			
54:4	3 Ne. 22:4	C			
54:5	3 Ne. 22:5	SC			
54:6-8	3 Ne. 22:6-8	S			
54:9	3 Ne. 22:9	SC			
54:10	3 Ne. 22:10	SBM			JFS, *DS* 2:316-17
54:11- 12	3 Ne. 22:11- 12	S	Rev. 21:19- 21		
54:13	3 Ne. 22:13	S		45:58	
54:14	3 Ne. 22:14	S			
54:15	3 Ne. 22:15	SCBM			
54:16	3 Ne. 22:16	S			
54:17	3 Ne. 22:17	S		71:9-10 109:25	
55:1	2 Ne. 9:50	SC	Rev. 3:18; 21:6;		
	2 Ne. 26:25	SC	22:17		
			John 4: 13:14; 6:47-51		
55:2	2 Ne. 9:51	C			
55:3			Acts 13:34		
55:4-5					
55:6-7				88:62-63	JAC, CR 10/71:89
55:8-9	Jacob 4:8				BKP, CR 4/67:129-30
55:10-13					
56:1-6					
56:7			Matt. 21:13		
			Mark 11:17		
			Luke 19:46		
56:8-12					
57:1-4					
57:5		SC			

Isaiah	*Book of Mormon*	*JST*	*New Testament*	*D&C*	*General Authorities*
57:6-18					
57:19-21			Eph. 2:17		HBL, CR 10/73:4
58:1-3					
58:4-12					JHV, CR 4/63:28-29; VLB, *Ensign* 11/77:83
58:13-14					
59:1-2					MEP, CR 10/64:122
59:3-6					
59:7			Rom. 3:15-16		
59:8-16					
59:17			Eph. 6: 13-17 1 Thes. 5:8	27:15-18	
59:18-19					
59:20-21			Rom. 11: 26-27		OC, *MA*, Oct. 1835, p. 199 (quotes Moroni) OP, *JD* 14:64
60:1					OP, *JD* 16:78
60:2				112:23 45:62-75	*TPJS*, pp. 47, 160-61; OP, *JD* 14:355
60:3			Matt. 2:2		OP, *JD* 18:153
60:4-5					
60:6			Matt. 2:11		
60:7					
60:8-10					JL, CR 4/64:116
60:11			Rev. 21:25		OP, *JD* 14:355
60:12					SWK, CR 10/75:8
60:13-16					
60:17					OP, *JD* 18:154
60:18					
60:19-20			Rev. 21:23, 25		OP, *JD* 14:355-56
60:21					
60:22		C		133:58	OP, *JD* 18:153
61:1			Luke 4: 18-19; 7:22; Matt. 11:5 1 Pet. 3:19	128:22	*TPJS*, p. 77
61:2-9					
61:10-11			Rev. 19:7-9; 21:2		

Isaiah	Book of Mormon	JST	New Testament	D&C	General Authorities
62:1-2					
62:3				133:32	
62:4		C		133:23-24	
62:5		C			
62:6-9					
62:10-12					OP, *JD* 18:183-84; 16:86; 14:69
63:1-2			Rev. 19:13, 15; 14:20	133:46-48	
63:3				133:50-51 76:107 88:106	JT, *JD* 10:115
63:4				133:51-52	
63:5-6					
63:7				133:52	
63:8					
63:9				133:53	
63:10-16					
63:17		C			
63:18-19					
64:1				133:40	
64:2				133:41-42; 34:8	
64:3				133:43-44	
64:4			1 Cor. 2:9		
64:5-6		C			
64:7-12					
65:1-2		C	Rom. 10: 20-21		
65:3					
65:4		SC			
65:5-16					
65:17	3 Ne. 26:3		2 Pet. 3: 10-13	101:25	JFS, *ST*, pp. 36-37; *DS* 3:94; OP, *JD* 21:327
65:18-19				101:27-29	
65:20		C		101:30-31 63:50-51 101:101	JFS, *DS* 3:63-64; *AQ* 2: 20-21; 5:141-42
65:21-22					
65:23					LR, CR 10/73:75-76; CR 10/74:73

Isaiah	*Book of Mormon*	*JST*	*New Testament*	*D&C*	*General Authorities*
65:24				101:32-34	
65:25				101:26	JFS (1838), *Gospel Doctrine*, pp. 265-66
66:1-2			Acts 7: 47-50	38:17	
66:3-6					
66:7			Rev. 12:1-5		BRM, *DNTC* 3:516
66:8-17					
66:18-21	3 Ne. 21:1-6		Rom. 15:16		OP, *JD* 18:16-17
66:22			Rev. 21:1	29:23	
66:23					
66:24			Mark 9:44, 46, 48; Luke 16:24	76:44	

Appendix C
Isaiah in the Book of Mormon

There are sixty-six chapters, containing a total of 1292 verses, in the present-day KJV text of Isaiah.[1] Nineteen of the sixty-six chapters are quoted in their entirety in the Book of Mormon, and two other chapters are quoted in their entirety except for 2 verses in each chapter. The first 2 verses of one other chapter are quoted in the Book of Mormon, and 1 verse from each of two other chapters. Eight chapters of Isaiah have verses quoted from them more than once, either completely or partially. Not counting these duplications, 425 of the 1292 verses of Isaiah are quoted in the Book of Mormon. Of these 425 verses, 229 are quoted differently from those in the King James text, while 196 are identical.

BOOK OF MORMON, QUOTATIONS FROM ISAIAH

Isaiah Reference	*B. of M. Reference*	*Quoted by*	*Number of Verses Quoted*	*Verses Quoted Differently*
chap. 2	2 Ne. 12	Nephi	22	14
3	2 Ne. 13	Nephi	26	15
4	2 Ne. 14	Nephi	6	4
5	2 Ne. 15	Nephi	30	15
6	2 Ne. 16	Nephi	13	7
7	2 Ne. 17	Nephi	25	12
8	2 Ne. 18	Nephi	22	6
9	2 Ne. 19	Nephi	21	7
10	2 Ne. 20	Nephi	34	13
11	2 Ne. 21	Nephi	16	4

1. Four of these 66 chapters and 90 of these 1292 verses are not actually the writings of Isaiah, but are historical chapters from the book of 2 Kings. Therefore, Isaiah's writings, as found in the KJV, include only 62 chapters and 1202 verses.

Isaiah Reference	B. of M. Reference	Quoted by	Number of Verses Quoted	Verses Quoted Differently
12	2 Ne. 22	Nephi	6	1
13	2 Ne. 23	Nephi	22	10
14	2 Ne. 24	Nephi	32	15
28:10	2 Ne. 28:30[2]	Nephi	1	1
29: 3-5	2 Ne. 26:15-18[3]	Nephi	3	3
29: 6-24	2 Ne. 27:2-35[4]	Nephi	19	16
40:3	1 Ne. 10:8[5]	Nephi (Lehi)	1	1
48	1 Ne. 20	Nephi	22	21
49	1 Ne. 21	Nephi	26	19
50	2 Ne. 7	Jacob	11	8
51	2 Ne. 8	Jacob	23	16
52: 1-3, 6-15	3 Ne. 20:32-45[6]	Jesus	13	9
53	Mos. 14	Abinadi	12	6
54	3 Ne. 22	Jesus	17	4
55: 1-2	2 Ne. 9:50-51[7]	Jacob	2	2
Totals:	24 chapters[8]		425	229

There are three chapters in Isaiah from which verses are quoted more than once. Some of the same verses are quoted four times from one of these chapters. A total of 21 of these duplicate verses are quoted completely; 8 of those 21 are quoted differently than in Isaiah.

Duplicate Quotations in the Book of Mormon

Isaiah Reference	B. of M. Reference	Quoted by	Number of Verses Quoted	Verses Quoted Differently
chap. 11:	2 Ne. 30:9-16	Nephi[9]	5	2

2. Not identified as Isaiah. 2 Nephi 28:31 may also be part of Isaiah.

3. Not identified as Isaiah. Includes one verse not in Isaiah.

4. Not identified as Isaiah. Includes 14 additional verses.

5. Not identified as Isaiah.

6. Quoted in a different sequence than found in Isaiah.

7. Not identified as Isaiah.

8. Four of the 24 chapters not identified as Isaiah.

9. Includes one verse not in Isaiah. Isaiah 11:4 is different here, but not in 2 Nephi 21.

Isaiah Reference	*B. of M. Reference*	*Quoted by*	*Number of Verses Quoted*	*Verses Quoted Differently*
4-9				
49: 23-26	2 Ne. 6:7, 16-18	Jacob[10]	4	3
52: 1-2	2 Ne. 8:24-25	Jacob	2	1
52: 7-10	Mos. 12:21-24	Priests of Noah[11]	4	0
52: 8-10	Mos. 15:29-31	Abinadi[12]	3	1
52: 8-10	3 Ne. 16:18-20	Jesus[13]	3	1
Totals:	3 chapters duplicated		21	8

If these duplicate verses are added to the other quotations in the Book of Mormon, a total of 446 verses of Isaiah are quoted in the Book of Mormon, 237 of which are quoted differently than in the KJV. Some of these differences are due to the fact that the person quoting them was applying them to the situation of which he was speaking.

Several phrases from the book of Isaiah were also quoted by various Book of Mormon prophets and the Savior as they were commenting upon Isaiah's message. Only those which are obvious are included below; there are many others which are possible paraphrases, but these are not included.

Isaiah Reference	*B. of M. Reference*	*Quoted by*
chap. 5:26	2 Ne. 29:2	Nephi
11: 11	2 Ne. 6:14	Jacob
	2 Ne. 25:17	Nephi
	2 Ne. 29:1	Nephi
	Jacob 6:2	Jacob
29:	2 Ne. 25:17-18	Nephi

10. Isaiah 49:24 is different here, but not in 1 Nephi 21.

11. Isaiah 52:7-10 is the same here, but different in 3 Nephi 20.

12. Verse 8 is different here, but not in Mosiah 12.

13. Verse 10 is slightly different than in Mosiah 12 and 15.

Isaiah Reference	*B. of M. Reference*	*Quoted by*
14		
49:	2 Ne. 29:1-2	Nephi
23		
	2 Ne. 6:13	Jacob
52:1	Moro. 10:31	Moroni
52:	3 Ne. 21:8, 10	Jesus
14-15		
53:7	Mos. 15:6	Abinadi
53:	Mos. 15:10	Abinadi
10		
54:2	Moro. 10:31	Moroni
55:1	2 Ne. 26:25	Nephi

There are four persons in the Book of Mormon who quote extensively from Isaiah. These are Nephi, Jacob, Abinadi, and Jesus. The priests of Noah also quoted a passage from Isaiah and asked Abinadi to explain its meaning. Moroni did not actually quote Isaiah, but he did quote short phrases and commanded his readers to search Isaiah's prophecies, indicating that he could not write them (see Mormon 8:23).

Number of Verses of Isaiah Quoted by Various People

Person	*Verses*	*Verses Changed*	*Comments*
Nephi	352[14]	186	5 verses are duplicates, including 2 changes
Jacob	42	30	
Abinadi	15	7	
Jesus	33	14	3 verses are duplicates, including 1 change
Totals:	442	237	(Does not include 4 verses quoted by the priests of Noah)

14. One of these verses is taken from Nephi's abridgment of his father's record, in which Levi "spake concerning the prophets" and was apparently quoting or paraphrasing Isaiah (see 1 Nephi 10:8; compare Isaiah 40:3).

There are also twenty-one additional verses quoted by Nephi which are possibly from Isaiah. These are either introduced with "saith the prophet" following some quotation from Isaiah, or are sandwiched between other verses quoted from Isaiah. These additional verses are listed below. (The verses from 2 Nephi 27 are included in the JST reading of the Isaiah text.)

1 Nephi 22:15-17	Possibly from Isaiah 49 and 50 or elsewhere; especially verses 15 and 17.
2 Nephi 26:17	Possibly from Isaiah 29.
2 Nephi 27:6-14	From Isaiah 29 (included in JST).
2 Nephi 27:16	From Isaiah 29 (included in JST).
2 Nephi 27:20-24	From Isaiah 29 (included in JST).
2 Nephi 28:31	Possibly from Isaiah 28.
2 Nephi 30:10	Possibly from Isaiah 49 and 50, although inserted in Isaiah 11:4-9.

Appendix D
Isaiah in the Doctrine and Covenants

The Lord said that the proclamation of the restored gospel was in fulfillment of the prophets (see D&C 1:18). There are at least sixty-six quotations or paraphrases from the prophet Isaiah in the Doctrine and Covenants. Some of these are full verses, and some are only phrases. Only those which are obviously based on Isaiah have been included. Represented within the sixty-six passages are thirty-one different chapters of Isaiah. Fourteen of these chapters are from so-called First Isaiah, nine are from so-called Second Isaiah, and eight are from so-called Third Isaiah (although Isaiah is not specifically named as the author of any of these quotations). This is another evidence of the unity and the single authorship of the book of Isaiah.

Isaiah		*D&C*	*Common Phrase or Concept*
1.	1:19	64:34	"shall eat the good of the land"
2.	2:2-3	133:12-13	"unto the mountain of the Lord's house"
3.	4:5	45:63-75	"upon every dwelling place of mount Zion"
4.	4:6	115:6	"a place of refuge . . . from storm"
5.	5:1-7	101:43-62	"built a tower . . . break down the wall thereof"
6.	8:16	88:84; 133:72[1]	"Bind up the testimony, seal the law"
7.	11:1-5	113:1-4	"a rod out of the stem of Jesse"
8.	11:4	19:15	"smite the earth with the rod of his mouth"

1. The Doctrine and Covenants references reverse the words "testimony" and "law."

Isaiah		*D&C*	*Common Phrase or Concept*
9.	11:10	113:5-6	"a root of Jesse"
10.	11:16	133:26-29	"And there shall be an highway"
11.	13:1	133:14	"The burden of Babylon"
12.	13:10	29:14; 34:9; 45:42; 88:87; 133:49[2]	"the sun shall be darkened"
13.	13:13	21:6; 35:24	"I will shake the heavens"
14.	14:12	76:26	"Lucifer, son of the morning"
15.	24:5	1:15	"they have changed the ordinance, broken the everlasting covenant"
16.	24:20	49:23; 88:87	"The earth shall reel to and fro like a drunkard"
17.	25:6	58:8	"a feast of fat things"
18.	28:10	98:12; 128:21	"precept upon precept; line upon line"
19.	28:15, 18	45:31; 5:19; 97:23	"overflowing scourge"
20.	28:21	95:4; 101:95	"bring to pass . . . his strange act"
21.	29:14	4:1; 6:1; 11:1; 12:1; 14:1; 18:44	"a marvellous work and a wonder"
22.	34:5	1:13	"my sword shall be bathed in heaven"
23.	35:1-2	49:24-25; 117:7	"the solitary place shall... blossom as the rose"
24.	35:3	81:5	"Strengthen ye the weak hands, and confirm the feeble knees"
25.	35:7-10	133:27-33	"the ransomed of the Lord shall return"
26.	35:10	45:71; 66:11	"with songs and everlasting joy"
27.	40:3	88:66	"The voice of him that crieth in the wilderness"
28.	40:3	33:10; 65:1	"Prepare ye the way of the Lord"
29.	40:4	133:22	"Every valley shall be exalted, and every mountain . . . made low"
30.	40:5	101:23	"all flesh shall see it together"
31.	40:31	89:20	"run, and not be weary . . . walk, and not faint"
32.	42:7	128:22	"bring out the prisoners from the prison"
33.	43:11	76:1	"beside me there is no saviour"
34.	45:23	76:110; 88:104	"every knee shall bow, every tongue shall swear"
35.	49:2	6:2; 11:2; 12:2; 14:2; 15:2; 16:2; 33:1	"my mouth like a sharp sword"
36.	49:2	86:9	"in the shadow of his hand hath he hid me"

2. The Doctrine and Covenants quotations are closer to the wording of Joel 2:31, but the Isaiah text is very similar.

Isaiah		*D&C*	*Common Phrase or Concept*
37.	49:6	86:11	"a light to the Gentiles"
38.	49:22	45:9; 115:5	"my standard to the people"
39.	50:2-3	133:66-69	"when I came, was there no man?"
40.	50:11	133:70	"ye shall lie down in sorrow"
41.	51:9-11	101:18	"the redeemed shall return"
42.	52:1	113:7-8; 82:14	"put on thy strength, O Zion"
43.	52:2	113:9-10	"loose thyself from the bands of thy neck"
44.	52:7	19:29; 31:3; 113:10	"good tidings of good"
45.	52:8	84:98-99; 113:10	"they shall see eye to eye"
46.	52:10	133:3; 113:10	"made bare his holy arm in the eyes of all the nations"
47.	52:11	38:42; 133:5	"be ye clean, that bear the vessels of the Lord"
48.	52:12	133:15	"ye shall not go out with haste"
49.	52:15	101:94	"that which they had not heard shall they consider"
50.	54:2	82:14; 133:9	"Enlarge the place of thy tent"
51.	54:17	71:9; 109:25	"No weapon that is formed against thee shall prosper"
52.	55:6	88:62-63	"call ye upon him while he is near"
53.	59:17	27:15-18	"put on righteousness as a breastplate"
54.	60:2	112:23	"darkness shall cover the earth, and gross darkness the people"
55.	60:22	133:58	"a small one a strong nation"
	61:1	(see no. 32)	———
56.	62:4	133:23-24	"thy land shall be married"
57.	63:1-2	133:46-48	"Who is this that cometh . . . with dyed garments . . .?"
58.	63:3-6	133:50-52; 76:107; 88:106	"I have trodden the winepress alone"
59.	63:7-9	133:52-53	"will mention the loving kindnesses of the Lord"
60.	64:1-2	133:40-42; 34:8	"Oh that thou wouldest rend the heavens"
61.	64:3-5	133:43-45	"When thou didst terrible things"
62.	65:17	29:23	"I create new heavens and a new earth"
63.	65:20	101:30; 63:51	"no more thence an infant of days"
64.	65:21-22	101:101	"they shall build houses, and inhabit them"
65.	66:1	38:17	"the earth is my footstool"
66.	66:24	76:44	"their worm shall not die, neither shall their fire be quenched"

Appendix E
Isaiah in the New Testament

The most oft-quoted prophet in the New Testament is the prophet Isaiah. There are forty-two different passages of Isaiah which are definitely identifiable, as well as many others which are apparently from Isaiah. The forty-two passages do not include duplications, such as those found in the synoptic gospels. In the list that folows, those passages which are definitely identifiable as quotations of Isaiah are asterisked; others which appear to be from Isaiah are also listed. There are several additional New Testament passages which are allusions to Isaiah's writing, or shadows of his thought, but these are not included here.

Isaiah	*New Testament*	*By Whom*	*Introduction*
*1:9	Rom. 9:29	Paul	"as *Esaias* [Isaiah] said before"
1:16-17	1 Pet. 3:11		
2:10a, 19, 21	Rev. 6:15-16		
2:10b, 19, 21	2 Thes. 1:9		
	Luke 23:30		
6:1-3	Rev. 4:2, 8		
6:4	Rev. 15:8		
*6:9-10	Matt. 13:14-15	Jesus	"the prophecy of *Esaias*, which saith"
	Mark 4:12	Jesus	None
	Luke 8:10	Jesus	None
	John 12:40	Jesus	"*Esaias* said again"
	Acts 28:26-27	Paul	"Well spake the Holy Ghost by *Esaias* the prophet"

Isaiah	*New Testament*	*By Whom*	*Introduction*
	Rom. 11:8	Paul	"According as it is written"
*7:14	Matt. 1:23	Matthew	"which was spoken of the Lord by the prophet, saying"
*8:14	1 Pet. 2:8	Peter	"it is contained in the scripture"
	1 Cor. 1:23	Paul	None
	Rom. 9:33	Paul	"As it is written"
*8:18a	Heb. 2:13	Paul	"Saying . . . And again"
*9:1-2	Matt. 4:15-16	Matthew	"which was spoken by *Esaias* the prophet, saying"
	Luke 1:79	Zacharias	"As he spake by the mouth of his holy prophets"
9:7	Luke 1:32; 2:10-11		
*10:22-23	Rom. 9:27-28	Paul	"*Esaias* also crieth"
11:1	Rev. 5:5		
11:4	Rev. 2:16; 19:15		
*11:10	Rom. 15:12	Paul	"And again, Esaias saith"
	Rev. 5:5		
12:2	Heb. 2:13		
12:3	John 7:38		
	Rev. 21:6		
13:10	Matt. 24:29		
16:5	Luke 1:32		
21:9	Rev. 14:8		
22:13	1 Cor. 15:32		
22:22	Rev. 3:7		
23:8	Rev. 18:23		
24:5	Heb. 13:20		
24:8	Rev. 18:22		
24:23	Rev. 21:23		
*25:8	1 Cor. 15:54	Paul	"the saying that is written"
	Rev. 7:17; 21:4		
26:17	John 16:21		
*28:11-12	1 Cor. 14:21	Paul	"In the law it is written"
*28:16	Rom. 9:33; 10:11	Paul	"As it is written" "For the scripture saith"
	1 Pet. 2:6	Peter	"it is contained in the scripture"
28:22	Rom. 9:28		
29:1-3	Luke 19:43		
29:10	Rom. 11:8		

Isaiah	*New Testament*	*By Whom*	*Introduction*
*29:13-14	Matt. 15:7-9	Jesus	"well did *Esaias* prophesy of you, saying"
	Mark 7:6-7	Jesus	"Well hath *Esaias* prophesied . . . as it is written"
	1 Cor. 1:19-20	Paul	"For it is written"
29:16	Rom. 9:20		
30:26	Rev. 21:23		
33:18	1 Cor. 1:20		
34:4	2 Pet. 3:10-13 Rev. 6:14		
34:10	Rev. 14:11		
35:3	Heb. 12:12		
*40:3	Matt. 3:3	Matthew	"spoken of by the prophet *Esaias*, saying"
	Mark 1:3	Mark	"As it is written in the prophets"
	Luke 1:76	Zacharias	"As he spake by the mouth of his holy prophets"
	John 1:23	John the Baptist	"as said the prophet *Esaias*"
*40:3-5	Luke 3:4-6	Luke	"As it is written in the book of the words of *Esaias* the prophet"
*40:6-8	1 Pet. 1:24-25	Peter	None
40:8	Mark 13:31		
40:10	Rev. 22:12		
*40:13-14	Rom. 11:34-35	Paul	None
41:4	Rev. 1:8, 17; 22:13		
*42:1-3	Matt. 12:18	Matthew	"which was spoken by *Esaias* the prophet, saying"
*42:6	Luke 2:32	Simeon	None
42:7	Acts 26:18 1 Pet. 3:19		
44:3	John 7:30		
44:6	Rev. 1:8, 17; 22:13		
45:5	Mark 12:32		
45:9	Rom. 9:20		
45:14	1 Cor. 14:25		
45:22	Mark 12:32		
*45:23	Rom. 14:11 Philip. 2:10-11	Paul	"For it is written"
47:7-9	Rev. 18:7-8		

Isaiah	*New Testament*	*By Whom*	*Introduction*
47:15	Rev. 18:3		
48:12	Rev. 1:8, 17; 22:13		
49:2	Rev. 1:16		
*49:6	Acts 13:47	Paul and Barnabas	"For so hath the Lord commanded us, saying"
49:7	1 Cor. 1:9		
*49:8	2 Cor. 6:2	Paul	"For he saith"
49:10	Rev. 7:16		
51:6	Matt. 24:6 2 Pet. 3:10-13		
*52:5	Rom. 2:24	Paul	"as it is written"
*52:7	Rom. 10:14-15	Paul	"as it is written"
52:10	Luke 2:30		
*52:11	2 Cor. 6:17	Paul	"saith the Lord"
	Rev. 18:4	John	"And I heard another voice from heaven, saying"
*52:15	Rom. 15:21	Paul	"But as it is written"
*53:1	John 12:38	John	"the saying of *Esaias* the prophet . . . which he spake"
	Rom. 10:16	Paul	"For *Esaias* saith"
53:3-9	Matt. 27:26-31, 38, 59-60 Mark 14:61; 15:3-4 John 18:28; 19:16		
*53:4	Matt. 8:17	Matthew	"which was spoken by *Esaias* the prophet, saying"
*53:4-7, 9	1 Pet. 2:22-25	Peter	None
53:5-6	Rom. 4:25		
53:7	Luke 23:8-11		
*53:7-8	Acts 8:32-33	(Ethiopian eunuch, with Philip)	"read the prophet *Esaias*"
53:11-12	Matt. 20:28		
*53:12	Mark 15:28	Mark	"And the scripture was fulfilled, which saith"
	Luke 22:37	Jesus	"this that is written"
*54:1	Gal. 4:27	Paul	"For it is written"
54:5	Rev. 21:2		
54:11	Rev. 21:19		
*54:13	John 6:45	Jesus	"It is written in the prophets"

Isaiah	*New Testament*	*By Whom*	*Introduction*
55:1	Rev. 3:18; 21:6; 22:17		
*55:3b	Acts 13:34	Paul	"he said on this wise"
*56:7	Matt. 21:13	Jesus	"It is written"
	Mark 11:17	Jesus	"Is it not written"
	Luke 19:46	Jesus	"It is written"
*57:19	Eph. 2:17	Paul	None
*59:7-8	Rom. 3:15-17	Paul	"As it is written"
59:17	Eph. 6:14-17 1 Thes. 5:8		
*59:20-21	Rom. 11:26-27	Paul	"as it is written"
60:3	Matt. 2:2		
60:6	Matt. 2:11		
60:11	Rev. 21:25		
60:19-20	Rev. 21:23, 25		
*61:1-2	Luke 4:18-19; 7:22	Jesus	"the book of the prophet *Esaias*"
	Matt. 11:5	Jesus	None
	1 Pet. 3:19	Peter	None
61:10	Rev. 19:7-9; 21:2		
63:2-3	Rev. 19:13, 15; 14:20		
*64:4	1 Cor. 2:9	Paul	"as it is written"
*65:1-2	Rom. 10:20-21	Paul	"But *Esaias* is very bold, and saith"
65:17	2 Pet. 3:10-13 Rev. 21:1		
*66:1-2	Acts 7:49-50	Stephen	"as saith the prophet"
66:7	Rev. 12:2		
66:20	Rom. 15:16		
66:22	2 Pet. 3:10-13 Rev. 21:1		
*66:24	Mark 9:44, 46, 48	Jesus	None
	Luke 16:24	Jesus	None

The forty-two asterisked quotations in the foregoing list come from twenty-five different chapters of Isaiah. Twelve of these forty-two quotations come from ten different chapters of so-called First Isaiah (chapters 1-35); twenty-one come from eight different chapters of so-called Second Isaiah (chapters 40-55); and nine come from seven chapters of so-called Third Isaiah (chapters 56-66). These facts witness against the theories claiming multiple authorship of Isaiah.

Fourteen of the forty-two asterisked passages are specifically identified as the words of the prophet Isaiah ("Esaias"). These fourteen quotations come from eleven separate chapters — six chapters in First Isaiah, three in Second Isaiah, and two in Third Isaiah, as they are called. Twenty-one of the forty-two quotations are identified as scripture, though Isaiah is not named as their author. These also are representative of all areas of the book of Isaiah: six are from so-called First Isaiah, ten from Second Isaiah, and five from Third Isaiah. The remainder of the forty-two passages are seven obvious quotations from Isaiah which are identified neither as Isaiah's words nor as scripture; five of these are from Second Isaiah, and two are from Third Isaiah.

Distribution of New Testament Isaiah Quotations Throughout So-called First, Second, and Third Isaiah

(The numbers of chapters from which the passages are quoted are shown in parentheses.)

	"First" Isaiah (ch. 1-35) Passages		*"Second" Isaiah (ch. 40-55) Passages*		*"Third" Isaiah (ch. 56-66) Passages*		*Totals*	
Identified as Isaiah's words	6	(6)	6	(3)	2	(2)	14	(11)
Identified as scripture but not as Isaiah	6	(4)	10	(5)[1]	5	(4)	21	(13)[1]
Quoted without identification			5	(4)[1]	2	(2)[1]	7	(6)[1]
Totals	12	(10)	21	(12)	9	(8)	42	(30)[1]

The following table will show the distribution of quotations specifically attributed to Isaiah by various New Testament characters. As can be seen, either Jesus or his apostles named Isaiah as the author of passages from all three of the scholars' divisions of the book which bears his name.

1. Includes duplications. There are only 25 separate chapters from which quotations are taken.

IDENTIFICATION OF ISAIAH AUTHORSHIP
BY NEW TESTAMENT CHARACTERS

Quoted by	*Quotations from "First" Isaiah*	*Quotations from "Second" Isaiah*	*Quotations from "Third" Isaiah*	*Totals*
Jesus	2		1	3
Paul	4	1	1	6
Matthew	1	3		4
John		1		1
John the Baptist		1		1
Luke		1		1
Ethiopian eunuch with Philip		1		1
Totals	7[2]	8[2]	2	17[2]

There are eleven different people who actually quoted the prophet Isaiah in the New Testament, though not all of them mention his name: Paul quoted far more frequently than did other new Testament writers. Jesus quoted seven different passages of Isaiah, not counting the duplications in the synoptic gospels. Peter quoted Isaiah four times, which was a considerable number in light of the small amount of his writings which we have today.

The apostle John paraphrased Isaiah extensively in his writings, especially in the book of Revelation. There are at least forty paraphrases of Isaiah in John's writings. Paul also paraphrased or partially quoted Isaiah at least twenty-one times, in addition to his twenty-five quotations. Peter partially quoted or paraphrased Isaiah eight times, in addition to his four quotations. In addition to Jesus and others whose statements are recorded in the gospels, all of the gospel writers themselves relied upon Isaiah as well.

2. Includes duplications. There are only 14 separate passages explicitly attributed to Isaiah.

Distribution of Quotations and Paraphrases of Isaiah Among New Testament Characters

Quoted by	*Quotations*	*Paraphrases or Partial Quotations*	*Totals*
Jesus	7	0	7
Peter	4	8	12
John	1	40	41
Matthew	3	7	10
Mark	2	4	6
Luke	1	10	11
Paul	25[3]	21	46
John the Baptist	1	0	1
Stephen	1	0	1
Simeon	1	0	1
Ethiopian eunuch with Philip	1	0	1
Totals	47	90	137

3. Includes one quotation attributed to both Paul and Barnabas.

Appendix F
The Prophet Joseph Smith and Isaiah

Joseph Smith was called to give the Lord's word to "this generation," the dispensation of the fulness of times (see D&C 5:10). Unfortunately, many of his sermons were not recorded, and some of those which were recorded were not verbatim accounts, but rather summaries produced by various clerks assigned to take notes on the Prophet's discourses. In spite of these limitations, a review of his teachings discloses that in fulfilling the charge to declare the Lord's word, Joseph Smith often quoted from the prophet Isaiah. The following tabulation of his recorded quotations from Isaiah, taken from the book *Teachings of the Prophet Joseph Smith* (compiled in 1938 by Elder Joseph Fielding Smith), shows that throughout his lifetime the Prophet quoted from many parts of the book of Isaiah (the quotations included in this list were taken from twenty-one different chapters in Isaiah).

Isaiah	*TPJS Page*	*Approx. Date*	*Description of Comment*
2:2-3	367	May 2, 1844	Paraphrase and commentary
2:3	252	July 15, 1842	Partial quotation
2:4	248, 251	July 15, 1842	Partial quotation and commentary
8:20	373-74	June 16, 1844	Paraphrase
11:6-8	71	May 26, 1834	Paraphrase and commentary
11:6-9a	316	July 23, 1843	Paraphrase and commentary
11:9b	93	Jan. 6, 1836	Paraphrase and commentary
11:11	14-15	Jan. 4, 1833	Paraphrase and commentary
13:10, 13	71	Apr. 21, 1834	Paraphrase and commentary
13:13	29	Nov. 19, 1833	Paraphrase and commentary
24:5	15	Jan. 4, 1833	Partial quotation and commentary
24:20	29	Nov. 19, 1833	Paraphrase and commentary
24:20-22	219	Apr. 15, 1842	Quotation and commentary

Isaiah	*TPJS Page*	*Approx. Date*	*Description of Comment*
26:20-21	17	Jan. 4, 1833	Reference and commentary
28:19	87	Nov. 1835	Partial quotation and commentary
28:21	267	Sept. 15, 1842	Paraphrase and commentary
29:21	124, 315 341	Dec. 16, 1838 July 23, 1843; Mar. 24, 1844	Paraphrase and commentary
33:14	361	Apr. 6, 1844	Paraphrase and commentary
33:20	33	Dec. 5, 1833	Paraphrase and commentary
33:22	252	July 15, 1842	Paraphrase and commentary
34:4	29	Nov. 19, 1833	Paraphrase and commentary
35:10	17, 34, 78	Jan. 4, 1833 Dec. 10, 1833; June 1835	Partial quotation and commentary
40:3	319, 335	Aug. 13, 1843; May 10, 1844	Paraphrase and commentary
40:4	13	Aug. 1832	Paraphrase and commentary
40:6	274	Jan. 22, 1843	Paraphrase
42:7	219, 222	Apr. 15, 1842	Partial quotation and commentary
43:5-6	183	Jan. 8, 1841	Paraphrase and commentary
45:22-24	82	Sept. 1, 1835	Quotation
51:3	249	July 15, 1842	Paraphrase
52:8	79-80	Sept. 1, 1835	Quotation and commentary
54:2	363	Apr. 1844	Allusion
59:20	13	Aug. 1832	Paraphrase and commentary
60:2	47	Jan. 22, 1834	Paraphrase and commentary
60:10-11	227	Apr. 28, 1842	Paraphrase and commentary
61:1-2	77	June 1835	Paraphrase

Other comments by the Prophet Joseph Smith which are helpful to an understanding of the text of Isaiah, but are not quotations or paraphrases, have been quoted earlier in this work. These are listed below; the Prophet's statements can be found in the "Notes and Commentary" corresponding to the references indicated in the left-hand column.

Isaiah	*TPJS Page*	*Isaiah*	*TPJS Page*
10:24-25	262	45:8 (Moses 7:62)	84
11:1	151	49:2	304
14:9-11	297	49:14-15	362
14:12-14	297-98	51:3	362
16:5	339	60:1-2	160-61
Intro-duction to chapters 36-39	365		

Also, Joseph Smith — History 1:17-19 is an important passage related to Isaiah 29:13-14.

Index

This index does not include references to the text of the book of Isaiah. For those references a regular Bible concordance should be consulted.

— A —

— B —

— C —